Cloud Native w
Kubernetes

Deploy, configure, and run modern cloud native applications on Kubernetes

Alexander Raul

BIRMINGHAM—MUMBAI

Cloud Native with Kubernetes

Commissioning Editor: Karan Sadawana

Acquisition Editor: Rahul Nair

Senior Editor: Arun Nadar

Content Development Editor: Pratik Andrade

Technical Editor: Soham Amburle

Copy Editor: Safis Editing

Project Coordinator: Neil Dmello

Proofreader: Safis Editing

Indexer: Manju Arasan

Production Designer: Prashant Ghare

First published: January 2021

Production reference: 1031220

Published by Packt Publishing Ltd.

Livery Place

35 Livery Street

Birmingham

B3 2PB, UK.

ISBN 978-1-83882-307-8

www.packt.com

To my team at Rackner, my family, and my friends for their support in the process. To my girlfriend, for dealing with all the late nights of writing. And to the late Dan Kohn, in memoriam, for introducing me to and evangelizing the amazing Kubernetes community.

– Alexander Raul

Packt.com

Subscribe to our online digital library for full access to over 7,000 books and videos, as well as industry leading tools to help you plan your personal development and advance your career. For more information, please visit our website.

Why subscribe?

- Spend less time learning and more time coding with practical eBooks and Videos from over 4,000 industry professionals

- Improve your learning with Skill Plans built especially for you

- Get a free eBook or video every month

- Fully searchable for easy access to vital information

- Copy and paste, print, and bookmark content

Did you know that Packt offers eBook versions of every book published, with PDF and ePub files available? You can upgrade to the eBook version at packt.com and as a print book customer, you are entitled to a discount on the eBook copy. Get in touch with us at customercare@packtpub.com for more details.

At www.packt.com, you can also read a collection of free technical articles, sign up for a range of free newsletters, and receive exclusive discounts and offers on Packt books and eBooks.

Contributors

About the author

Alexander Raul is CEO of Rackner, an innovative consultancy that builds, runs, and secures Kubernetes and the cloud for clients ranging from highly funded start-ups to Fortune and Global 500 enterprises. With Rackner, he has personally built and managed large Kubernetes-based platforms and implemented end-to-end DevSecOps for incredible organizations. Though his background and education are technical (he received an aerospace degree from the University of Maryland), he is well versed in the business and strategic arguments for the cloud and Kubernetes – as well as the issues around the adoption of these technologies. Alexander lives in Washington, D.C. – and when he isn't working with clients, he's mountaineering, skiing, or running.

About the reviewer

Zihao Yu is a senior staff software engineer at HBO in New York City. He has been instrumental in Kubernetes and other cloud-native practices and CI/CD projects within the company. He was a keynote speaker at KubeCon North America 2017. He holds a Master of Science degree in computer engineering from Rutgers, The State University of New Jersey, and a Bachelor of Engineering degree from Nanjing University of Science and Technology in China.

Packt is searching for authors like you

If you're interested in becoming an author for Packt, please visit `authors.packtpub.com` and apply today. We have worked with thousands of developers and tech professionals, just like you, to help them share their insight with the global tech community. You can make a general application, apply for a specific hot topic that we are recruiting an author for, or submit your own idea.

Table of Contents

2

Setting Up Your Kubernetes Cluster

3

Running Application Containers on Kubernetes

Section 2:
Configuring and Deploying Applications on Kubernetes

4
Scaling and Deploying Your Application

5
Services and Ingress – Communicating with the Outside World

6
Kubernetes Application Configuration

7
Storage on Kubernetes

8

Pod Placement Controls

Section 3:
Running Kubernetes in Production

9

Observability on Kubernetes

10
Troubleshooting Kubernetes

11
Template Code Generation and CI/CD on Kubernetes

12
Kubernetes Security and Compliance

Section 4: Extending Kubernetes

13
Extending Kubernetes with CRDs

14

Service Meshes and Serverless

15

Stateful Workloads on Kubernetes

Assessments

Other Books You May Enjoy

Index

Preface

The aim of this book is to give you the knowledge and the broad set of tools needed to build cloud-native applications using Kubernetes. Kubernetes is a powerful technology that gives engineers powerful tools to build cloud-native platforms using containers. The project itself is constantly evolving and contains many different tools to tackle common scenarios.

For the layout of this book, rather than sticking to any one niche area of the Kubernetes toolset, we will first give you a thorough summary of the most important parts of default Kubernetes functionality – giving you all the skills you need in order to run applications on Kubernetes. Then, we'll give you the tools you need in order to deal with security and troubleshooting for Kubernetes in a day 2 scenario. Finally, we'll go past the boundaries of Kubernetes itself and look at some powerful patterns and technologies to build on top of Kubernetes – such as service meshes and serverless.

Who this book is for

This book is for beginners to Kubernetes, but you should be well acquainted with containers and DevOps principles in order to get the most out of this book. A solid grounding in Linux will help but is not completely necessary.

What this book covers

Chapter 1, *Communicating with Kubernetes*, introduces you to the concept of container orchestration and the fundamentals of how Kubernetes works. It also gives you the basic tools you need in order to communicate with and authenticate with a Kubernetes cluster.

Chapter 2, *Setting Up Your Kubernetes Cluster*, walks you through creating a Kubernetes cluster in a few different popular ways, both on your local machine and on the cloud.

Chapter 3, *Running Application Containers on Kubernetes*, introduces you to the most basic building block of running applications on Kubernetes – the Pod. We cover how to create a Pod, as well as the specifics of the Pod lifecycle.

Chapter 4, *Scaling and Deploying Your Application*, reviews higher-level controllers, which allow the scaling and upgrading of multiple Pods of an application, including autoscaling.

Chapter 5, *Services and Ingress – Communicating with the Outside World,* introduces several approaches to exposing applications running in a Kubernetes cluster to users on the outside.

Chapter 6, *Kubernetes Application Configuration*, gives you the skills you need to provide configuration (including secure data) to applications running on Kubernetes.

Chapter 7, *Storage on Kubernetes*, reviews methods and tools to provide persistent and non-persistent storage to applications running on Kubernetes.

Chapter 8, *Pod Placement Controls*, introduces several different tools and strategies for controlling and influencing Pod placement on Kubernetes Nodes.

Chapter 9, *Observability on Kubernetes*, covers multiple tenets of observability in the context of Kubernetes, including metrics, tracing, and logging.

Chapter 10, *Troubleshooting Kubernetes*, reviews some key ways Kubernetes clusters can fail – as well as how to effectively triage issues on Kubernetes.

Chapter 11, *Template Code Generation and CI/CD on Kubernetes*, introduces Kubernetes YAML templating tooling and some common patterns for CI/CD on Kubernetes.

Chapter 12, *Kubernetes Security and Compliance*, covers the basics of security on Kubernetes, including some recent security issues with the Kubernetes project, and tooling for cluster and container security.

Chapter 13, *Extending Kubernetes with CRDs*, introduces Custom Resource Definitions (CRDs) along with other ways to add custom functionality to Kubernetes, such as operators.

Chapter 14, *Service Meshes and Serverless*, reviews some advanced patterns on Kubernetes, teaching you how to add a service mesh to your cluster and enable serverless workloads.

Chapter 15, *Stateful Workloads on Kubernetes*, walks you through the specifics of running stateful workloads on Kubernetes, including a tutorial on running some powerful stateful applications from the ecosystem.

To get the most out of this book

Since Kubernetes is based on containers, some examples in this book may use containers that have changed since publishing. Other illustrative examples may use containers that do not publicly exist in Docker Hub. These examples should be used as a basis for running your own application containers.

Software/Hardware covered in the book	OS Requirements
Docker	Windows, macOS, and Linux (any)
Kubernetes	Can be run locally with Minikube on macOS or Linux. Full Kubernetes clusters support Linux for the control plane components (see *Chapter 2, Setting Up Your Kubernetes Cluster*, for more information).
Helm	Windows, macOS, and Linux (any)

In some cases, open source software like Kubernetes can have breaking changes. The book is up to date with Kubernetes 1.19, but always check the documentation (for Kubernetes and for any of the other open source projects covered in the book) for the most up-to-date information and specifications.

If you are using the digital version of this book, we advise you to type the code yourself or access the code via the GitHub repository (link available in the next section). Doing so will help you avoid any potential errors related to the copying and pasting of code.

Download the example code files

You can download the example code files for this book from GitHub at `https://github.com/PacktPublishing/Cloud-Native-with-Kubernetes`. In case there's an update to the code, it will be updated on the existing GitHub repository.

We also have other code bundles from our rich catalog of books and videos available at `https://github.com/PacktPublishing/`. Check them out!

Download the color images

We also provide a PDF file that has color images of the screenshots/diagrams used in this book. You can download it here: `http://www.packtpub.com/sites/default/files/downloads/9781838823078_ColorImages.pdf`.

Conventions used

There are a number of text conventions used throughout this book.

`Code in text`: Indicates code words in text, database table names, folder names, filenames, file extensions, pathnames, dummy URLs, user input, and Twitter handles. Here is an example: "In our case, we want to let every authenticated user on the cluster create privileged Pods, so we bind to the `system:authenticated` group."

A block of code is set as follows:

```
apiVersion: networking.k8s.io/v1
kind: NetworkPolicy
metadata:
  name: full-restriction-policy
  namespace: development
spec:
  policyTypes:
  - Ingress
  - Egress
  podSelector: {}
```

When we wish to draw your attention to a particular part of a code block, the relevant lines or items are set in bold:

```
spec:
  privileged: false
  allowPrivilegeEscalation: false
  volumes:
    - 'configMap'
    - 'emptyDir'
    - 'projected'
    - 'secret'
    - 'downwardAPI'
    - 'persistentVolumeClaim'
  hostNetwork: false
  hostIPC: false
  hostPID: false
```

Any command-line input or output is written as follows:

```
helm install falco falcosecurity/falco
```

Bold: Indicates a new term, an important word, or words that you see onscreen. For example, words in menus or dialog boxes appear in the text like this. Here is an example: "Prometheus also provides an **Alerts** tab for configuring Prometheus alerts."

> **Tips or important notes**
> Appear like this.

Get in touch

Feedback from our readers is always welcome.

General feedback: If you have questions about any aspect of this book, mention the book title in the subject of your message and email us at customercare@packtpub.com.

Errata: Although we have taken every care to ensure the accuracy of our content, mistakes do happen. If you have found a mistake in this book, we would be grateful if you would report this to us. Please visit www.packtpub.com/support/errata, selecting your book, clicking on the Errata Submission Form link, and entering the details.

Piracy: If you come across any illegal copies of our works in any form on the Internet, we would be grateful if you would provide us with the location address or website name. Please contact us at copyright@packt.com with a link to the material.

If you are interested in becoming an author: If there is a topic that you have expertise in and you are interested in either writing or contributing to a book, please visit authors.packtpub.com.

Reviews

Please leave a review. Once you have read and used this book, why not leave a review on the site that you purchased it from? Potential readers can then see and use your unbiased opinion to make purchase decisions, we at Packt can understand what you think about our products, and our authors can see your feedback on their book. Thank you!

For more information about Packt, please visit packt.com.

Section 1: Setting Up Kubernetes

In this section, you'll learn what Kubernetes is for, how it is architected, and the basics of communicating with, and creating, a simple cluster, as well as how to run a basic workload.

This part of the book comprises the following chapters:

- *Chapter 1, Communicating with Kubernetes*
- *Chapter 2, Setting Up Your Kubernetes Cluster*
- *Chapter 3, Running Application Containers on Kubernetes*

1
Communicating with Kubernetes

This chapter contains an explanation of container orchestration, including its benefits, use cases, and popular implementations. We'll also review Kubernetes briefly, including a layout of the architectural components, and a primer on authorization, authentication, and general communication with Kubernetes. By the end of this chapter, you'll know how to authenticate and communicate with the Kubernetes API.

In this chapter, we will cover the following topics:

- A container orchestration primer
- Kubernetes' architecture
- Authentication and authorization on Kubernetes
- Using kubectl and YAML files

Technical requirements

In order to run the commands detailed in this chapter, you will need a computer running Linux, macOS, or Windows. This chapter will teach you how to install the kubectl command-line tool that you will use in all later chapters.

The code used in this chapter can be found in the book's GitHub repository at the following link:

```
https://github.com/PacktPublishing/Cloud-Native-with-
Kubernetes/tree/master/Chapter1
```

Introducing container orchestration

We cannot talk about Kubernetes without an introduction of its purpose. Kubernetes is a container orchestration framework, so let's review what that means in the context of this book.

What is container orchestration?

Container orchestration is a popular pattern for running modern applications both in the cloud and the data center. By using containers – preconfigured application units with bundled dependencies – as a base, developers can run many instances of an application in parallel.

Benefits of container orchestration

There are quite a few benefits that container orchestration offers, but we will highlight the main ones. First, it allows developers to easily build **high-availability** applications. By having multiple instances of an application running, a container orchestration system can be configured in a way that means it will automatically replace any failed instances of the application with new ones.

This can be extended to the cloud by having those multiple instances of the application spread across physical data centers, so if one data center goes down, other instances of the application will remain, and prevent downtime.

Second, container orchestration allows for highly **scalable** applications. Since new instances of the application can be created and destroyed easily, the orchestration tool can auto-scale up and down to meet demand. Either in a cloud or data center environment, new **Virtual Machines** (**VMs**) or physical machines can be added to the orchestration tool to give it a bigger pool of compute to manage. This process can be completely automated in a cloud setting to allow for completely hands-free scaling, both at the micro and macro level.

Popular orchestration tools

There are several highly popular container orchestration tools available in the ecosystem:

- **Docker Swarm**: Docker Swarm was created by the team behind the Docker container engine. It is easier to set up and run compared to Kubernetes, but somewhat less flexible.

- **Apache Mesos**: Apache Mesos is a lower-level orchestration tool that manages compute, memory, and storage, in both data center and cloud environments. By default, Mesos does not manage containers, but Marathon – a framework that runs on top of Mesos – is a fully fledged container orchestration tool. It is even possible to run Kubernetes on top of Mesos.

- **Kubernetes**: As of 2020, much of the work in container orchestration has consolidated around Kubernetes (koo-bur-net-ees), often shortened to k8s. Kubernetes is an open source container orchestration tool that was originally created by Google, with learnings from internal orchestration tools Borg and Omega, which had been in use at Google for years. Since Kubernetes became open source, it has risen in popularity to become the de facto way to run and orchestrate containers in an enterprise environment. There are a few reasons for this, including that Kubernetes is a mature product that has an extremely large open source community. It is also simpler to operate than Mesos, and more flexible than Docker Swarm.

The most important thing to take away from this comparison is that although there are multiple relevant options for container orchestration and some are indeed better in certain ways, Kubernetes has emerged as the de facto standard. With this in mind, let's take a look at how Kubernetes works.

Kubernetes' architecture

Kubernetes is an orchestration tool that can run on cloud VMs, on VMs running in your data center, or on bare metal servers. In general, Kubernetes runs on a set of nodes, each of which can each be a VM or a physical machine.

Kubernetes node types

Kubernetes nodes can be many different things – from a VM, to a bare metal host, to a Raspberry Pi. Kubernetes nodes are split into two distinct categories: first, the master nodes, which run the Kubernetes control plane applications; second, the worker nodes, which run the applications that you deploy onto Kubernetes.

In general, for high availability, a production deployment of Kubernetes should have a minimum of three master nodes and three worker nodes, though most large deployments have many more workers than masters.

The Kubernetes control plane

The Kubernetes control plane is a suite of applications and services that run on the master nodes. There are several highly specialized services at play that form the core of Kubernetes functionality. They are as follows:

- **kube-apiserver**: This is the Kubernetes API server. This application handles instructions sent to Kubernetes.

- **kube-scheduler**: This is the Kubernetes scheduler. This component handles the work of deciding which nodes to place workloads on, which can become quite complex.

- **kube-controller-manager**: This is the Kubernetes controller manager. This component provides a high-level control loop that ensures that the desired configuration of the cluster and applications running on it is implemented.

- **etcd**: This is a distributed key-value store that contains the cluster configuration.

Generally, all of these components take the form of system services that run on every master node. They can be started manually if you wanted to bootstrap your cluster entirely by hand, but through the use of a cluster creation library or cloud provider-managed service such as **Elastic Kubernetes Service (EKS)**, this will usually be done automatically in a production setting.

The Kubernetes API server

The Kubernetes API server is a component that accepts HTTPS requests, typically on port 443. It presents a certificate, which can be self-signed, as well as authentication and authorization mechanisms, which we will cover later in this chapter.

When a configuration request is made to the Kubernetes API server, it will check the current cluster configuration in etcd and change it if necessary.

The Kubernetes API is generally a RESTful API, with endpoints for each Kubernetes resource type, along with an API version that is passed in the query path; for instance, /api/v1.

For the purposes of extending Kubernetes (see *Chapter 13, Extending Kubernetes with CRDs*), the API also has a set of dynamic endpoints based on API groups, which can expose the same RESTful API functionality to custom resources.

The Kubernetes scheduler

The Kubernetes scheduler decides where instances of a workload should be run. By default, this decision is influenced by workload resource requirements and node status. You can also influence the scheduler via placement controls that are configurable in Kubernetes (see *Chapter 8, Pod Placement Controls*). These controls can act on node labels, which other pods are already running on a node, and many other possibilities.

The Kubernetes controller manager

The Kubernetes controller manager is a component that runs several controllers. Controllers run control loops that ensure that the actual state of the cluster matches that stored in the configuration. By default, these include the following:

- The node controller, which ensures that nodes are up and running

- The replication controller, which ensures that each workload is scaled properly

- The endpoints controller, which handles communication and routing configuration for each workload (see *Chapter 5, Services and Ingress – Communicating with the Outside World*)

- Service account and token controllers, which handle the creation of API access tokens and default accounts

etcd

etcd is a distributed key-value store that houses the configuration of the cluster in a highly available way. An `etcd` replica runs on each master node and uses the Raft consensus algorithm, which ensures that a quorum is maintained before allowing any changes to the keys or values.

The Kubernetes worker nodes

Each Kubernetes worker node contains components that allow it to communicate with the control plane and handle networking.

First, there is the **kubelet**, which makes sure that containers are running on the node as dictated by the cluster configuration. Second, **kube-proxy** provides a network proxy layer to workloads running on each node. And finally, the **container runtime** is used to run the workloads on each node.

kubelet

The kubelet is an agent that runs on every node (including master nodes, though it has a different configuration in that context). Its main purpose is to receive a list of PodSpecs (more on those later) and ensure that the containers prescribed by them are running on the node. The kubelet gets these PodSpecs through a few different possible mechanisms, but the main way is by querying the Kubernetes API server. Alternately, the kubelet can be started with a file path, which it will monitor for a list of PodSpecs, an HTTP endpoint to monitor, or its own HTTP endpoint to receive requests on.

kube-proxy

kube-proxy is a network proxy that runs on every node. Its main purpose is to do TCP, UDP, and SCTP forwarding (either via stream or round-robin) to workloads running on its node. kube-proxy supports the Kubernetes `Service` construct, which we will discuss in *Chapter 5, Services and Ingress – Communicating with the Outside World*.

The container runtime

The container runtime runs on each node and is the component that actually runs your workloads. Kubernetes supports CRI-O, Docker, containerd, rktlet, and any valid **Container Runtime Interface (CRI)** runtime. As of Kubernetes v1.14, the RuntimeClass feature has been moved from alpha to beta and allows for workload-specific runtime selection.

Addons

In addition to the core cluster components, a typical Kubernetes installation includes addons, which are additional components that provide cluster functionality.

For example, **Container Network Interface (CNI)** plugins such as `Calico`, `Flannel`, or `Weave` provide overlay network functionality that adheres to Kubernetes' networking requirements.

CoreDNS, on the other hand, is a popular addon for in-cluster DNS and service discovery. There are also tools such as Kubernetes Dashboard, which provides a GUI for viewing and interacting with your cluster.

At this point, you should have a high-level idea of the major components of Kubernetes. Next, we will review how a user interacts with Kubernetes to control those components.

Authentication and authorization on Kubernetes

Namespaces are an extremely important concept in Kubernetes, and since they can affect API access as well as authorization, we'll cover them now.

Namespaces

A namespace in Kubernetes is a construct that allows you to group Kubernetes resources in your cluster. They are a method of separation with many possible uses. For instance, you could have a namespace in your cluster for each environment – dev, staging, and production.

By default, Kubernetes will create the default namespace, the `kube-system` namespace, and the `kube-public` namespace. Resources created without a specified namespace will be created in the default namespace. `kube-system` contains the cluster services such as `etcd`, the scheduler, and any resource created by Kubernetes itself and not users. `kube-public` is readable by all users by default and can be used for public resources.

Users

There are two types of users in Kubernetes – regular users and service accounts.

Regular users are generally managed by a service outside the cluster, whether they be private keys, usernames and passwords, or some form of user store. Service accounts however are managed by Kubernetes and restricted to specific namespaces. To create a service account, the Kubernetes API may automatically make one, or they can be made manually through calls to the Kubernetes API.

There are three possible types of requests to the Kubernetes API – those associated with a regular user, those associated with a service account, and anonymous requests.

Authentication methods

In order to authenticate requests, Kubernetes provides several different options: HTTP basic authentication, client certificates, bearer tokens, and proxy-based authentication.

To use HTTP authentication, the requestor sends requests with an `Authorization` header that will have the value bearer `"token value"`.

In order to specify which tokens are valid, a CSV file can be provided to the API server application when it starts using the `--token-auth-file=filename` parameter. A new beta feature (as of the writing of this book), called *Bootstrap Tokens*, allows for the dynamic swapping and changing of tokens while the API server is running, without restarting it.

Basic username/password authentication is also possible via the `Authorization` token, by using the header value `Basic base64encoded(username:password)`.

Kubernetes' certificate infrastructure for TLS and security

In order to use client certificates (X.509 certificates), the API server must be started using the `--client-ca-file=filename` parameter. This file needs to contain one or more **Certificate Authorities (CAs)** that will be used when validating certificates passed with API requests.

In addition to the **CA**, a **Certificate Signing Request (CSR)** must be created for each user. At this point, user `groups` can be included, which we will discuss in the *Authorization options* section.

For instance, you can use the following:

```
openssl req -new -key myuser.pem -out myusercsr.pem -subj "/
CN=myuser/O=dev/O=staging"
```

This will create a CSR for the user `myuser` who is part of groups named `dev` and `staging`.

Once the CA and CSR are created, the actual client and server certificates can be created using `openssl`, `easyrsa`, `cfssl`, or any certificate generation tool. TLS certificates for the Kubernetes API can also be created at this point.

Since our aim is to get you started running workloads on Kubernetes as soon as possible, we will leave all the various possible certificate configurations out of this book – but both the Kubernetes documentation and the article *Kubernetes The Hard Way* have some great tutorials on setting up a cluster from scratch. In the majority of production settings, you will not be doing these steps manually.

Authorization options

Kubernetes provides several authorization methods: nodes, webhooks, RBAC, and ABAC. In this book, we will focus on RBAC and ABAC as they are the ones used most often for user authorization. If you extend your cluster with other services and/or custom features, the other authorization modes may become more important.

RBAC

RBAC stands for **Role-Based Access Control** and is a common pattern for authorization. In Kubernetes specifically, the roles and users of RBAC are implemented using four Kubernetes resources: Role, ClusterRole, RoleBinding, and ClusterRoleBinding. To enable RBAC mode, the API server can be started with the --authorization-mode=RBAC parameter.

Role and ClusterRole resources specify a set of permissions, but do not assign those permissions to any specific users. Permissions are specified using resources and verbs. Here is a sample YAML file specifying a Role. Don't worry too much about the first few lines of the YAML file – we'll get to those soon. Focus on the resources and verbs lines to see how the actions can be applied to resources:

Read-only-role.yaml

```
apiVersion: rbac.authorization.k8s.io/v1
kind: Role
metadata:
  namespace: default
  name: read-only-role
rules:
- apiGroups: [""]
  resources: ["pods"]
  verbs: ["get", "list"]
```

The only difference between a Role and ClusterRole is that a Role is restricted to a particular namespace (in this case, the default namespace), while a ClusterRole can affect access to all resources of that type in the cluster, as well as cluster-scoped resources such as nodes.

RoleBinding and ClusterRoleBinding are resources that associate a
Role or ClusterRole with a user or a list of users. The following file represents
a RoleBinding resource to connect our read-only-role with a user,
readonlyuser:

Read-only-rb.yaml

```
apiVersion: rbac.authorization.k8s.io/v1namespace.
kind: RoleBinding
metadata:
  name: read-only
  namespace: default
subjects:
- kind: User
  name: readonlyuser
  apiGroup: rbac.authorization.k8s.io
roleRef:
  kind: Role
  name: read-only-role
  apiGroup: rbac.authorization.k8s.io
```

The subjects key contains a list of all entities to associate a role with; in this case, the
user alex. roleRef contains the name of the role to associate, and the type (either
Role or ClusterRole).

ABAC

ABAC stands for **Attribute-Based Access Control**. ABAC works using *policies* instead
of roles. The API server is started in ABAC mode with a file called an authorization
policy file, which contains a list of JSON objects called policy objects. To enable ABAC
mode, the API server can be started with the --authorization-mode=ABAC and
--authorization-policy-file=filename parameters.

In the policy file, each policy object contains information about a single policy: firstly,
which subjects it corresponds to, which can be either users or groups, and secondly, which
resources can be accessed via the policy. Additionally, a Boolean readonly value can be
included to limit the policy to list, get, and watch operations.

A secondary type of policy is associated not with a resource, but with types of
non-resource requests, such as calls to the /version endpoint.

When a request to the API is made in ABAC mode, the API server will check the user and any group it is a part of against the list in the policy file, and see if any policies match the resource or endpoint that the user is trying to access. On a match, the API server will authorize the request.

You should have a good understanding now of how the Kubernetes API handles authentication and authorization. The good news is that while you can directly access the API, Kubernetes provides an excellent command-line tool to simply authenticate and make Kubernetes API requests.

Using kubectl and YAML

kubectl is the officially supported command-line tool for accessing the Kubernetes API. It can be installed on Linux, macOS, or Windows.

Setting up kubectl and kubeconfig

To install the newest release of kubectl, you can use the installation instructions at `https://kubernetes.io/docs/tasks/tools/install-kubectl/`.

Once kubectl is installed, it needs to be set up to authenticate with one or more clusters. This is done using the `kubeconfig` file, which looks like this:

Example-kubeconfig

```
apiVersion: v1
kind: Config
preferences: {}

clusters:
- cluster:
    certificate-authority: fake-ca-file
    server: https://1.2.3.4
  name: development

users:
- name: alex
  user:
    password: mypass
    username: alex
```

```
contexts:
- context:
    cluster: development
    namespace: frontend
    user: developer
  name: development
```

This file is written in YAML and is very similar to other Kubernetes resource specifications that we will get to shortly – except that this file lives only on your local machine.

There are three sections to a `Kubeconfig` YAML file: `clusters`, `users`, and `contexts`:

- The `clusters` section is a list of clusters that you will be able to access via kubectl, including the CA filename and server API endpoint.

- The `users` section lists users that you will be able to authorize with, including any user certificates or username/password combinations for authentication.

- Finally, the `contexts` section lists combinations of a cluster, a namespace, and a user that combine to make a context. Using the `kubectl config use-context` command, you can easily switch between contexts, which allows easy switching between cluster, user, and namespace combinations.

Imperative versus declarative commands

There are two paradigms for talking to the Kubernetes API: imperative and declarative. Imperative commands allow you to dictate to Kubernetes "what to do" – that is, "spin up two copies of Ubuntu," "scale this application to five copies," and so on.

Declarative commands, on the other hand, allow you to write a file with a specification of what should be running on the cluster, and have the Kubernetes API ensure that the configuration matches the cluster configuration, updating it if necessary.

Though imperative commands allow you to quickly get started with Kubernetes, it is far better to write some YAML and use a declarative configuration when running production workloads, or workloads of any complexity. The reason for this is that it makes it easier to track changes, for instance via a GitHub repo, or introduce Git-driven **Continous Integration/Continuous** Delivery (**CI/CD**) to your cluster.

Some basic kubectl commands

kubectl provides many convenient commands for checking the current state of your cluster, querying resources, and creating new ones. kubectl is structured so most commands can access resources in the same way.

First, let's learn how to see Kubernetes resources in your cluster. You can do this by using `kubectl get resource_type` where `resource_type` is the full name of the Kubernetes resource, or alternately, a shorter alias. A full list of aliases (and `kubectl` commands) can be found in the kubectl documentation at `https://kubernetes. io/docs/reference/kubectl/overview`.

We already know about nodes, so let's start with that. To find which nodes exist in a cluster, we can use `kubectl get nodes` or the alias `kubectl get no`.

kubectl's `get` commands return a list of Kubernetes resources that are currently in the cluster. We can run this command with any Kubernetes resource type. To add additional information to the list, you can add the `wide` output flag: `kubectl get nodes -o wide`.

Listing resources isn't enough, of course – we need to be able to see the details of a particular resource. For this, we use the `describe` command, which works similarly to `get`, except that we can optionally pass the name of a specific resource. If this last parameter is omitted, Kubernetes will return the details of all resources of that type, which will probably result in a lot of scrolling in your terminal.

For example, `kubectl describe nodes` will return details for all nodes in the cluster, while `kubectl describe nodes node1` will return a description of the node named `node1`.

As you've probably noticed, these commands are all in the imperative style, which makes sense since we're just fetching information about existing resources, not creating new ones. To create a Kubernetes resource, we can use the following:

- `kubectl create -f /path/to/file.yaml`, which is an imperative command
- `kubectl apply -f /path/to/file.yaml`, which is declarative

Both commands take a path to a file, which can be either YAML or JSON – or you can just use `stdin`. You can also pass in the path to a folder instead of a file, which will create or apply all YAML or JSON files in that folder. `create` works imperatively, so it will create a new resource, but if you run it again with the same file, the command will fail since the resource already exists. `apply` works declaratively, so if you run it the first time it will create the resource, and subsequent runs will update the running resource in Kubernetes with any changes. You can use the `--dry-run` flag to see the output of the `create` or `apply` commands (that is, what resources will be created, or any errors if they exist).

To update existing resources imperatively, use the `edit` command like so: `kubectl edit resource_type resource_name` – just like with our `describe` command. This will open up the default terminal editor with the YAML of the existing resource, regardless of whether you created it imperatively or declaratively. You can edit this and save as usual, which will trigger an automatic update of the resource in Kubernetes.

To update existing resources declaratively, you can edit your local YAML resource file that you used to create the resource in the first place, then run `kubectl apply -f /path/to/file.yaml`. Deleting resources is best accomplished via the imperative command `kubectl delete resource_type resource_name`.

The last command we'll talk about in this section is `kubectl cluster-info`, which will show the IP addresses where the major Kubernetes cluster services are running.

Writing Kubernetes resource YAML files

For communicating with the Kubernetes API declaratively, formats of both YAML and JSON are allowed. For the purposes of this book, we will stick to YAML since it is a bit cleaner and takes up less space on the page. A typical Kubernetes resource YAML file looks like this:

resource.yaml

```
apiVersion: v1
kind: Pod
```

```
metadata:
  name: my-pod
spec:
  containers:
  - name: ubuntu
    image: ubuntu:trusty
    command: ["echo"]
    args: ["Hello Readers"]
```

A valid Kubernetes YAML file has four top-level keys at a minimum. They are `apiVersion`, `kind`, `metadata`, and `spec`.

`apiVersion` dictates which version of the Kubernetes API will be used to create the resource. `kind` specifies what type of resource the YAML file is referencing. `metadata` provides a location to name the resource, as well as adding annotations and name-spacing information (more on that later). And finally, the `spec` key will contain all the resource-specific information that Kubernetes needs to create the resource in your cluster.

Don't worry about `kind` and `spec` quite yet – we'll get to what a `Pod` is in *Chapter 3, Running Application Containers on Kubernetes.*

Summary

In this chapter, we learned the background behind container orchestration, an architectural overview of a Kubernetes cluster, how a cluster authenticates and authorizes API calls, and how to communicate with the API via imperative and declarative patterns using kubectl, the officially supported command-line tool for Kubernetes.

In the next chapter, we'll learn several ways to get started with a test cluster, and master harnessing the kubectl commands you've learned so far.

Questions

1. What is container orchestration?
2. What are the constituent parts of the Kubernetes control plane, and what do they do?
3. How would you start the Kubernetes API server in ABAC authorization mode?
4. Why is it important to have more than one master node for a production Kubernetes cluster?

5.   What is the difference between `kubectl apply` and `kubectl create`?

6.   How would you switch between contexts using `kubectl`?

7.   What are the downsides of creating a Kubernetes resource declaratively and then editing it imperatively?

Further reading

- The official Kubernetes documentation: `https://kubernetes.io/docs/home/`

- *Kubernetes The Hard Way*: `https://github.com/kelseyhightower/kubernetes-the-hard-way`

2
Setting Up Your Kubernetes Cluster

This chapter contains a review of some of the possibilities for creating a Kubernetes cluster, which we'll need to be able to learn the rest of the concepts in this book. We'll start with minikube, a tool to create a simple local cluster, then touch on some additional, more advanced (and production-ready) tools and review the major managed Kubernetes services from public cloud providers, before we finally introduce the strategies for creating a cluster from scratch.

In this chapter, we will cover the following topics:

- Options for creating your first cluster
- minikube – an easy way to start
- Managed services – EKS, GKE, AKS, and more
- Kubeadm – simple conformance
- Kops – infrastructure bootstrapping
- Kubespray – Ansible-powered cluster creation
- Creating a cluster completely from scratch

Technical requirements

In order to run the commands in this chapter, you will need to have the kubectl tool installed. Installation instructions are available in *Chapter 1, Communicating with Kubernetes.*

If you are actually going to create a cluster using any of the methods in this chapter, you will need to review the specific technical requirements for each method in the relevant project's documentation. For minikube specifically, most machines running Linux, macOS, or Windows will work. For large clusters, please review the specific documentation of the tool you plan to use.

The code used in this chapter can be found in the book's GitHub repository at the following link:

```
https://github.com/PacktPublishing/Cloud-Native-with-
Kubernetes/tree/master/Chapter2
```

Options for creating a cluster

There are many ways to create a Kubernetes cluster, ranging from simple local tools all the way to fully creating a cluster from scratch.

If you're just getting started with learning Kubernetes, you'll probably want to spin up a simple local cluster with a tool such as minikube.

If you're looking to build a production cluster for an application, you have several options:

- You can use a tool such as Kops, Kubespray, or Kubeadm to create the cluster programmatically.
- You can use a managed Kubernetes service.
- You can create a cluster completely from scratch on VMs or physical hardware.

Unless you have extremely specific demands in terms of cluster configuration (and even then), it is not usually recommended to create your cluster completely from scratch without using a bootstrapping tool.

For most use cases, the decision will be between using a managed Kubernetes service on a cloud provider and using a bootstrapping tool.

In air-gapped systems, using a bootstrapping tool is the only way to go – but some are better than others for particular use cases. In particular, Kops is aimed at making it easier to create and manage clusters on cloud providers such as AWS.

> **Important note**
>
> Not included in this section is a discussion of alternative third-party managed services or cluster creation and administration tools such as Rancher or OpenShift. When making a selection for running clusters in production, it is important to take into account a large variety of factors including the current infrastructure, business requirements, and much more. To keep things simple, in this book we will focus on production clusters, assuming no other infrastructure or hyper-specific business needs – a "clean slate," so to speak.

minikube – an easy way to start

minikube is the easiest way to get started with a simple local cluster. This cluster won't be set up for high availability, and is not aimed at production uses, but it is a great way to get started running workloads on Kubernetes in minutes.

Installing minikube

minikube can be installed on Windows, macOS, and Linux. What follows is the installation instructions for all three platforms, which you can also find by navigating to `https://minikube.sigs.k8s.io/docs/start`.

Installing on Windows

The easiest installation method on Windows is to download and run the minikube installer from `https://storage.googleapis.com/minikube/releases/latest/minikube-installer.exe`.

Installing on macOS

Use the following command to download and install the binary. You can find it in the code repository as well:

Minikube-install-mac.sh

```
    curl -LO https://storage.googleapis.com/minikube/releases/
latest/minikube-darwin-amd64 \
&& sudo install minikube-darwin-amd64 /usr/local/bin/minikube
```

Installing on Linux

Use the following command to download and install the binary:

Minikube-install-linux.sh

```
curl -LO https://storage.googleapis.com/minikube/releases/
latest/minikube-linux-amd64 \
&& sudo install minikube-linux-amd64 /usr/local/bin/minikube
```

Creating a cluster on minikube

To get started with a cluster on minikube, simply run `minikube start`, which will create a simple local cluster with the default VirtualBox VM driver. minikube also has several additional configuration options that can be reviewed at the documentation site.

Running the `minikube start` command will automatically configure your `kubeconfig` file so you can run `kubectl` commands without any further configuration on your newly created cluster.

Managed Kubernetes services

The number of managed cloud providers that offer a managed Kubernetes service is always growing. However, for the purposes of this book, we will focus on the major public clouds and their particular Kubernetes offerings. This includes the following:

- **Amazon Web Services (AWS) – Elastic Kubernetes Service (EKS)**
- Google Cloud – **Google Kubernetes Engine (GKE)**
- Microsoft Azure – **Azure Kubernetes Service (AKS)**

> **Important note**
>
> The number and implementation of managed Kubernetes services is always changing. AWS, Google Cloud, and Azure were selected for this section of the book because they are very likely to continue working in the same manner. Whatever managed service you use, make sure to check the official documentation provided with the service to ensure that the cluster creation procedure is still the same as what is presented in this book.

Benefits of managed Kubernetes services

Generally, the major managed Kubernetes service offerings provide a few benefits. Firstly, all three of the managed service offerings we're reviewing provide a completely managed Kubernetes control plane.

This means that when you use one of these managed Kubernetes services, you do not need to worry about your master nodes. They are abstracted away and may as well not exist. All three of these managed clusters allow you to choose the number of worker nodes when creating a cluster.

Another benefit of a managed cluster is seamless upgrades from one version of Kubernetes to another. Generally, once a new version of Kubernetes (not always the newest version) is validated for the managed service, you should be able to upgrade using a push button or a reasonably simple procedure.

Drawbacks of managed Kubernetes services

Although a managed Kubernetes cluster can make operations easier in many respects, there are also some downsides.

For many of the managed Kubernetes services available, the minimum cost for a managed cluster far exceeds the cost of a minimal cluster created manually or with a tool such as Kops. For production use cases, this is generally not as much of an issue because a production cluster should contain a minimum amount of nodes anyway, but for development environments or test clusters, the additional cost may not be worth the ease of operations depending on the budget.

Additionally, though abstracting away master nodes makes operations easier, it also prevents fine tuning or advanced master node functionality that may otherwise be available on clusters with defined masters.

AWS – Elastic Kubernetes Service

AWS' managed Kubernetes service is called EKS, or Elastic Kubernetes Service. There are a few different ways to get started with EKS, but we'll cover the simplest way.

Getting started

In order to create an EKS cluster, you must provision the proper **Virtual Private Cloud (VPC)** and **Identity and Access Management (IAM)** role settings – at which point you can create a cluster through the console. These settings can be created manually through the console, or through infrastructure provisioning tools such as CloudFormation and Terraform. Full instructions for creating a cluster through the console can be found at `https://docs.aws.amazon.com/en_pv/eks/latest/userguide/getting-started-console.html`.

Assuming you're creating a cluster and VPC from scratch, however, you can instead use a tool called `eksctl` to provision your cluster.

To install `eksctl`, you can find installation instructions for macOS, Linux, and Windows at `https://docs.aws.amazon.com/eks/latest/userguide/getting-started-eksctl.html`.

Once you have `eksctl` installed, creating a cluster is as simple as using the `eksctl create cluster` command:

Eks-create-cluster.sh

```
eksctl create cluster \
  --name prod \
  --version 1.17 \
  --nodegroup-name standard-workers \
  --node-type t2.small \
  --nodes 3 \
  --nodes-min 1 \
  --nodes-max 4 \
  --node-ami auto
```

This will create a cluster of three `t2.small` instances as worker nodes set up in an autoscaling group with a minimum of one node and a maximum of four. The Kubernetes version that is used will be `1.17`. Importantly, `eksctl` starts with a default region, and depending on the number of nodes chosen, they will be spread throughout multiple availability zones in that region.

`eksctl` will also automatically update your `kubeconfig` file, so you should be able to run `kubectl` commands immediately after the cluster creation process is finished.

Test the configuration with the following code:

```
kubectl get nodes
```

You should see a list of your nodes and their associated IPs. Your cluster is ready! Next, let's take a look at Google's GKE setup process.

Google Cloud – Google Kubernetes Engine

GKE is Google Cloud's managed Kubernetes service. With the gcloud command-line tool, it is very easy to quickly spin up a GKE cluster.

Getting started

To create a cluster on GKE using gcloud, you can either use Google Cloud's Cloud Shell service, or run the commands locally. If you want to run the commands locally, you must install the gcloud CLI via the Google Cloud SDK. See https://cloud.google.com/sdk/docs/quickstarts for installation instructions.

Once you have gcloud installed, you need to ensure that you have activated the GKE API in your Google Cloud account.

To easily accomplish this, navigate to https://console.cloud.google.com/apis/library, then search for kubernetes in the search bar. Click on **Kubernetes Engine API** and then click **Enable**.

Now that the API is activated, set your project and compute zone in Google Cloud by using the following commands:

```
gcloud config set project proj_id
gcloud config set compute/zone compute_zone
```

In the commands, proj_id corresponds to the project ID in Google Cloud that you want to create your cluster in, and compute_zone corresponds to your desired compute zone in Google Cloud.

There are actually three types of clusters on GKE, each with different (increasing) levels of reliability and fault tolerance:

- Single-zone clusters
- Multi-zonal clusters
- Regional clusters

A **single-zone** cluster in GKE means a cluster that has a single control plane replica and one or more worker nodes running in the same Google Cloud zone. If something happens to the zone, both the control plane and the workers (and thus the workloads) will go down.

A **multi-zonal** cluster in GKE means a cluster that has a single control plane replica and two or more worker nodes running in different Google Cloud zones. This means that if a single zone (even the zone containing the control plane) goes down, the workloads running in the cluster will still persist, but the Kubernetes API will be unavailable until the control plane zone comes back up.

Finally, a **regional cluster** in GKE means a cluster that has both a multi-zonal control plane and multi-zonal worker nodes. If any zone goes down, both the control plane and the workloads on the worker nodes will persist. This is the most expensive and reliable option.

Now, to actually create your cluster, you can run the following command to create a cluster named `dev` with the default settings:

```
gcloud container clusters create dev \
    --zone [compute_zone]
```

This command will create a single-zone cluster in your chosen compute zone.

In order to create a multi-zonal cluster, you can run the following command:

```
gcloud container clusters create dev \
    --zone [compute_zone_1]
    --node-locations [compute_zone_1],[compute_zone_2],[etc]
```

Here, `compute_zone_1` and `compute_zone_2` are disparate Google Cloud zones. In addition, more zones can be added via the `node-locations` flag.

Finally, to create a regional cluster, you can run the following command:

```
gcloud container clusters create dev \
    --region [region] \
    --node-locations [compute_zone_1],[compute_zone_2],[etc]
```

In this case, the `node-locations` flag is actually optional. If left out, the cluster will be created with worker nodes in all the zones within the region. If you'd like to change this default behavior, you can override it using the `node-locations` flag.

Now that you have a cluster running, you need to configure your `kubeconfig` file to communicate with the cluster. To do this, simply pass the cluster name into the following command:

```
gcloud container clusters get-credentials [cluster_name]
```

Finally, test the configuration with the following command:

```
kubectl get nodes
```

As with EKS, you should see a list of all your provisioned nodes. Success! Finally, let's take a look at Azure's managed offering.

Microsoft Azure – Azure Kubernetes Service

Microsoft Azure's managed Kubernetes service is called AKS. Creating a cluster on AKS can be done via the Azure CLI.

Getting started

To create a cluster on AKS, you can use the Azure CLI tool and run the following command to create a service principal (a role that the cluster will use to access Azure resources):

```
az ad sp create-for-rbac --skip-assignment --name
myClusterPrincipal
```

The result of this command will be a JSON object with information on the service principal, which we will use in the next step. This JSON object looks like the following:

```
{
  "appId": "559513bd-0d99-4c1a-87cd-851a26afgf88",
  "displayName": "myClusterPrincipal",
  "name": "http://myClusterPrincipal",
  "password": "e763725a-5eee-892o-a466-dc88d980f415",
  "tenant": "72f988bf-90jj-41af-91ab-2d7cd011db48"
}
```

Now, you can use the values from the previous JSON command to actually create your AKS cluster:

Aks-create-cluster.sh

```
az aks create \
    --resource-group devResourceGroup \
    --name myCluster \
    --node-count 2 \
    --service-principal <appId> \
    --client-secret <password> \
    --generate-ssh-keys
```

This command assumes a resource group named `devResourceGroup`, and a cluster named `devCluster`. For `appId` and `password`, use the values from the service principal creation step.

Finally, to generate the proper `kubectl` configuration on your machine, you can run the following command:

```
az aks get-credentials --resource-group devResourceGroup --name myCluster
```

At this point, you should be able to properly run `kubectl` commands. Test the configuration with the `kubectl get nodes` command.

Programmatic cluster creation tools

There are several tools available that will bootstrap a Kubernetes cluster in various non-managed environments. We'll focus on three of the most popular: Kubeadm, Kops, and Kubespray. Each tool is aimed at a different use case and generally works by a different method.

Kubeadm

Kubeadm is a tool created by the Kubernetes community to simplify cluster creation on infrastructure that is already provisioned. Unlike Kops, Kubeadm does not have the ability to provision infrastructure on cloud services. It simply creates a best-practices cluster that will pass Kubernetes conformance tests. Kubeadm is agnostic to infrastructure – it should work anywhere you can run Linux VMs.

Kops

Kops is a popular cluster provisioning tool. It provisions the underlying infrastructure for your cluster, installs all cluster components, and validates the functionality of your cluster. It can also be used to perform various cluster operations such as upgrades, node rotations, and more. Kops currently supports AWS, with (as of the time of writing this book) beta support for Google Compute Engine and OpenStack, and alpha support for VMware vSphere and DigitalOcean.

Kubespray

Kubespray is different to both Kops and Kubeadm. Unlike Kops, Kubespray does not inherently provision cluster resources. Instead, Kubespray allows you to choose between Ansible and Vagrant in order to perform provisioning, orchestration, and node setup.

When compared to Kubeadm, Kubespray has far fewer integrated cluster creation and life cycle processes. Newer versions of Kubespray allow you to use Kubeadm specifically for cluster creation after node setup.

> **Important note**
>
> Since creating a cluster with Kubespray requires some Ansible-specific domain knowledge, we will keep that discussion out of this book – but a guide to all things Kubespray can be found at `https://github.com/kubernetes-sigs/kubespray/blob/master/docs/getting-started.md`.

Creating a cluster with Kubeadm

To create a cluster with Kubeadm, you will need your nodes provisioned ahead of time. As with any other Kubernetes cluster, we'll need VMs or bare-metal servers running Linux.

For the purposes of this book, we will show how to bootstrap a Kubeadm cluster with only a single master node. For highly available setups, you'll need to run additional join commands on the other master nodes, which you can find at `https://kubernetes.io/docs/setup/production-environment/tools/kubeadm/high-availability/`.

Installing Kubeadm

First things first – you'll need to install Kubeadm on all nodes. The installation instructions for each supported operating system can be found at `https://kubernetes.io/docs/setup/production-environment/tools/kubeadm/install-kubeadm`.

For each node, also make sure to check that all the required ports are open, and that you've installed your intended container runtime.

Starting the master nodes

To quickly start master nodes with Kubeadm, you only need to run a single command:

```
kubeadm init
```

This initialization command can take in several optional arguments – depending on your preferred cluster setup, networking, and so on, you may need to use them.

In the output of the `init` command, you'll see a `kubeadm join` command. Make sure to save this command.

Starting the worker nodes

In order to bootstrap the worker nodes, you need to run the `join` command you saved. The command will be of the following form:

```
kubeadm join --token [TOKEN] [IP ON MASTER]:[PORT ON MASTER]
--discovery-token-ca-cert-hash sha256:[HASH VALUE]
```

The token in this command is a bootstrap token. It is used to authenticate nodes with each other and join new nodes to the cluster. With access to this token comes the power to join new nodes to the cluster, so treat it as such.

Setting up kubectl

With Kubeadm, kubectl will already be properly set up on the master node. However, to use kubectl from any other machine or outside the cluster, you can copy the config from the master to your local machine:

```
scp root@[IP OF MASTER]:/etc/kubernetes/admin.conf .
kubectl --kubeconfig ./admin.conf get nodes
```

This `kubeconfig` will be the cluster administrator config – in order to specify other users (and permissions), you will need to add new service accounts and generate `kubeconfig` files for them.

Creating a cluster with Kops

Since Kops will provision infrastructure for you, there is no need to pre-create any nodes. All you need to do is install Kops, ensure your cloud platform credentials are working, and create your cluster all at once. Kops can be installed on Linux, macOS, and Windows.

For this tutorial, we will go through creating a cluster on AWS, but you can find instructions for other supported Kops platforms in the Kops documentation at `https://github.com/kubernetes/kops/tree/master/docs`.

Installing on macOS

On OS X, the easiest way to install Kops is using Homebrew:

```
brew update && brew install kops
```

Alternatively, you can grab the newest stable Kops binary from the Kops GitHub page at `https://github.com/kubernetes/kops/releases/tag/1.12.3`.

Installing on Linux

On Linux, you can install Kops via the following command:

Kops-linux-install.sh

```
curl -LO https://github.com/kubernetes/kops/releases/
download/$(curl -s https://api.github.com/repos/kubernetes/
kops/releases/latest | grep tag_name | cut -d '"' -f 4)/kops-
linux-amd64
chmod +x kops-linux-amd64
sudo mv kops-linux-amd64 /usr/local/bin/kops
```

Installing on Windows

To install Kops on Windows, you'll need to download the newest Windows release from `https://github.com/kubernetes/kops/releases/latest`, rename it to `kops.exe`, and add it to your `path` variable.

Setting up credentials for Kops

In order for Kops to work, you'll need AWS credentials on your machine with a few required IAM permissions. To do this safely, you will want to create an IAM user specifically for Kops.

First, create an IAM group for the kops user:

```
aws iam create-group --group-name kops_users
```

Then, attach the required roles for the kops_users group. To function properly, Kops will need AmazonEC2FullAccess, AmazonRoute53FullAccess, AmazonS3FullAccess, IAMFullAccess, and AmazonVPCFullAccess. We can accomplish this by running the following commands:

Provide-aws-policies-to-kops.sh

```
aws iam attach-group-policy --policy-arn
arn:aws:iam::aws:policy/AmazonEC2FullAccess --group-name kops
```
```
aws iam attach-group-policy --policy-arn
arn:aws:iam::aws:policy/AmazonRoute53FullAccess --group-name
kops
```
```
aws iam attach-group-policy --policy-arn
arn:aws:iam::aws:policy/AmazonS3FullAccess --group-name kops
```
```
aws iam attach-group-policy --policy-arn
arn:aws:iam::aws:policy/IAMFullAccess --group-name kops
```
```
aws iam attach-group-policy --policy-arn
arn:aws:iam::aws:policy/AmazonVPCFullAccess --group-name kops
```

Finally, create the kops user, add it to the kops_users group, and create programmatic access keys, which you should save:

```
aws iam create-user --user-name kops
```
```
aws iam add-user-to-group --user-name kops --group-name kops_
users
```
```
aws iam create-access-key --user-name kops
```

To allow Kops to access your new IAM credentials, you can use the following commands to configure your AWS CLI with the access key and secret from the previous command (`create-access-key`):

```
aws configure
export AWS_ACCESS_KEY_ID=$(aws configure get aws_access_key_id)
export AWS_SECRET_ACCESS_KEY=$(aws configure get aws_secret_access_key)
```

Setting up state storage

With the proper credentials set up, we can start creating our cluster. In this case, we're going to build a simple gossip-based cluster so we won't need to mess around with DNS. To see the possible DNS setups, you can look at the Kops documentation (`https://github.com/kubernetes/kops/tree/master/docs`).

First, we'll need a location to store our cluster spec. S3 is perfect for this since we're on AWS.

As usual with S3, bucket names need to be unique. You can easily create a bucket using the AWS SDK (make sure to replace `my-domain-dev-state-store` with your desired S3 bucket name):

```
aws s3api create-bucket \
    --bucket my-domain-dev-state-store \
    --region us-east-1
```

It's a best practice to enable bucket encryption and versioning as well:

```
aws s3api put-bucket-versioning --bucket prefix-example-com-state-store  --versioning-configuration Status=Enabled
aws s3api put-bucket-encryption --bucket prefix-example-com-state-store --server-side-encryption-configuration '{"Rules":[{"ApplyServerSideEncryptionByDefault": {"SSEAlgorithm":"AES256"}}]}'
```

Finally, to set up variables for Kops, use the following commands:

```
export NAME=devcluster.k8s.local
export KOPS_STATE_STORE=s3://my-domain-dev-cluster-state-store
```

> **Important note**
>
> Kops supports several state storage locations such as AWS S3, Google Cloud Storage, Kubernetes, DigitalOcean, OpenStack Swift, Alibaba Cloud, and memfs. However, you can just save the Kops state to a local file and use that instead. The benefit of having a cloud-based state store is the ability for multiple infrastructure developers to access and update it with versioning controls.

Creating clusters

With Kops, we can deploy clusters of any size. For the purposes of this guide, we will deploy a production-ready cluster by having both worker and master nodes span three availability zones. We're going to use the US-East-1 region, and both the masters and workers will be t2.medium instances.

To create the config for this cluster, you can run the following kops create command:

Kops-create-cluster.sh

```
kops create cluster \
    --node-count 3 \
    --zones us-east-1a,us-east-1b,us-east-1c \
    --master-zones us-east-1a,us-east-1b,us-east-1c \
    --node-size t2.medium \
    --master-size t2.medium \
    ${NAME}
```

To see the config that has been created, use the following command:

```
kops edit cluster ${NAME}
```

Finally, to create our cluster, run the following command:

```
kops update cluster ${NAME} --yes
```

The cluster creation process may take some time, but once it is complete, your kubeconfig should be properly configured to use kubectl with your new cluster.

Creating a cluster completely from scratch

Creating a Kubernetes cluster entirely from scratch is a multi-step endeavor that could likely span multiple chapters of this book. However, since our purpose is to get you up and running with Kubernetes as quickly as possible, we will refrain from describing the entire process.

If you are interested in creating a cluster from scratch, either for educational reasons or a need to finely customize your cluster, a great guide is *Kubernetes The Hard Way*, which is a full cluster creation tutorial written by *Kelsey Hightower*. It can be found at `https://github.com/kelseyhightower/kubernetes-the-hard-way`.

Now that we've gotten that out of the way, we can proceed with an overview of the manual cluster creation process.

Provisioning your nodes

First things first – you'll need some infrastructure to run Kubernetes on. Generally, VMs are a good candidate for this, though Kubernetes can be run on bare metal as well. If you're working in an environment where you cannot easily add nodes (which removes many of the scaling benefits of the cloud, but is definitely possible in enterprise settings), you'll need enough nodes to meet your application demands. This is more likely to be an issue in air-gapped environments.

Some of your nodes will be used for the master control plane, while others will solely be used as workers. There is no need to make the master and worker nodes identical from a memory or CPU perspective – you could even have some weaker and some more powerful workers. This pattern results in a non-homogeneous cluster, in which certain nodes are better suited to particular workloads.

Creating the Kubernetes certificate authority for TLS

In order to function properly, all major control plane components will need a TLS certificate. To create these, a **Certificate Authority (CA)** needs to be created, which will in turn create the TLS certificates.

To create the CA, a **Public Key Infrastructure (PKI)** needs to be bootstrapped. For this task, you can use any PKI tool, but the one used in the Kubernetes docs is cfssl.

Once the PKI, CA, and TLS certificates have been created for all components, the next step is to create config files for the control plane and worker node components.

Creating config files

Config files need to be created for the `kubelet`, `kube-proxy`, `kube-controller-manager`, and `kube-scheduler` components. They will use the certificates in these config files to authenticate with `kube-apiserver`.

Creating an etcd cluster and configuring encryption

Creating the data encryption config is handled via a YAML file with a data encryption secret. At this point, it is required to start the `etcd` cluster.

To do this, `systemd` files are created on each node with the `etcd` process config. Then `systemctl` is used on each node to start the `etcd` servers.

Here is a sample `systemd` file for `etcd`. The `systemd` files for the other control plane components will be similar to this:

Example-systemd-control-plane

```
[Unit]
Description=etcd
Documentation=https://github.com/coreos

[Service]
Type=notify
ExecStart=/usr/local/bin/etcd \\
  --name ${ETCD_NAME} \\
  --cert-file=/etc/etcd/kubernetes.pem \\
  --key-file=/etc/etcd/kubernetes-key.pem \\
  --peer-cert-file=/etc/etcd/kubernetes.pem \\
  --peer-key-file=/etc/etcd/kubernetes-key.pem \\
  --trusted-ca-file=/etc/etcd/ca.pem \\
  --peer-trusted-ca-file=/etc/etcd/ca.pem \\
  --peer-client-cert-auth \\
  --initial-cluster-state new \\
  --data-dir=/var/lib/etcd
Restart=on-failure
```

```
RestartSec=5

[Install]
WantedBy=multi-user.target
```

This service file provides a runtime definition for our etcd component, which will be started on each master node. To actually start etcd on our node, we run the following command:

```
{
    sudo systemctl daemon-reload
    sudo systemctl enable etcd
    sudo systemctl start etcd
}
```

This enables the etcd service along with automatic restarts when the node is restarted.

Bootstrapping the control plane component

Bootstrapping the control plane components on the master nodes is similar to the process used to create the etcd cluster. systemd files are created for each component – the API server, the controller manager, and the scheduler – and then a systemctl command is used to start each component.

The previously created config files and certificates also need to be included on each master node.

Let's take a look at our service file definition for the kube-apiserver component, broken down into its sections as follows. The Unit section is just a quick description of our systemd file:

```
[Unit]
Description=Kubernetes API Server
Documentation=https://github.com/kubernetes/kubernetes
```

Api-server-systemd-example

This second piece is the actual start command for the services, along with any variables to be passed to the services:

```
[Service]
ExecStart=/usr/local/bin/kube-apiserver \\
```

```
--advertise-address=${INTERNAL_IP} \\
--allow-privileged=true \\
--apiserver-count=3 \\
--audit-log-maxage=30 \\
--audit-log-maxbackup=3 \\
--audit-log-maxsize=100 \\
--audit-log-path=/var/log/audit.log \\
--authorization-mode=Node,RBAC \\
--bind-address=0.0.0.0 \\
--client-ca-file=/var/lib/kubernetes/ca.pem \\
--enable-admission-plugins=NamespaceLifecycle,NodeRestrictio
n,LimitRanger,ServiceAccount,DefaultStorageClass,ResourceQuota
\\
--etcd-cafile=/var/lib/kubernetes/ca.pem \\
--etcd-certfile=/var/lib/kubernetes/kubernetes.pem \\
--etcd-keyfile=/var/lib/kubernetes/kubernetes-key.pem \\
--etcd-
--service-account-key-file=/var/lib/kubernetes/service-
account.pem \\
--service-cluster-ip-range=10.10.0.0/24 \\
--service-node-port-range=30000-32767 \\
--tls-cert-file=/var/lib/kubernetes/kubernetes.pem \\
--tls-private-key-file=/var/lib/kubernetes/kubernetes-key.pem
\\
--v=2
```

Finally, the `Install` section allows us to specify a `WantedBy` target:

```
Restart=on-failure
RestartSec=5
[Install]
WantedBy=multi-user.target
```

The service files for `kube-scheduler` and `kube-controller-manager` will be very similar to the `kube-apiserver` definition, and once we're ready to start the components on the node, the process is easy:

```
{
    sudo systemctl daemon-reload
```

```
   sudo systemctl enable kube-apiserver kube-controller-manager
kube-scheduler
   sudo systemctl start kube-apiserver kube-controller-manager
kube-scheduler
}
```

Similarly to etcd, we want to ensure the services restart on a node shutdown.

Bootstrapping the worker node

It's a similar story on the worker nodes. Service specs for kubelet, the container runtime, cni, and kube-proxy need to be created and run using systemctl. The kubelet config will specify the aforementioned TLS certificate so that it can communicate with the control plane via the API server.

Let's take a look at what our kubelet service definition looks like:

Kubelet-systemd-example

```
[Unit]
Description=Kubernetes Kubelet
Documentation=https://github.com/kubernetes/kubernetes
After=containerd.service
Requires=containerd.service

[Service]
ExecStart=/usr/local/bin/kubelet \\
  --config=/var/lib/kubelet/kubelet-config.yaml \\
  --container-runtime=remote \\
  --container-runtime-endpoint=unix:///var/run/containerd/
containerd.sock \\
  --image-pull-progress-deadline=2m \\
  --kubeconfig=/var/lib/kubelet/kubeconfig \\
  --network-plugin=cni \\
  --register-node=true \\
  --v=2
Restart=on-failure
RestartSec=5
```

```
[Install]
WantedBy=multi-user.target
```

As you can see, this service definition references `cni`, the container runtime, and the `kubelet-config` file. The `kubelet-config` file contains the TLS information we need for our workers.

After bootstrapping the workers and master, the cluster should be functional via the use of the admin `kubeconfig` file that was created as part of the TLS setup.

Summary

In this chapter, we reviewed several methods for creating a Kubernetes cluster. We looked at minimal local cluster creation using minikube, setting up clusters on managed Kubernetes services on Azure, AWS, and Google Cloud, creating clusters using the Kops provisioning tool, and finally, manually creating a cluster from scratch.

Now that we have the skills to create a Kubernetes cluster in several different environments, we can move on to using Kubernetes to run applications.

In the next chapter, we will learn how to start running applications on Kubernetes. The knowledge you've gained about how Kubernetes works at the architectural level should make it much easier to understand the concepts in the next few chapters.

Questions

1. What purpose does minikube serve?

2. What are some downsides to using a managed Kubernetes service?

3. How does Kops compare to Kubeadm? What are the major differences?

4. Which platforms does Kops support?

5. When manually creating a cluster, how are the major cluster components specified? How are they run on each node?

Further reading

- The official Kubernetes documentation: `https://kubernetes.io/docs/home/`

- *Kubernetes The Hard Way*: `https://github.com/kelseyhightower/kubernetes-the-hard-way`

3
Running Application Containers on Kubernetes

This chapter contains a comprehensive overview of the smallest Lego block that Kubernetes provides – the Pod. Included is an explanation of the PodSpec YAML format and possible configurations, and a quick discussion of how Kubernetes handles and schedules Pods. The Pod is the most basic way to run applications on Kubernetes and is used in all higher-order application controllers.

In this chapter, we will cover the following topics:

- What is a Pod?
- Namespaces
- The Pod life cycle
- The Pod resource spec
- Pod scheduling

Technical requirements

In order to run the commands detailed in this chapter, you will need a computer that supports the kubectl command-line tool, along with a working Kubernetes cluster. See *Chapter 1, Communicating with Kubernetes,* for several methods for getting up and running with Kubernetes quickly, and for instructions on how to install the kubectl tool.

The code used in this chapter can be found in the book's GitHub repository at the following link:

https://github.com/PacktPublishing/Cloud-Native-with-Kubernetes/tree/master/Chapter3

What is a Pod?

The Pod is the simplest compute resource in Kubernetes. It specifies one or more containers to be started and run by the Kubernetes scheduler on a node. Pods have many potential configurations and extensions but remain the most basic way to run applications on Kubernetes.

> **Important note**
>
> A Pod by itself is not a very good way to run applications on Kubernetes. Pods should be treated like fdisposable things in order to take advantage of the true capabilities of a container orchestrator like Kubernetes. This means treating containers (and therefore Pods) like cattle, not pets. To really make use of containers and Kubernetes, applications should be run in self-healing, scalable groups. The Pod is the building block of these groups, and we'll get into how to configure applications this way in later chapters.

Implementing Pods

Pods are implemented using Linux isolation tenets such as groups and namespaces, and generally can be thought of as a logical host machine. Pods run one or more containers (which can be based on Docker, CRI-O, or other runtimes) and these containers can communicate with each other in the same ways that different processes on a VM can communicate.

In order for containers within two different Pods to communicate, they need to access the other Pod (and container) via its IP. By default, only containers running on the same Pod can use lower-level methods of communication, though it is possible to configure different Pods with the availability to talk to each other via host IPC.

Pod paradigms

At the most basic level, there are two types of Pods:

- Single-container Pods
- Multi-container Pods

It is generally a best practice to include a single container per Pod. This approach allows you to scale the different parts of your application separately, and generally keeps things simple when it comes to creating a Pod that starts and runs without issues.

Multi-container Pods, on the other hand, are more complex but can be useful in various circumstances:

- If there are multiple parts of your application that run in separate containers but are tightly coupled, you can run them both inside the same Pod to make communication and filesystem access seamless.

- When implementing the *sidecar* pattern, where utility containers are injected alongside your main application to handle logging, metrics, networking, or advanced functionality such as a Service Mesh (more on this in *Chapter 14, Service Meshes and Serverless*).

The following diagram shows a common sidecar implementation:

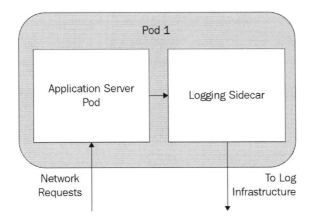

Figure 3.1 – Common sidebar implementation

In this example, we have a single Pod with two containers: our application container running a web server, and a logging application that pulls logs from our server Pod and forwards them to our logging infrastructure. This is a very applicable use of the sidecar pattern, though many log collectors work at the node level, not at the Pod level, so this is not a universal way of collecting logs from our app containers in Kubernetes.

Pod networking

As we just mentioned, Pods have their own IP addresses that can be used in inter-pod communication. Each Pod has an IP address as well as ports, which are shared among the containers running in a Pod if there is more than one container.

Within a Pod, as we mentioned before, containers can communicate without calling the wrapping Pod's IP – instead they can simply use localhost. This is because containers within a Pod share a network namespace – in essence, they communicate via the same *bridge*, which is implemented using a virtual network interface.

Pod storage

Storage in Kubernetes is a large topic on its own, and we will review it in depth in *Chapter 7, Storage on Kubernetes* – but for now, you can think of Pod storage as either persistent or non-persistent volumes attached to a Pod. Non-persistent volumes can be used by a Pod to store data or files depending on the type, but they are deleted when the Pod shuts down. Persistent-type volumes will remain past Pod shutdown and can even be used to share data between multiple Pods or applications.

Before we can continue with our discussion of Pods, we will take a quick moment to discuss namespaces. Since we'll be working with kubectl commands during our work with Pods, it's important to know how namespaces tie into Kubernetes and kubectl, since it can be a big "gotcha."

Namespaces

We talked briefly about namespaces in the section on authorization in *Chapter 1, Communicating with Kubernetes*, but we will reiterate and expand on their purpose here. Namespaces are a way to logically separate different areas within your cluster. A common use case is having a namespace per environment – one for dev, one for staging, one for production – all living inside the same cluster.

As we mentioned in the *Authorization* section, it is possible to specify user permissions on a per-namespace basis – for instance, letting a user deploy new applications and resources to the dev namespace but not to production.

In your running cluster, you can see what namespaces exist by running `kubectl get namespaces` or `kubectl get ns`, which should result in the following output:

NAME	STATUS	AGE
default	Active	1d
kube-system	Active	1d
kube-public	Active	1d

To create a namespace imperatively, you can simply run `kubectl create namespace staging`, or run `kubectl apply -f /path/to/file.yaml` with the following YAML resource spec:

Staging-ns.yaml

```
apiVersion: v1
kind: Namespace
metadata:
  name: staging
```

As you can see, a `Namespace` spec is very simple. Let's move on to something more complex – the PodSpec itself.

The Pod life cycle

To quickly see which Pods are running in your cluster, you can run `kubectl get pods` or `kubectl get pods --all-namespaces` to get Pods in either the current namespace (defined by your `kubectl` context, or the default namespace if none is specified) or all namespaces, respectively.

The output of `kubectl get pods` looks like this:

NAME	READY	STATUS	RESTARTS	AGE
my-pod	1/1	Running	0	9s

As you can see, Pods have a STATUS value that tells us in which state the Pod currently is.

The values for Pod state are as follows:

- **Running**: In the Running status, a Pod has successfully spun up its container(s) without any issues. If the Pod has a single container, and it's in Running status, then the container has not completed or exited its process. It could also currently be restarting, which you can tell by checking the READY column. If, for instance, the READY value is 0/1, that means that the container in the Pod is currently not passing health checks. This could be for a variety of reasons: the container could still be spinning up, a database connection could be non-functional, or some important configuration could be preventing the application process from starting.

- **Succeeded**: If your Pod container(s) are set to run a command that can complete or exit (not a long-running command, such as starting a web server), the Pod will show the Succeeded state if those containers have completed their process command.

- **Pending**: Pending statuses designate that at least one container in the Pod is waiting for its image. This is likely because the container image is still being fetched from an external repository, or because the Pod itself is waiting to be scheduled by kube-scheduler.

- **Unknown**: The Unknown status means that Kubernetes cannot tell what state the Pod is actually in. This usually means that the node that the Pod lives on is experiencing some form of error. It may be out of disk space, disconnected from the rest of the cluster, or otherwise be encountering problems.

- **Failed**: In the Failed status, one or more of the containers in the Pod has terminated with a failure status. Additionally, the other containers in the Pod must have terminated in either success or failure. This can happen for a variety of reasons due to the cluster removing Pods or something inside the container application breaking the process.

Understanding the Pod resource spec

Since the Pod resource spec is the first one we've really dug into, we will spend our time detailing the various parts of the YAML file and how they fit together.

Let's start things off with a fully spec'd-out Pod file, which we can then pick apart and review:

Simple-pod.yaml

```
apiVersion: v1
kind: Pod
```

```
metadata:
  name: myApp
  namespace: dev
  labels:
    environment: dev
  annotations:
    customid1: 998123hjhsad
spec:
  containers:
  - name: my-app-container
    image: busybox
```

This Pod YAML file is somewhat more complicated than the one that we looked at in the first chapter. It exposes some new Pod functionality that we will review shortly.

API version

Let's start at line 1: `apiVersion`. As we mentioned in *Chapter 1, Communicating with Kubernetes*, `apiVersion` tells Kubernetes which version of the API to look at when creating and configuring your resource. Pods have been around for a long time in Kubernetes, so the PodSpec is solidified into API version `v1`. Other resource types may contain group names in addition to version names – for instance, a CronJob resource in Kubernetes uses `batch/v1beta1 apiVersion`, while the Job resource uses the `batch/v1 apiVersion`. In both of these, `batch` corresponds to the API group name.

Kind

The `kind` value corresponds to the actual name of the resource type in Kubernetes. In this case, we're trying to spec out a Pod, so that's what we put. The `kind` value is always in camel case, such as `Pod`, `ConfigMap`, `CronJob`, and so on.

> **Important note**
> For a full list of `kind` values, check the official Kubernetes documentation at `https://kubernetes.io/docs/home/`. New Kubernetes `kind` values are added in new releases so the ones reviewed in this book may not be an exhaustive list.

Metadata

Metadata is a top-level key that can have several different values underneath. First of all, name is the resource name, which is what the resource will display as via kubectl and what it is stored as in etcd. namespace corresponds to the namespace that the resource should be created in. If no namespace is specified in the YAML spec, the resource will be created in the default namespace – unless a namespace is specified in the apply or create commands.

Next, labels are key-value pairs that are used to add metadata to a resource. labels are special compared to other metadata because they are used by default in Kubernetes native selectors to filter and select resources – but they can also be used for custom functionality.

Finally, the metadata block can play host to multiple annotations which, like labels, can be used by controllers and custom Kubernetes functionality to provide additional configuration and feature-specific data. In this PodSpec, we have several annotations specified in our metadata:

pod-with-annotations.yaml

```
apiVersion: v1
kind: Pod
metadata:
  name: myApp
  namespace: dev
  labels:
    environment: dev
  annotations:
    customid1: 998123hjhsad
    customid2: 1239808908sd
spec:
  containers:
  - name: my-app-container
    image: busybox
```

Generally, it is better to use labels for Kubernetes-specific functionality and selectors while using annotations for adding data or extension functionality – this is just a convention.

Spec

`spec` is the top-level key that contains the resource-specific configuration. In this case, since our `kind` value is `Pod`, we'll add some configuration that is specific to our Pod. All further keys will be indented under this `spec` key and will represent our Pod configuration.

Containers

The `containers` key expects a list of one or more containers that will run within a Pod. Each container spec will expose its own configuration values, which are indented under the container list item in your resource YAML. We will review some of these configurations here, but for a full list, check the Kubernetes documentation (`https://kubernetes.io/docs/home/`).

Name

Inside a container spec, `name` pertains to what the container will be named within a Pod. Container names can be used to specifically access the logs of a particular container using the `kubectl logs` command, but we'll get to that later. For now, ensure you choose a clear name for each container in your Pod to make things easier when it comes to debugging.

Image

For each container, `image` is used to specify the name of the Docker (or other runtime) image that should be started within the Pod. Images will be pulled from the configured repository, which is the public Docker Hub by default, but can be a private repository as well.

And that's it – that's all you need to specify a Pod and run it in Kubernetes. Everything from this point on in the `Pod` section falls under the *additional configuration* umbrella.

Pod resource specifications

Pods can be configured to have specific amounts of memory and compute allocated to them. This prevents particularly hungry applications from impacting cluster performance and can also help prevent memory leaks. There are two possible resources that can be specified – `cpu` and `memory`. For each of these, there are two different types of specifications, `Requests` and `Limits`, for a total of four possible resource specification keys.

Memory requests and limits can be configured with any typical memory number suffix, or its power-of-two equivalent – for instance, 50 Mi (mebibytes), 50 MB (megabytes), or 1 Gi (gibibytes).

CPU requests and limits can be configured either by using m which corresponds to 1 milli-CPU, or by just using a decimal number. So 200m is equivalent to 0.2, which equals 20% or one fifth of a logical CPU. This quantity will be the same amount of compute power regardless of the number of cores. 1 CPU equals a virtual core in AWS or a core in GCP. Let's look at how these resource requests and limits look in our YAML file:

pod-with-resource-limits.yaml

```
apiVersion: v1
kind: Pod
metadata:
  name: myApp
spec:
  containers:
  - name: my-app-container
    image: mydockername
    resources:
      requests:
        memory: "50Mi"
        cpu: "100m"
      limits:
        memory: "200Mi"
        cpu: "500m"
```

In this Pod, we have a container running a Docker image that is specified with both requests and limits on cpu and memory. In this case, our container image name, mydockername, is a placeholder - but if you want to test the Pod resource limits in this example, you can use the busybox image.

Container start commands

When a container starts in a Kubernetes Pod, it runs the default start script for the container – for instance, the script specified in the Docker container spec. In order to override this functionality with different commands or additional arguments, you can provide the command and args keys. Let's look at a container configured with a start command and some arguments:

pod-with-start-command.yaml

```
apiVersion: v1
kind: Pod
metadata:
  name: myApp
spec:
  containers:
  - name: my-app-container
    image: mydockername
    command: ["run"]
    args: ["--flag", "T", "--run-type", "static"]
```

As you can see, we specify a command as well as a list of arguments as an array of strings, separated with commas where spaces would be.

Init containers

init containers are special containers within a Pod that start, run, and shut down before the normal Pod container(s) start.

init containers can be used for many different use cases, such as initializing files before an application starts or ensuring that other applications or services are running before starting a Pod.

If multiple init containers are specified, they will run in order until all init containers have shut down. For this reason, init containers must run a script that completes and has an endpoint. If your init container script or application keeps running, the normal container(s) in your Pod will not start.

In the following Pod, the `init` container is running a loop to check that our `config-service` exists via `nslookup`. Once it sees that `config-service` is up, the script ends, which triggers our `my-app` app container to start:

pod-with-init-container.yaml

```yaml
apiVersion: v1
kind: Pod
metadata:
  name: myApp
spec:
  containers:
  - name: my-app
    image: mydockername
    command: ["run"]
  initContainers:
  - name: init-before
    image: busybox
    command: ['sh', '-c', 'until nslookup config-service; do echo config-service not up; sleep 2; done;']
```

> **Important note**
> When an `init` container fails, Kubernetes will automatically restart the Pod, similar to the usual Pod startup functionality. This functionality can be changed by changing `restartPolicy` at the Pod level.

Here's a diagram showing the typical Pod startup flow in Kubernetes:

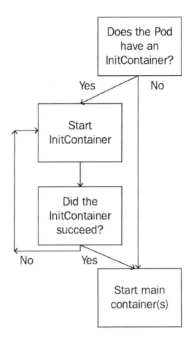

Figure 3.2 – Init container flowchart

If a Pod has more than one initContainer, they will be invoked sequentially. This is valuable for times where you set up initContainers with modular steps that must be executed in order. The following YAML shows this:

pod-with-multiple-init-containers.yaml

```
apiVersion: v1
kind: Pod
metadata:
  name: myApp
spec:
  containers:
  - name: my-app
    image: mydockername
    command: ["run"]
  initContainers:
  - name: init-step-1
    image: step1-image
    command: ['start-command']
```

```
  - name: init-step-2
    image: step2-image
    command: ['start-command']
```

For instance, in this `Pod` YAML file, the `step-1 init` container needs to succeed before `init-step-2` is invoked, and both need to show success before the `my-app` container will be started.

Introducing different types of probes in Kubernetes

In order to know when a container (and therefore a Pod) has failed, Kubernetes needs to know how to test that the container is functioning. We do this by defining `probes`, which Kubernetes can run at a specified interval to determine whether the container is working.

There are three types of probes that Kubernetes lets us configure – readiness, liveness, and startup.

Readiness probes

First off, readiness probes can be used to determine whether a container is ready to perform a function such as accepting traffic via HTTP. These probes are helpful in the beginning stages of a running application, where it may still be fetching the configuration, for instance, and not yet be ready to accept connections.

Let's take a look at what a Pod with a readiness probe configured looks like. What follows is a PodSpec with a readiness probe attached:

pod-with-readiness-probe.yaml

```
apiVersion: v1
kind: Pod
metadata:
  name: myApp
spec:
  containers:
  - name: my-app
    image: mydockername
    command: ["run"]
    ports:
    - containerPort: 8080
    readinessProbe:
```

```
        exec:
          command:
          - cat
          - /tmp/thisfileshouldexist.txt
        initialDelaySeconds: 5
        periodSeconds: 5
```

For starters, as you can see, probes are defined per container, not per Pod. Kubernetes will run all probes per container and use that to determine the total health of the Pod.

Liveness probes

Liveness probes can be used to determine whether an application has failed for some reason (for instance, due to a memory error). For application containers that run a long time, liveness probes can come in handy as a method to help Kubernetes recycle old and broken Pods for new ones. Though probes in and of themselves won't cause a container to restart, other Kubernetes resources and controllers will check the probe status and use it to restart Pods when necessary. Here is a PodSpec with a liveness probe definition attached to it:

pod-with-liveness-probe.yaml

```
apiVersion: v1
kind: Pod
metadata:
  name: myApp
spec:
  containers:
  - name: my-app
    image: mydockername
    command: ["run"]
    ports:
    - containerPort: 8080
    livenessProbe:
      exec:
        command:
        - cat
        - /tmp/thisfileshouldexist.txt
      initialDelaySeconds: 5
```

```
        failureThreshold: 3
        periodSeconds: 5
```

As you can see, our liveness probe is specified in the same way as our readiness probe, with one addition – `failureThreshold`.

The `failureThreshold` value will determine how many times Kubernetes will attempt the probe before taking action. For liveness probes, Kubernetes will restart the Pod once the `failureThreshold` is crossed. For readiness probes, Kubernetes will simply mark the Pod as `Not Ready`. The default value for this threshold is 3, but it can be changed to any value greater than or equal to 1.

In this case, we are using the `exec` mechanism with our probe. We will review the various probe mechanisms available shortly.

Startup probes

Finally, startup probes are a special type of probe that will only run once, on container startup. Some (often older) applications will take a long time to start up in a container, so by providing some extra leeway when a container starts up the first time, you can prevent the liveness or readiness probes failing and causing a restart. Here's a startup probe configured with our Pod:

pod-with-startup-probe.yaml

```
apiVersion: v1
kind: Pod
metadata:
  name: myApp
spec:
  containers:
  - name: my-app
    image: mydockername
    command: ["run"]
    ports:
    - containerPort: 8080
    startupProbe:
      exec:
        command:
        - cat
```

```
    - /tmp/thisfileshouldexist.txt
  initialDelaySeconds: 5
  successThreshold: 2
  periodSeconds: 5
```

Startup probes provide a benefit greater than simply extending the time between liveness or readiness probes – they allow Kubernetes to maintain a quick reaction time when addressing problems that happen after startup and (more importantly) to prevent slow-starting applications from restarting constantly. If your application takes many seconds or even a minute or two to start up, you will have a much easier time implementing a startup probe.

`successThreshold` is just what it seems, the opposite side of the coin to `failureThreshold`. It specifies how many successes in a row are required before a container is marked `Ready`. For applications that can go up and down on startup before stabilizing (like some self-clustering applications), changing this value can be useful. The default is 1, and for liveness probes the only possible value is 1, but we can change the value for readiness and startup probes.

Probe mechanism configuration

There are multiple mechanisms to specify any of the three probes: `exec`, `httpGet`, and `tcpSocket`.

The `exec` method allows you to specify a command that will be run inside the container. A successfully executed command will result in a passed probe, while a command that fails will result in a fail on the probe. All the probes we've configured so far have used the `exec` method, so configuration should be self-evident. If the chosen command (with any arguments specified in comma-separated list form) fails, the probe will fail.

The `httpGet` method for probes allows you to specify a URL on the container that will be hit with an HTTP GET request. If the HTTP request returns a code anywhere between 200 to 400, it will result in a success on the probe. Any other HTTP code will result in a failure.

The configuration for `httpGet` looks like this:

pod-with-get-probe.yaml

```
apiVersion: v1
kind: Pod
metadata:
```

```
    name: myApp
spec:
  containers:
  - name: my-app
    image: mydockername
    command: ["run"]
    ports:
    - containerPort: 8080
    livenessProbe:
      httpGet:
        path: /healthcheck
        port: 8001
        httpHeaders:
        - name: My-Header
          value: My-Header-Value
      initialDelaySeconds: 3
      periodSeconds: 3
```

Finally, the `tcpSocket` method will try to open the specified socket on the container and will use the result to dictate a success or failure. The `tcpSocket` configuration looks like this:

pod-with-tcp-probe.yaml

```
apiVersion: v1
kind: Pod
metadata:
  name: myApp
spec:
  containers:
  - name: my-app
    image: mydockername
    command: ["run"]
    ports:
    - containerPort: 8080
    readinessProbe:
      tcpSocket:
```

```
        port: 8080
        initialDelaySeconds: 5
        periodSeconds: 10
```

As you can see, this type of probe takes in a port, which will be pinged every time the check occurs.

Common Pod transitions

Failing Pods in Kubernetes tend to transition between statuses quite a bit. For a first-time user, this can be intimidating, so it is valuable to break down how the Pod statuses we listed earlier interact with probe functionality. Just to reiterate, here are our statuses:

- `Running`

- `Succeeded`

- `Pending`

- `Unknown`

- `Failed`

A common flow is to run `kubectl get pods -w` (the `-w` flag adds a watch to the command) and see offending Pods transitioning between `Pending` and `Failed`. Typically, what is occurring is that the Pods (and their containers) are spinning up and pulling images – which is the `Pending` state since the health checks have not yet started.

Once the initial probe timeout (which as we saw in the previous section is configurable) elapses, the first probe fails. This can continue for seconds or even minutes depending on how high the failure threshold is, with the status still pinned at `Pending`.

Finally, our failure threshold is reached, and our Pod status transitions to `Failed`. At this point, one of two things can happen, and the decision is based purely on the `RestartPolicy` on the PodSpec, which can either be `Always`, `Never`, or `OnFailure`. If a Pod fails and the `restartPolicy` is `Never`, the Pod will stay in the failed status. If it is one of the other two options, the Pod will restart automatically, and go back to `Pending`, which is the root cause of our never-ending transition cycle.

For a different example, you may see Pods stuck forever in the `Pending` status. This can be due to the Pod failing to be scheduled on any node. This could be due to resource request constraints (which we will cover in depth later in this book, in *Chapter 8, Pod Placement Controls*), or other issues such as nodes being unreachable.

Finally, with Unknown, typically the node that the Pod is scheduled on is unreachable for some reason – the node might have shut down, for instance, or is unreachable via the network.

Pod scheduling

The complexities of Pod scheduling and the ways the Kubernetes lets you influence and control it will be saved for our *Chapter 8, Pod Placement Controls* – but for now we will review the basics.

When deciding where to schedule a Pod, Kubernetes takes many factors into account, but the most important to consider (when not delving into the more complex controls that Kubernetes lets us use) are Pod priority, node availability, and resource availability.

The Kubernetes scheduler operates a constant control loop that monitors the cluster for unbound (unscheduled) Pods. If one or more unbound Pods is found, the scheduler will use the Pod priority to decide which one to schedule first.

Once the scheduler has decided on a Pod to schedule, it will perform several rounds and types of checks in order to find the local optima of a node for where to schedule the Pod. The latter rounds of checks are dictated by granular scheduling controls, which we'll get into in the *Chapter 8, Pod Placement Controls*. We'll worry about the first couple of checks for now.

First, Kubernetes checks to see which nodes are even schedulable at the current moment. Nodes may be non-functioning or otherwise encountering issues that would prevent new Pods from being scheduled.

Secondly, Kubernetes filters schedulable nodes by checking to see which of those nodes match the minimum resource requirement stated in the PodSpec.

At this point, in the absence of any other placement controls, the scheduler will make its decision and assign our new Pod to a node. When the kubelet on that node sees that it has a new Pod assigned to it, the Pod will be spun up.

Summary

In this chapter, we learned that Pods are the most basic building block we have to work with in Kubernetes. It's important to have a strong understanding of Pods and all their subtleties because all compute on Kubernetes uses Pods as a building block. It's probably pretty obvious by now, but Pods are very small, individual things that are not very sturdy. Running an application as a single Pod on Kubernetes with no controller is a bad decision, and any issue with your Pod will result in downtime.

In the next chapter, we'll see how to prevent this by using Pod controllers to run multiple replicas of an application at once.

Questions

1. How could you use namespaces to separate application environments?

2. What is a possible reason for a Pod status to be listed as Unknown?

3. What could be a reason for constraining Pod memory resources?

4. If an application running on Kubernetes often does not start in time before a failed probe restarts the Pod, which probe type should you tune? Readiness, liveness, or startup?

Further reading

*   The official Kubernetes documentation: https://kubernetes.io/docs/home/

*   *Kubernetes The Hard Way*: https://github.com/kelseyhightower/kubernetes-the-hard-way

Section 2: Configuring and Deploying Applications on Kubernetes

In this section, you'll learn how to configure and deploy applications on Kubernetes, as well as provisioning storage and exposing your application outside of the cluster.

This part of the book comprises the following chapters:

4

Scaling and Deploying Your Application

In this chapter, we will learn about the higher-level Kubernetes resources that are used to run applications and control Pods. First, we'll cover the drawbacks of the Pod, before moving on to the simplest Pod controller, ReplicaSets. From there we will move on to Deployments, the most popular method for deploying applications to Kubernetes. Then we'll cover special resources to help you deploy specific types of applications – Horizontal Pod Autoscalers, DaemonSets, StatefulSets, and Jobs. Finally, we'll put it all together with a full example of how to run a complex application on Kubernetes.

In this chapter, we will cover the following topics:

- Understanding Pod drawbacks and their solutions
- Using ReplicaSets
- Controlling Deployments
- Harnessing the Horizontal Pod Autoscaler

- Implementing DaemonSets

- Reviewing StatefulSets and Jobs

- Putting it all together

Technical requirements

In order to run the commands detailed in this chapter, you will need a computer that supports the kubectl command-line tool along with a working Kubernetes cluster. See *Chapter 1*, *Communicating with Kubernetes*, for several methods to get up and running with Kubernetes quickly, and for instructions on how to install the kubectl tool.

The code used in this chapter can be found in the book's GitHub repository at https://github.com/PacktPublishing/Cloud-Native-with-Kubernetes/tree/master/Chapter4.

Understanding Pod drawbacks and their solutions

As we reviewed in the previous chapter, *Chapter 3*, *Running Application Containers on Kubernetes*, a Pod in Kubernetes is an instance of one or more application containers that run on a node. Creating just one Pod is enough to run an application the same way you would in any other container.

That being said, using a single Pod to run an application ignores many of the benefits of running containers in the first place. Containers allow us to treat each instance of our application as a stateless item that can be scaled up or down to meet demand by spinning up new instances of the application.

This has the benefits of both allowing us to scale our application easily and making our application more available by providing multiple instances of our application at a given time. If one of our instances crashes, the application will still continue to function, and will automatically scale to pre-crash levels. The way we do this on Kubernetes is by using a Pod controller resource.

Pod controllers

Kubernetes provides several choices for Pod controllers out of the box. The simplest option is to use a ReplicaSet, which maintains a given number of Pod instances for a particular Pod. If one instance fails, the ReplicaSet will spin up a new instance to replace it.

Secondly, there are Deployments, which themselves control a ReplicaSet. Deployments are the most popular controller when it comes to running an application on Kubernetes, and they make it easy to upgrade applications using a rolling update across a ReplicaSet.

Horizontal Pod Autoscalers take Deployments to the next level by allowing applications to autoscale to different numbers of instances based on performance metrics.

Finally, there are a few specialty controllers that may be valuable in certain situations:

- DaemonSets, which run an instance of the application on each node and maintain them

- StatefulSets, where the Pod identity is kept static to assist in running stateful workloads

- Jobs, which start, run to completion, and then shut down on a specified number of Pods

The actual behavior of a controller, be it a default Kubernetes controller like a ReplicaSet or a custom controller (for instance, the PostgreSQL Operator), should be easy to predict. A simplified view of the standard control loop looks something like the following diagram:

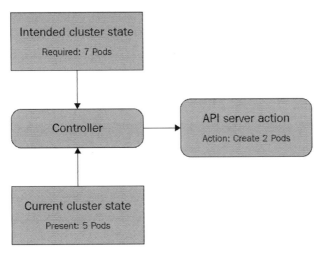

Figure 4.1 – A basic control loop for a Kubernetes controller

As you can see, the controller constantly checks the **Intended cluster state** (we want seven Pods of this app) against the **Current cluster state** (we have five Pods of this app running). When the intended state does not match the current state, the controller will take action via the API to correct the current state to match the intended state.

By now, you should understand why controllers are necessary on Kubernetes: the Pod itself is not a powerful enough primitive when it comes to delivering highly available applications. Let's move on to the simplest such controller: the ReplicaSet.

Using ReplicaSets

ReplicaSets are the simplest Kubernetes Pod controller resource. They replace the older ReplicationController resource.

The major difference between a ReplicaSet and a ReplicationController is that a ReplicationController uses a more basic type of *selector* – the filter that determines which Pods should be controlled.

While ReplicationControllers use simple equity-based (*key=value*) selectors, ReplicaSets use a selector with multiple possible formats, such as `matchLabels` and `matchExpressions`, which will be reviewed in this chapter.

> **Important note**
> There shouldn't be any reason to use a ReplicationController over a ReplicaSet – just stick with ReplicaSets unless you have a really good reason not to.

ReplicaSets allow us to inform Kubernetes to maintain a certain number of Pods for a particular Pod spec. The YAML for a ReplicaSet is very similar to that for a Pod. In fact, the entire Pod spec is nested in the ReplicaSet YAML, under the `template` key.

There are also a few other key differences, which can be observed in the following code block:

replica-set.yaml

```
apiVersion: apps/v1
kind: ReplicaSet
metadata:
  name: myapp-group
  labels:
    app: myapp
```

```
spec:
  replicas: 3
  selector:
    matchLabels:
      app: myapp
  template:
    metadata:
      labels:
        app: myapp
    spec:
      containers:
      - name: myapp-container
        image: busybox
```

As you can see, in addition to the `template` section, which is essentially a Pod definition, we have a `selector` key and a `replicas` key in our ReplicaSet spec. Let's start with `replicas`.

Replicas

The `replicas` key specifies a replica count, which our ReplicaSet will ensure is always running at a given time. If a Pod dies or stops working, our ReplicaSet will create a new Pod to take its place. This makes the ReplicaSet a self-healing resource.

How does a ReplicaSet controller decide when a Pod stops working? It looks at the Pod's status. If the Pod's current status isn't "*Running*" or "*ContainerCreating*", the ReplicaSet will attempt to start a new Pod.

As we discussed in *Chapter 3, Running Application Containers on Kubernetes*, the Pod's status after container creation is driven by the liveness, readiness, and startup probes, which can be configured specifically for a Pod. This means that you can set up application-specific ways to know whether a Pod is broken in some way, and your ReplicaSet can jump in and start a new one in its place.

Selector

The `selector` key is important because of the way a ReplicaSet works – it is a controller that is implemented with the selector at its core. The ReplicaSet's job is to ensure that the number of running Pods that match its selector is correct.

Let's say, for instance, that you have an existing Pod running your application, `MyApp`. This Pod is labeled with a `selector` key as `App=MyApp`.

Now let's say you want to create a ReplicaSet with the same app, which will add an additional three instances of your application. You create a ReplicaSet with the same selector, and specify three replicas, with the intent of running four instances in total, since you already have one running.

What will happen once you start the ReplicaSet? You'll find that the total number of Pods running that application will be three, not four. This is because a ReplicaSet has the ability to adopt orphaned Pods and bring them under its reign.

When the ReplicaSet starts up, it sees that there is already an existing Pod matching its `selector` key. Depending on the number of replicas required, a ReplicaSet will shut down existing Pods or start new Pods that match the `selector` in order to create the correct number.

Template

The `template` section contains the Pod and supports all the same fields as Pod YAMLs do, including the metadata section and the spec itself. Most other controllers follow this pattern – they allow you to define the Pod spec within the larger overall controller YAML.

You should now understand the various parts of the ReplicaSet spec and what they do. Let's move on to actually running applications using our ReplicaSet.

Testing a ReplicaSet

Now, let's deploy our ReplicaSet.

Copy the `replica-set.yaml` file listed previously and run it on your cluster using the following command in the same folder as your YAML file:

```
kubectl apply -f replica-set.yaml
```

To check that the ReplicaSet has been created properly, run `kubectl get pods` to fetch the Pods in the default namespace.

Since we haven't specified a namespace for our ReplicaSet, it will be created by default. The `kubectl get pods` command should give you the following:

NAME AGE	READY	STATUS	RESTARTS
myapp-group-192941298-k705b	1/1	Running	0

```
1m
myapp-group-192941298-o9sh8      1/1      Running     0
1m
myapp-group-192941298-n8gh2      1/1      Running     0
1m
```

Now, try deleting one of the ReplicaSet Pods by using the following command:

```
kubectl delete pod myapp-group-192941298-k705b
```

A ReplicaSet will always try to keep the specified number of replicas online.

Let's use our `kubectl get` command to see our running pods again:

```
NAME                            READY   STATUS             RESTARTS
AGE
myapp-group-192941298-u42s0   1/1     ContainerCreating  0
1m
myapp-group-192941298-o9sh8   1/1     Running            0
2m
myapp-group-192941298-n8gh2   1/1     Running            0
2m
```

As you can see, our ReplicaSet controller is starting a new pod to keep our number of replicas at three.

Finally, let's delete our ReplicaSet using the following command:

```
kubectl delete replicaset myapp-group
```

With our cluster a bit cleaner, let's move on to a more complex controller – Deployments.

Controlling Deployments

Though ReplicaSets contain much of the functionality you would want to run a high availability application, most of the time you will want to use Deployments to run applications on Kubernetes.

Deployments have a few advantages over ReplicaSets, and they actually work by owning and controlling a ReplicaSet.

The main advantage of a Deployment is that it allows you to specify a `rollout` procedure – that is, how an application upgrade is deployed to the various pods in the Deployment. This lets you easily configure controls to stop bad upgrades in their tracks.

Before we review how to do this, let's look at the entire spec for a Deployment:

deployment.yaml

```yaml
apiVersion: apps/v1
kind: Deployment
metadata:
  name: myapp-deployment
  labels:
    app: myapp
spec:
  replicas: 3
  strategy:
    type: RollingUpdate
    rollingUpdate:
      maxSurge: 25%
      maxUnavailable: 25%
  selector:
    matchLabels:
      app: myapp
  template:
    metadata:
      labels:
        app: myapp
    spec:
      containers:
      - name: myapp-container
        image: busybox
```

As you can see, this is very similar to the spec for a ReplicaSet. The difference we see here is a new key in the spec: `strategy`.

Using the `strategy` setting, we can tell our Deployment which way to upgrade our application, either via a `RollingUpdate`, or `Recreate`.

`Recreate` is a very basic deployment method: all Pods in the Deployment will be deleted at the same time, and new Pods will be created with the new version. `Recreate` doesn't give us much control against a bad Deployment – if the new Pods don't start for some reason, we're stuck with a completely non-functioning application.

With `RollingUpdate` on the other hand, Deployments are slower but far more controlled. Firstly, the new application will be rolled out bit by bit, Pod by Pod. We can specify values for `maxSurge` and `maxUnavailable` to tune the strategy.

A rolling update works like this – when the Deployment spec is updated with a new version of the Pod container, the Deployment will take down one Pod at a time, create a new Pod with the new application version, wait for the new Pod to register `Ready` as determined by the readiness check, and then move on to the next Pod.

The `maxSurge` and `maxUnavailable` parameters allow you to speed up or slow down this process. `maxUnavailable` allows you to tune the maximum number of unavailable Pods during the rollout process. This can be either a percentage or a fixed number. `maxSurge` allows you to tune the maximum number of Pods over the Deployment replica number that can be created at any given time. Like with `maxUnavailable`, this can be a percentage or a fixed number.

The following diagram shows the `RollingUpdate` procedure:

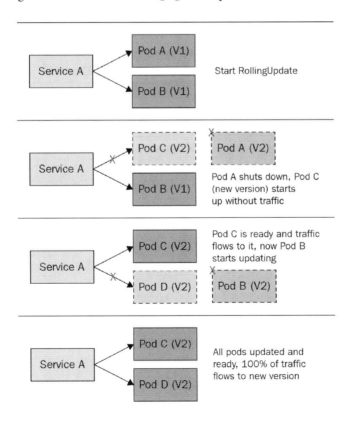

Figure 4.2 – RollingUpdate process for a Deployment

As you can see, the `RollingUpdate` procedure follows several key steps. The Deployment attempts to update Pods, one by one. Only after a Pod is successfully updated does the update proceed to the next Pod.

Controlling Deployments with imperative commands

As we've discussed, we can change our Deployment by simply updating its YAML using declarative methods. However, Kubernetes also gives us some special commands in `kubectl` for controlling several aspects of Deployments.

First off, Kubernetes lets us manually scale a Deployment – that is, we can edit the amount of replicas that should be running.

To scale our `myapp-deployment` up to five replicas, we can run the following:

```
kubectl scale deployment myapp-deployment --replicas=5
```

Similarly, we can roll back our `myapp-deployment` to an older version if required. To demonstrate this, first let's manually edit our Deployment to use a new version of our container:

```
Kubectl set image deployment myapp-deployment myapp-
container=busybox:1.2 -record=true
```

This command tells Kubernetes to change the version of our container in our Deployment to 1.2. Then, our Deployment will go through the steps in the preceding figure to roll out our change.

Now, let's say that we want to go back to our previous version before we updated the container image version. We can easily do this using the `rollout undo` command:

```
Kubectl rollout undo deployment myapp-deployment
```

In our previous case, we only had two versions, the initial one and our version with the updated container, but if we had others, we could specify them in the `undo` command like this:

```
Kubectl rollout undo deployment myapp-deployment -
to-revision=10
```

This should give you a glimpse into why Deployments are so valuable – they give us fine-tuned control over rollout for new versions of our application. Next, we'll discuss a smart scaler for Kubernetes that works in concert with Deployments and ReplicaSets.

Harnessing the Horizontal Pod Autoscaler

As we've seen, Deployments and ReplicaSets allow you to specify a total number of replicas that should be available at a certain time. However, neither of these structures allow automatic scaling – they must be scaled manually.

Horizontal Pod Autoscalers (HPA) provide this functionality by existing as a higher-level controller that can change the replica count of a Deployment or ReplicaSet based on metrics such as CPU and memory usage.

By default, an HPA can autoscale based on CPU utilization, but by using custom metrics this functionality can be extended.

The YAML file for an HPA looks like this:

hpa.yaml

```
apiVersion: autoscaling/v1
kind: HorizontalPodAutoscaler
metadata:
  name: myapp-hpa
spec:
  maxReplicas: 5
  minReplicas: 2
  scaleTargetRef:
    apiVersion: apps/v1
    kind: Deployment
    name: myapp-deployment
  targetCPUUtilizationPercentage: 70
```

In the preceding spec, we have the `scaleTargetRef`, which specifies what should be autoscaled by the HPA, and the tuning parameters.

The definition of `scaleTargetRef` can be a Deployment, ReplicaSet, or ReplicationController. In this case, we've defined the HPA to scale our previously created Deployment, `myapp-deployment`.

For tuning parameters, we're using the default CPU utilization-based scaling, so we can use `targetCPUUtilizationPercentage` to define the intended CPU utilization of each Pod running our application. If the average CPU usage of our Pods increases past 70%, our HPA will scale the Deployment spec up, and if it drops below for long enough, it will scale the Deployment down.

A typical scaling event looks like this:

1. The average CPU usage of a Deployment exceeds 70% on three replicas.

2. The HPA control loop notices this increase in CPU utilization.

3. The HPA edits the Deployment spec with a new replica count. This count is calculated based on CPU utilization, with the intent of a steady state per-node CPU usage under 70%.

4. The Deployment controller spins up a new replica.

5. This process repeats itself to scale the Deployment up or down.

In summary, the HPA keeps track of CPU and memory utilization and initiates a scaling event when boundaries are exceeded. Next, we will review DaemonSets, which provide a very specific type of Pod controller.

Implementing DaemonSets

From now until the end of the chapter, we will be reviewing more niche options when it comes to running applications with specific requirements.

We'll start with DaemonSets, which are similar to ReplicaSets except that the number of replicas is fixed at one replica per node. This means that each node in the cluster will keep one replica of the application active at any time.

> **Important note**
>
> It's important to keep in mind that this functionality will only create one replica per node in the absence of additional Pod placement controls, such as Taints or Node Selectors, which we will cover in greater detail in *Chapter 8, Pod Placement Controls*.

This ends up looking like the following diagram for a typical DaemonSet:

Figure 4.3 – DaemonSet spread across three nodes

As you can see in the preceding figure, each node (represented by a box) contains one Pod of the application, as controlled by the DaemonSet.

This makes DaemonSets great for running applications that collect metrics at the node level or provide networking processes on a per-node basis. A DaemonSet spec looks like this:

daemonset-1.yaml

```
apiVersion: apps/v1
kind: DaemonSet
metadata:
  name: log-collector
spec:
  selector:
    matchLabels:
      name: log-collector
  template:
    metadata:
      labels:
        name: log-collector
    spec:
      containers:
      - name: fluentd
        image: fluentd
```

As you can see, this is very similar to your typical ReplicaSet spec, except that we do not specify the number of replicas. This is because a DaemonSet will try to run a Pod on each node in your cluster.

If you want to specify a subset of nodes to run your application, you can do this using a node selector as shown in the following file:

daemonset-2.yaml

```
apiVersion: apps/v1
kind: DaemonSet
metadata:
  name: log-collector
spec:
```

```
    selector:
        matchLabels:
            name: log-collector
    template:
        metadata:
            labels:
                name: log-collector
        spec:
            nodeSelector:
                type: bigger-node
            containers:
            - name: fluentd
                image: fluentd
```

This YAML will restrict our DaemonSet to nodes that match the `type=bigger-node` selector in their labels. We will learn much more about Node Selectors in *Chapter 8, Pod Placement Controls*. For now, let's discuss a type of controller well suited to running stateful applications such as databases – the StatefulSet.

Understanding StatefulSets

StatefulSets are very similar to ReplicaSets and Deployments, but with one key difference that makes them better for stateful workloads. StatefulSets maintain the order and identity of each Pod, even if the Pods are rescheduled onto new nodes.

For instance, in a StatefulSet of 3 replicas, there will always be Pod 1, Pod 2, and Pod 3, and those Pods will maintain their identity in Kubernetes and storage (which we'll get to in *Chapter 7, Storage on Kubernetes*), regardless of any rescheduling that happens.

Let's take a look at a simple StatefulSet configuration:

statefulset.yaml

```
apiVersion: apps/v1
kind: StatefulSet
metadata:
    name: stateful
spec:
    selector:
```

```
    matchLabels:
        app: stateful-app
  replicas: 5
  template:
    metadata:
      labels:
        app: stateful-app
    spec:
      containers:
      - name: app
        image: busybox
```

This YAML will create a StatefulSet with five replicas of our app.

Let's see how the StatefulSet maintains Pod identity differently than a typical Deployment or ReplicaSet. Let's fetch all Pods using the command:

```
kubectl get pods
```

The output should look like the following:

NAME	READY	STATUS	RESTARTS	AGE
stateful-app-0	1/1	Running	0	55s
stateful-app-1	1/1	Running	0	48s
stateful-app-2	1/1	Running	0	26s
stateful-app-3	1/1	Running	0	18s
stateful-app-4	0/1	Pending	0	3s

As you can see, in this example, we have our five StatefulSet Pods, each with a numeric indicator of their identity. This property is extremely useful for stateful applications such as a database cluster. In the case of running a database cluster on Kubernetes, the identity of the master versus replica Pods is important, and we can use StatefulSet identities to easily manage that.

Another point of interest is that you can see the final Pod is still starting up, and that the Pod ages increase as numeric identity increases. This is because StatefulSet Pods are created one at a time, in order.

StatefulSets are valuable in concert with persistent Kubernetes storage in order to run stateful applications. We'll learn more about this in *Chapter 7, Storage On Kubernetes*, but for now, let's discuss another controller with a very specific use: Jobs.

Using Jobs

The purpose of the Job resource in Kubernetes is to run tasks that can complete, which makes them not ideal for long-running applications, but great for batch jobs or similar tasks that can benefit from parallelism.

Here's what a Job spec YAML looks like:

job-1.yaml

```
apiVersion: batch/v1
kind: Job
metadata:
  name: runner
spec:
  template:
    spec:
      containers:
      - name: run-job
        image: node:lts-jessie
        command: ["node", "job.js"]
      restartPolicy: Never
  backoffLimit: 4
```

This Job will start a single Pod, and run a command, node job.js, until it completes, at which point the Pod will shut down. In this and the future examples, we assume that the container image used has a file, job.js, that runs the job logic. The node:lts-jessie container image will not have this by default. This is an example of a Job that runs without parallelism. As you are likely aware from Docker usage, multiple command arguments must be passed as an array of strings.

In order to create a Job that can run with parallelism (that is to say, multiple replicas running the Job at the same time), you need to develop your application code in a way that it can tell that the Job is completed before ending the process. In order to do this, each instance of the Job needs to contain code that ensures it does the right part of the greater batch task and prevents duplicate work from occurring.

There are several application patterns that can enable this, including a mutex lock and a Work Queue. In addition, the code needs to check the status of the entire batch task, which could again be handled by updating a value in a database. Once the Job code sees that the greater task is complete, it should exit.

Once you've done that, you can add parallelism to your job code using the `parallelism` key. The following code block shows this:

job-2.yaml

```
apiVersion: batch/v1
kind: Job
metadata:
  name: runner
spec:
  parallelism: 3
  template:
    spec:
      containers:
      - name: run-job
        image: node:lts-jessie
        command: ["node", "job.js"]
      restartPolicy: Never
  backoffLimit: 4
```

As you can see, we add the `parallelism` key with three replicas. Further, you can swap pure job parallelism for a specified number of completions, in which case Kubernetes can keep track of how many times the Job has been completed. You can still set parallelism for this case, but if you don't set it, it will default to 1.

This next spec will run a Job 4 times to completion, with 2 iterations running at any given time:

job-3.yaml

```
apiVersion: batch/v1
kind: Job
metadata:
  name: runner
spec:
  parallelism: 2
  completions: 4
  template:
    spec:
```

```
    containers:
    - name: run-job
      image: node:lts-jessie
      command: ["node", "job.js"]
      restartPolicy: Never
backoffLimit: 4
```

Jobs on Kubernetes provide a great way to abstract one-time processes, and many third-party applications link them into workflows. As you can see, they are very easy to use.

Next, let's look at a very similar resource, the CronJob.

CronJobs

CronJobs are a Kubernetes resource for scheduled job execution. This works very similarly to CronJob implementations you may find in your favorite programming language or application framework, with one key difference. Kubernetes CronJobs trigger Kubernetes Jobs, which provide an additional layer of abstraction that can be used, for instance, to trigger batch Jobs at night, every night.

CronJobs in Kubernetes are configured using a very typical cron notation. Let's take a look at the full spec:

cronjob-1.yaml

```
apiVersion: batch/v1beta1
kind: CronJob
metadata:
  name: hello
spec:
  schedule: "0 1 * * *"
  jobTemplate:
    spec:
      template:
        spec:
          containers:
          - name: run-job
            image: node:lts-jessie
            command: ["node", "job.js"]
          restartPolicy: OnFailure
```

This CronJob will, at 1 a.m. every day, create a Job that is identical to our previous Job spec. For a quick review of cron time notation, which will explain the syntax of our 1 a.m. job, read on. For a comprehensive review of cron notation, check `http://man7.org/linux/man-pages/man5/crontab.5.html`.

Cron notation consists of five values, separated by spaces. Each value can be a numeric integer, character, or combination. Each of the five values represents a time value with the following format, from left to right:

- Minute
- Hour
- Day of the month (such as `25`)
- Month
- Day of the week (where, for example, `3` = Wednesday)

The previous YAML assumes a non-parallel CronJob. If we wanted to increase the batch capacity of our CronJob, we could add parallelism as we did with our previous Job specs. The following code block shows this:

cronjob-2.yaml

```
apiVersion: batch/v1beta1
kind: CronJob
metadata:
  name: hello
spec:
  schedule: "0 1 * * *"
  jobTemplate:
    spec:
      parallelism: 3
      template:
        spec:
          containers:
            - name: run-job
              image: node:lts-jessie
              command: ["node", "job.js"]
          restartPolicy: OnFailure
```

Note that for this to work, the code in your CronJob container needs to gracefully handle parallelism, which could be implemented using a work queue or other such pattern.

We've now reviewed all the basic controllers that Kubernetes provides by default. Let's use our knowledge to run a more complex application example on Kubernetes in the next section.

Putting it all together

We now have a toolset for running applications on Kubernetes. Let's look at a real-world example to see how this could all be combined to run an application with multiple tiers and functionality spread across Kubernetes resources:

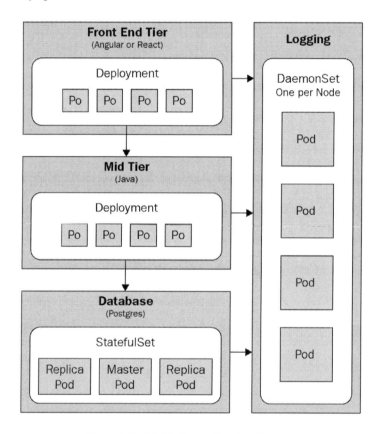

Figure 4.4 – Multi-tier application diagram

As you can see, our diagrammed application contains a web tier running a .NET Framework application, a mid-tier or service tier running Java, a database tier running Postgres, and finally a logging/monitoring tier.

Our controller choices for each of these tiers are dependent on the applications we plan to run on each tier. For both the web tier and the mid-tier, we're running stateless applications and services, so we can effectively use Deployments to handle rolling out updates, blue/green deploys, and more.

For the database tier, we need our database cluster to know which Pod is a replica and which is a master – so we use a StatefulSet. And finally, our log collector needs to run on every node, so we use a DaemonSet to run it.

Now, let's go through example YAML specs for each of our tiers.

Let's start with our JavaScript-based web app. By hosting this application on Kubernetes, we can do canary tests and blue/green Deployments. As a note, some of the examples in this section use container image names that aren't publicly available in DockerHub. To use this pattern, adapt the examples to your own application containers, or just use busybox if you want to run it without actual application logic.

The YAML file for the web tier could look like this:

example-deployment-web.yaml

```
apiVersion: apps/v1
kind: Deployment
metadata:
  name: webtier-deployment
  labels:
    tier: web
spec:
  replicas: 10
  strategy:
    type: RollingUpdate
    rollingUpdate:
      maxSurge: 50%
      maxUnavailable: 25%
  selector:
    matchLabels:
      tier: web
  template:
    metadata:
      labels:
```

```
        tier: web
    spec:
      containers:
      - name: reactapp-container
        image: myreactapp
```

In the preceding YAML, we're labeling our applications using the `tier` label and using that as our `matchLabels` selector.

Next up is the mid-tier service layer. Let's take a look at the relevant YAML:

example-deployment-mid.yaml

```
apiVersion: apps/v1
kind: Deployment
metadata:
  name: midtier-deployment
  labels:
    tier: mid
spec:
  replicas: 8
  strategy:
    type: RollingUpdate
    rollingUpdate:
      maxSurge: 25%
      maxUnavailable: 25%
  selector:
    matchLabels:
      tier: mid
  template:
    metadata:
      labels:
        tier: mid
    spec:
      containers:
      - name: myjavaapp-container
        image: myjavaapp
```

As you can see in the preceding code, our mid-tier application is pretty similar to the web tier setup, and we're using another Deployment.

Now comes the interesting part – let's look at the spec for our Postgres StatefulSet. We have truncated this code block somewhat in order to fit on the page, but you should be able to see the most important parts:

example-statefulset.yaml

```yaml
apiVersion: apps/v1
kind: StatefulSet
metadata:
  name: postgres-db
  labels:
    tier: db
spec:
  serviceName: "postgres"
  replicas: 2
  selector:
    matchLabels:
      tier: db
  template:
    metadata:
      labels:
        tier: db
    spec:
      containers:
      - name: postgres
        image: postgres:latest
        envFrom:
          - configMapRef:
              name: postgres-conf
        volumeMounts:
        - name: pgdata
          mountPath: /var/lib/postgresql/data
          subPath: postgres
```

In the preceding YAML file, we can see some new concepts that we haven't reviewed yet – ConfigMaps and volumes. We'll get a much closer look at how these work in *Chapters 6, Kubernetes Application Configuration*, and *Chapter 7, Storage on Kubernetes*, respectively, but for now let's focus on the rest of the spec. We have our `postgres` container as well as a port set up on the default Postgres port of `5432`.

Finally, let's take a look at our DaemonSet for our logging app. Here's a portion of the YAML file, which we've again truncated for length:

example-daemonset.yaml

```yaml
apiVersion: apps/v1
kind: DaemonSet
metadata:
  name: fluentd
  namespace: kube-system
  labels:
    tier: logging
spec:
  updateStrategy:
    type: RollingUpdate
  template:
    metadata:
      labels:
        tier: logging
    spec:
      tolerations:
      - key: node-role.kubernetes.io/master
        effect: NoSchedule
      containers:
      - name: fluentd
        image: fluent/fluentd-kubernetes-daemonset:v1-debian-papertrail
        env:
          - name: FLUENT_PAPERTRAIL_HOST
            value: "mycompany.papertrailapp.com"
          - name: FLUENT_PAPERTRAIL_PORT
            value: "61231"
```

```
    - name: FLUENT_HOSTNAME
      value: "DEV_CLUSTER"
```

In this DaemonSet, we're setting up FluentD (a popular open source log collector) to forward logs to Papertrail, a cloud-based log collector and search tool. Again, in this YAML file, we have some things we haven't reviewed before. For instance, the `tolerations` section for `node-role.kubernetes.io/master` will actually allow our DaemonSet to place Pods on master nodes, not just worker nodes. We'll review how this works in *Chapter 8, Pod Placement Controls*.

We're also specifying environment variables directly in the Pod spec, which is fine for relatively basic configurations, but could be improved by using Secrets or ConfigMaps (which we'll review in *Chapter 6, Kubernetes Application Configuration*) to keep it out of our YAML code.

Summary

In this chapter, we reviewed some methods of running applications on Kubernetes. To start, we reviewed why Pods themselves are not enough to guarantee application availability and introduced controllers. We then reviewed some simple controllers, including ReplicaSets and Deployments, before moving on to controllers with more specific uses such as HPAs, Jobs, CronJobs, StatefulSets, and DaemonSets. Finally, we took all our learning and used it to implement a complex application running on Kubernetes.

In the next chapter, we'll learn how to expose our applications (which are now running properly with high availability) to the world using Services and Ingress.

Questions

1. What is the difference between a ReplicaSet and a ReplicationController?

2. What's the advantage of a Deployment over a ReplicaSet?

3. What is a good use case for a Job?

4. Why are StatefulSets better for stateful workloads?

5. How might we support a canary release flow using Deployments?

Further reading

- The official Kubernetes documentation: `https://kubernetes.io/docs/home/`

- Documentation on the Kubernetes Job resource: `https://kubernetes.io/docs/concepts/workloads/controllers/job/`

- Docs for FluentD DaemonSet installation: `https://github.com/fluent/fluentd-kubernetes-daemonset`

- *Kubernetes The Hard Way*: `https://github.com/kelseyhightower/kubernetes-the-hard-way`

5

Services and Ingress – Communicating with the Outside World

This chapter contains a comprehensive discussion of the methods that Kubernetes provides to allow applications to communicate with each other, and with resources outside the cluster. You'll learn about the Kubernetes Service resource and all its possible types – ClusterIP, NodePort, LoadBalancer, and ExternalName – as well as how to implement them. Finally, you'll learn how to use Kubernetes Ingress.

In this chapter, we will cover the following topics:

- Understanding Services and cluster DNS
- Implementing ClusterIP
- Using NodePort

- Setting up a LoadBalancer Service

- Creating an ExternalName Service

- Configuring Ingress

Technical requirement

In order to run the commands detailed in this chapter, you will need a computer that supports the kubectl command-line tool along with a working Kubernetes cluster. Review *Chapter 1, Communicating with Kubernetes*, to see several methods for getting up and running with Kubernetes quickly, and for instructions on how to install the kubectl tool.

The code used in this chapter can be found in the book's GitHub repository at https://github.com/PacktPublishing/Cloud-Native-with-Kubernetes/tree/master/Chapter5.

Understanding Services and cluster DNS

In the last few chapters, we've talked about how to run applications effectively on Kubernetes using resources including Pods, Deployments, and StatefulSets. However, many applications, such as web servers, need to be able to accept network requests from outside their containers. These requests could come either from other applications or from devices accessing the public internet.

Kubernetes provides several types of resources to handle various scenarios when it comes to allowing resources outside and inside the cluster to access applications running on Pods, Deployments, and more.

These fall into two major resource types, Services and Ingress:

- **Services** have several subtypes – ClusterIP, NodePort, and LoadBalancer – and are generally used to provide simple access to a single application from inside or outside the cluster.

- **Ingress** is a more advanced resource that creates a controller that takes care of pathname- and hostname-based routing to various resources running inside the cluster. Ingress works by using rules to forward traffic to Services. You need to use Services to use Ingress.

Before we get started with our first type of Service resource, let's review how Kubernetes handles DNS inside the cluster.

Cluster DNS

Let's start by discussing which resources in Kubernetes get their own DNS names by default. DNS names in Kubernetes are restricted to Pods and Services. Pod DNS names contain several parts structured as subdomains.

A typical **Fully Qualified Domain Name (FQDN)** for a Pod running in Kubernetes looks like this:

```
my-hostname.my-subdomain.my-namespace.svc.my-cluster-domain.
example
```

Let's break it down, starting from the rightmost side:

- `my-cluster-domain.example` corresponds to the configured DNS name for the Cluster API itself. Depending on the tool used to set up the cluster, and the environment that it runs in, this can be an external domain name or an internal DNS name.

- `svc` is a section that will occur even in a Pod DNS name – so we can just assume it will be there. However, as you will see shortly, you won't generally be accessing Pods or Services through their FQDNs.

- `my-namespace` is pretty self-explanatory. This section of the DNS name will be whatever namespace your Pod is operating in.

- `my-subdomain` corresponds to the `subdomain` field in the Pod spec. This field is completely optional.

- Finally, `my-hostname` will be set to whatever the name of the Pod is in the Pod metadata.

Together, this DNS name allows other resources in the cluster to access a particular Pod. This generally isn't very helpful by itself, especially if you're using Deployments and StatefulSets that generally have multiple Pods. This is where Services come in.

Let's take a look at the A record DNS name for a Service:

```
my-svc.my-namespace.svc.cluster-domain.example
```

As you can see, it's very similar to the Pod DNS name, with the difference that we only have one value to the left of our namespace – which is the Service name (again, as with Pods, this is generated based on the metadata name).

One result of how these DNS names are handled is that within a namespace, you can access a Service or Pod via just its Service (or Pod) name, and the subdomain.

For instance, take our previous Service DNS name. From within the `my-namespace` namespace, the Service can be accessed simply by the DNS name `my-svc`. From outside the `my-namespace` namespace, you can access the Service via `my-svc.my-namespace`.

Now that we've learned how in-cluster DNS works, we can discuss how that translates to the Service proxy.

Service proxy types

Services, explained as simply as possible, provide an abstraction to forward requests to one or more Pods that are running an application.

When creating a Service, we define a selector that tells the Service which Pods to forward requests to. Through functionality in the `kube-proxy` component, when requests hit a Service, they will be forwarded to the various Pods that match the Service's selector.

There are three possible proxy modes that you can use in Kubernetes:

- **Userspace proxy mode**: The oldest proxy mode, available since Kubernetes version 1.0. This proxy mode will forward requests to the matched Pods in a round-robin fashion.

- **Iptables proxy mode**: Available since 1.1, and the default since 1.2. This offers a lower overhead than userspace mode and can use round robin or random selection.

- **IPVS proxy mode**: The newest option, available since 1.8. This proxy mode allows other load balancing options (not just Round Robin):

    a. Round Robin

    b. Least Connection (the least number of open connections)

    c. Source Hashing

    d. Destination Hashing

    e. Shortest Expected Delay

    f. Never Queue

Relevant to this list is a discussion of what round-robin load balancing is, for those not familiar.

Round-robin load balancing involves looping through the potential list of Service endpoints from beginning to end, per network request. The following diagram shows a simplified view of this process it pertains to Kubernetes Pods behind a Service:

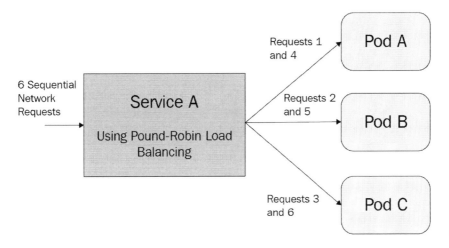

Figure 5.1 – A Service load-balancing to Pods

As you can see, the Service alternates which Pod it sends requests to. The first request goes to Pod A, the second goes to Pod B, the third goes to Pod C, and then it loops around. Now that we know how Services actually handle requests, let's review the major types of Services, starting with ClusterIP.

Implementing ClusterIP

ClusterIP is a simple type of Service exposed on an internal IP inside the cluster. This type of Service is not reachable from outside of the cluster. Let's take a look at the YAML file for our Service:

clusterip-service.yaml

```
apiVersion: v1
kind: Service
metadata:
  name: my-svc
Spec:
  type: ClusterIP
  selector:
    app: web-application
```

```
    environment: staging
ports:
  - name: http
    protocol: TCP
    port: 80
    targetPort: 8080
```

As with other Kubernetes resources, we have our metadata block with our name value. As you can recall from our discussion on DNS, this name value is how you can access your Service from elsewhere in the cluster. For this reason, ClusterIP is a great option for Services that only need to be accessed by other Pods within a cluster.

Next, we have our Spec, which consists of three major pieces:

- First, we have our type, which corresponds to the type of our Service. Since the default type is ClusterIP, you don't actually need to specify a type if you want a ClusterIP Service.

- Next, we have our selector. Our selector consists of key-value pairs that must match labels in the metadata of the Pods in question. In this case, our Service will look for Pods with app=web-application and environment=staging to forward traffic to.

- Finally, we have our ports block, where we can map ports on our Service to targetPort numbers on our Pods. In this case, port 80 (the HTTP port) on our Service will map to port 8080 on our application Pod. More than one port can be opened on our Service, but the name field is required when opening multiple ports.

Next, let's review the protocol options in depth, since these are important to our discussion of Service ports.

Protocol

In the case of our previous ClusterIP Service, we chose TCP as our protocol. Kubernetes currently (as of version 1.19) supports several protocols:

- **TCP**
- **UDP**
- **HTTP**
- **PROXY**
- **SCTP**

This is an area where new features are likely coming, especially where HTTP (L7) services are concerned. Currently, there is not full support of all of these protocols across environments or cloud providers.

> **Important note**
>
> For more information, you can check the main Kubernetes documentation (`https://kubernetes.io/docs/concepts/services-networking/service/`) for the current state of Service protocols.

Now that we've discussed the specifics of Service YAMLs with Cluster IP, we can move on to the next type of Service – NodePort.

Using NodePort

NodePort is an external-facing Service type, which means that it can actually be accessed from outside the Cluster. When creating a NodePort Service, a ClusterIP Service of the same name will automatically be created and routed to by the NodePort, so you will still be able to access the Service from inside the cluster. This makes NodePort a good option for external access to applications when a LoadBalancer Service is not feasible or possible.

NodePort sounds like what it is – this type of Service opens a port on every Node in the cluster on which the Service can be accessed. This port will be in a range that is by default between `30000-32767` and will be linked automatically on Service creation.

Here's what our NodePort Service YAML looks like:

nodeport-service.yaml

```
apiVersion: v1
kind: Service
metadata:
  name: my-svc
Spec:
  type: NodePort
  selector:
    app: web-application
  ports:
    - name: http
      protocol: TCP
```

```
    port: 80
    targetPort: 8080
```

As you can tell, the only difference from the ClusterIP Service is the Service type – however, it is important to note that our intended port 80 in the ports section will only be used when accessing the automatically created ClusterIP version of the Service. From outside the cluster, we'll need to see what the generated port link is to access the Service on our Node IP.

To do this, we can create our Service with the following command:

```
kubectl apply -f svc.yaml
```

And then run this command:

```
kubectl describe service my-svc
```

The result of the preceding command will be the following output:

Name:	my-svc
Namespace:	default
Labels:	app=web-application
Annotations:	<none>
Selector:	app=web-application
Type:	NodePort
IP:	10.32.0.8
Port:	<unset> 8080/TCP
TargetPort:	8080/TCP
NodePort:	<unset> 31598/TCP
Endpoints:	10.200.1.3:8080,10.200.1.5:8080
Session Affinity:	None
Events:	<none>

From this output, we look to the `NodePort` line to see that our assigned port for this Service is `31598`. Thus, this Service can be accessed on any node at `[NODE_IP]:[ASSIGNED_PORT]`.

Alternatively, we can manually assign a NodePort IP to the Service. The YAML for a manually assigned NodePort is as follows:

manual-nodeport-service.yaml

```
apiVersion: v1
kind: Service
metadata:
  name: my-svc
Spec:
  type: NodePort
  selector:
    app: web-application
  ports:
    - name: http
      protocol: TCP
      port: 80
      targetPort: 8080
      nodePort: 31233
```

As you can see, we have chosen a nodePort in the range 30000-32767, in this case, 31233. To see exactly how this NodePort Service works across Nodes, take a look at the following diagram:

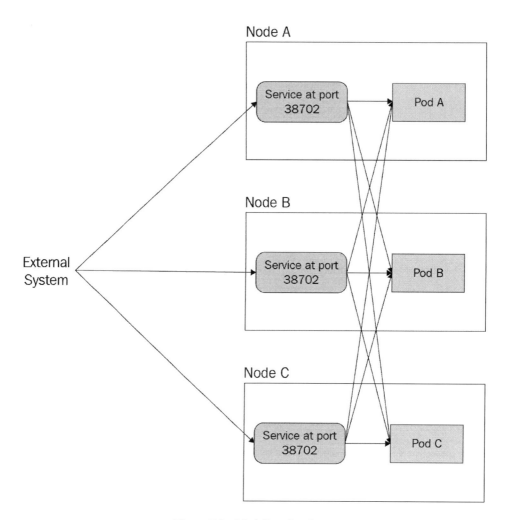

Figure 5.2 – NodePort Service

As you can see, though the Service is accessible at every Node in the cluster (Node A, Node B, and Node C), network requests are still load-balanced across the Pods in all Nodes (Pod A, Pod B, and Pod C), not just the Node that is accessed. This is an effective way to ensure that the application can be accessed from any Node. When using cloud services, however, you already have a range of tools to spread requests between servers. The next type of Service, LoadBalancer, lets us use those tools in the context of Kubernetes.

Setting up a LoadBalancer Service

LoadBalancer is a special Service type in Kubernetes that provisions a load balancer based on where your cluster is running. For instance, in AWS, Kubernetes will provision an Elastic Load Balancer.

> **Important note**
>
> For a full list of LoadBalancer services and configurations, check the documentation for Kubernetes Services at `https://kubernetes.io/docs/concepts/services-networking/service/#loadbalancer`.

Unlike with `ClusterIP` or NodePort, we can amend the functionality of a LoadBalancer Service in cloud-specific ways. Generally, this is done using an annotations block in the Service YAML file – which, as we've discussed before, is just a set of keys and values. To see how this is done for AWS, let's review the spec for a LoadBalancer Service:

loadbalancer-service.yaml

```
apiVersion: v1
kind: Service
metadata:
  name: my-svc
  annotations:
    service.beta.kubernetes.io/aws-load-balancer-ssl-cert:
arn:aws..
spec:
  type: LoadBalancer
  selector:
    app: web-application
  ports:
    - name: http
      protocol: TCP
      port: 80
      targetPort: 8080
```

Though we can create a LoadBalancer without any annotations, the supported AWS-specific annotations give us the ability (as seen in the preceding YAML code) to specify which TLS certificate (via its ARN in Amazon Certificate Manager) we want to be attached to our load balancer. AWS annotations also allow configuring logs for load balancers, and more.

Here are a few key annotations supported by the AWS Cloud Provider as of the writing of this book:

- `service.beta.kubernetes.io/aws-load-balancer-ssl-cert`

- `service.beta.kubernetes.io/aws-load-balancer-proxy-protocol`

- `service.beta.kubernetes.io/aws-load-balancer-ssl-ports`

> **Important note**
>
> A full list of annotations and explanations for all providers can be found on the **Cloud Providers** page in the official Kubernetes documentation, at `https://kubernetes.io/docs/tasks/administer-cluster/running-cloud-controller/`.

Finally, with LoadBalancer Services, we've covered the Service types you will likely use the most. However, for special cases where the Service itself runs outside of Kubernetes, we can use another Service type: ExternalName.

Creating an ExternalName Service

Services of type ExternalName can be used to proxify applications that are not actually running on your cluster, while still keeping the Service as a layer of abstraction that can be updated at any time.

Let's set the scene: you have a legacy production application running on Azure that you want to access from within your cluster. You can access this legacy application at `myoldapp.mydomain.com`. However, your team is currently working on containerizing this application and running it on Kubernetes, and that new version is currently working in your `dev` namespace environment on your cluster.

Instead of asking your other applications to talk to different places depending on the environment, you can always point to a Service called `my-svc` in both your production (`prod`) and development (`dev`) namespaces.

In dev, this Service could be a ClusterIP Service that leads to your newly containerized application on Pods. The following YAML shows how the in-development, containerized Service should work:

clusterip-for-external-service.yaml

```yaml
apiVersion: v1
kind: Service
metadata:
  name: my-svc
  namespace: dev
Spec:
  type: ClusterIP
  selector:
    app: newly-containerized-app
  ports:
    - name: http
      protocol: TCP
      port: 80
      targetPort: 8080
```

In the prod namespace, this Service would instead be an ExternalName Service:

externalname-service.yaml

```yaml
apiVersion: v1
kind: Service
metadata:
  name: my-svc
  namespace: prod
spec:
  type: ExternalName
  externalName: myoldapp.mydomain.com
```

Since our ExternalName Service is not actually forwarding requests to Pods, we don't need a selector. Instead, we specify an ExternalName, which is the DNS name we want the Service to direct to.

The following diagram shows how an `ExternalName` Service could be used in this pattern:

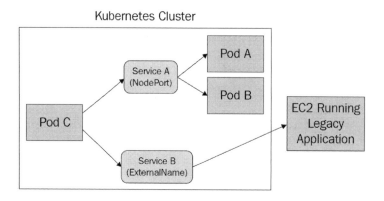

Figure 5.3 – ExternalName Service configuration

In the preceding diagram, our **EC2 Running Legacy Application** is an AWS VM, external to the cluster. Our **Service B** of type **ExternalName** will route requests out to the VM. That way, our **Pod C** (or any other Pod in the cluster) can access our external legacy application simply through the ExternalName services' Kubernetes DNS name.

With `ExternalName`, we've finished our review of all the Kubernetes Service types. Let's move on to a more complex method of exposing applications – the Kubernetes Ingress resource.

Configuring Ingress

As mentioned at the beginning of the chapter, Ingress provides a granular mechanism for routing requests into a cluster. Ingress does not replace Services but augments them with capabilities such as path-based routing. Why is this necessary? There are plenty of reasons, including cost. An Ingress with 10 paths to `ClusterIP` Services is a lot cheaper than creating a new LoadBalancer Service for each path – plus it keeps things simple and easy to understand.

Ingresses do not work like other Services in Kubernetes. Just creating the Ingress itself will do nothing. You need two additional components:

- An Ingress controller: you can choose from many implementations, built on tools such as Nginx or HAProxy.
- ClusterIP or NodePort Services for the intended routes.

First, let's discuss how to configure the Ingress controller.

Ingress controllers

Generally, clusters will not come configured with any pre-existing Ingress controllers. You'll need to select and deploy one to your cluster. `ingress-nginx` is likely the most popular choice, but there are several others – see `https://kubernetes.io/docs/concepts/services-networking/ingress-controllers/` for a full list.

Let's learn how to deploy an Ingress controller - for the purposes of this book, we'll stick with the Nginx Ingress controller created by the Kubernetes community, `ingress-nginx`.

Installation may differ from controller to controller, but for `ingress-nginx` there are two main parts. First, to deploy the main controller itself, run the following command, which may change depending on the target environment and newest Nginx Ingress version:

```
kubectl apply -f https://raw.githubusercontent.com/kubernetes/
ingress-nginx/controller-v0.41.2/deploy/static/provider/cloud/
deploy.yaml
```

Secondly, we may need to configure our Ingress depending on which environment we're running in. For a cluster running on AWS, we can configure the Ingress entry point to use an Elastic Load Balancer that we create in AWS.

> **Important note**
>
> To see all environment-specific setup instructions, see the `ingress-nginx` docs at `https://kubernetes.github.io/ingress-nginx/deploy/`.

The Nginx ingress controller is a set of Pods that will auto-update the Nginx configuration whenever a new Ingress resource (a custom Kubernetes resource) is created. In addition to the Ingress controller, we will need a way to route requests to the Ingress controller – known as the entry point.

Ingress entry point

The default `nginx-ingress` install will also create a singular Service that serves requests to the Nginx layer, at which point the Ingress rules take over. Depending on how you configure your Ingress, this can be a LoadBalancer or NodePort Service. In a cloud environment, you will likely use a cloud LoadBalancer Service as the entry point to the cluster Ingress.

Ingress rules and YAML

Now that we have our Ingress controller up and running, we can start configuring our Ingress rules.

Let's start with a simple example. We have two Services, service-a and service-b, that we want to expose on different paths via our Ingress. Once your Ingress controller and any associated Elastic Load Balancers are created (assuming we're running on AWS), let's first create our Services by working through the following steps:

1. First, let's look at how to create Service A in YAML. Let's call the file service-a.yaml:

service-a.yaml

```
apiVersion: v1
kind: Service
metadata:
  name: service-a
Spec:
  type: ClusterIP
  selector:
    app: application-a
  ports:
    - name: http
      protocol: TCP
      port: 80
      targetPort: 8080
```

2. You can create our Service A by running the following command:

```
kubectl apply -f service-a.yaml
```

3. Next, let's create our Service B, for which the YAML code looks very similar:

```
apiVersion: v1
kind: Service
metadata:
  name: service-b
Spec:
  type: ClusterIP
```

```
  selector:
    app: application-b
  ports:
  - name: http
    protocol: TCP
    port: 80
    targetPort: 8000
```

4. Create our Service B by running the following command:

```
kubectl apply -f service-b.yaml
```

5. Finally, we can create our Ingress with rules for each path. Here is the YAML code for our Ingress that will split requests as necessary based on path-based routing rules:

ingress.yaml

```
apiVersion: networking.k8s.io/v1
kind: Ingress
metadata:
  name: my-first-ingress
  annotations:
    nginx.ingress.kubernetes.io/rewrite-target: /
spec:
  rules:
  - host: my.application.com
    http:
      paths:
      - path: /a
        backend:
          serviceName: service-a
          servicePort: 80
      - path: /b
        backend:
          serviceName: service-b
          servicePort: 80
```

In our preceding YAML, the ingress has a singular `host` value, which would correspond to the host request header for traffic coming through the Ingress. Then, we have two paths, `/a` and `/b`, which lead to our two previously created `ClusterIP` Services. To put this configuration in a graphical format, let's take a look at the following diagram:

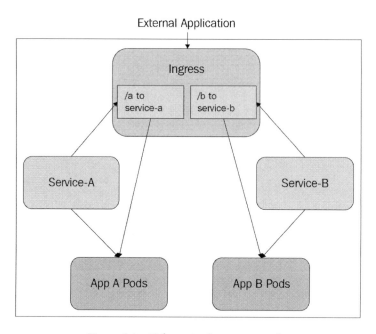

Figure 5.4 – Kubernetes Ingress example

As you can see, our simple path-based rules result in network requests getting routed directly to the proper Pods. This is because `nginx-ingress` uses the Service selector to get a list of Pod IPs, but does not directly use the Service to communicate with the Pods. Rather, the Nginx (in this case) config is automatically updated as new Pod IPs come online.

The `host` value isn't actually required. If you leave it out, any traffic that comes through the Ingress, regardless of the host header (unless it matches a different rule that specifies a host) will be routed according to the rule. The following YAML shows this:

ingress-no-host.yaml

```
apiVersion: networking.k8s.io/v1
kind: Ingress
metadata:
  name: my-first-ingress
```

```
    annotations:
        nginx.ingress.kubernetes.io/rewrite-target: /
spec:
    rules:
    - http:
        paths:
        - path: /a
          backend:
              serviceName: service-a
              servicePort: 80
        - path: /b
          backend:
              serviceName: service-b
              servicePort: 80
```

This previous Ingress definition will flow traffic to the path-based routing rules even if there is no host header value.

Similarly, it is possible to split traffic into multiple separate branching paths based on the host header, like this:

ingress-branching.yaml

```
apiVersion: networking.k8s.io/v1
kind: Ingress
metadata:
    name: multiple-branches-ingress
spec:
    rules:
    - host: my.application.com
      http:
          paths:
          - backend:
                serviceName: service-a
                servicePort: 80
    - host: my.otherapplication.com
      http:
          paths:
```

```
    - backend:
        serviceName: service-b
        servicePort: 80
```

Finally, you can also secure your Ingress with TLS in many cases, though this functionality differs on a per Ingress controller basis. For Nginx, this can be done by using a Kubernetes Secret. We'll get to this functionality in the next chapter but for now, check out the configuration on the Ingress side:

ingress-secure.yaml

```
apiVersion: networking.k8s.io/v1
kind: Ingress
metadata:
  name: secured-ingress
spec:
  tls:
  - hosts:
    - my.application.com
    secretName: my-tls-secret
  rules:
    - host: my.application.com
      http:
        paths:
        - path: /
          backend:
            serviceName: service-a
            servicePort: 8080
```

This configuration will look for a Kubernetes Secret named my-tls-secret in the default namespace to attach to the Ingress for TLS.

That ends our discussion of Ingress. A lot of Ingress functionality can be specific to which Ingress controller you decide to use, so check out the documentation for your chosen implementation.

Summary

In this chapter, we reviewed the various methods that Kubernetes provides in order to expose applications running on the cluster to the outside world. The major methods are Services and Ingress. Within Services, you can use ClusterIP Services for in-cluster routing and NodePort for access to a Service directly via ports on Nodes. LoadBalancer Services let you use existing cloud load-balancing systems, and ExternalName Services let you route requests out of the cluster to external resources.

Finally, Ingress provides a powerful tool to route requests in the cluster by path. To implement Ingress you need to install a third-party or open source Ingress controller on your cluster.

In the next chapter, we'll talk about how to inject configuration information into your applications running on Kubernetes using two resource types: ConfigMap and Secret.

Questions

1. What type of Service would you use for applications that are only accessed internally in a cluster?

2. How can you tell which port a NodePort Service is active on?

3. Why can Ingress be more cost-effective than purely Services?

4. Other than supporting legacy applications, how might ExternalName Services be useful on a cloud platform?

Further reading

*   Information on cloud providers, from the Kubernetes documentation: `https://kubernetes.io/docs/tasks/administer-cluster/running-cloud-controller/`

6
Kubernetes Application Configuration

This chapter describes the main configuration tools that Kubernetes provides. We'll start by discussing some best practices for injecting configuration into containerized applications. Next, we will discuss ConfigMaps, a Kubernetes resource aimed at providing applications with configuration data. Finally, we will cover Secrets, a secure way to store and provide sensitive data to applications running on Kubernetes. Altogether, this chapter should give you a great toolset for configuring your production applications on Kubernetes.

In this chapter, we will cover the following topics:

- Configuring containerized applications using best practices
- Implementing ConfigMaps
- Using Secrets

Technical requirements

In order to run the commands detailed in this chapter, you will need a computer that supports the kubectl command-line tool, along with a working Kubernetes cluster. Review *Chapter 1, Communicating with Kubernetes*, to find several methods for getting up and running with Kubernetes quickly, and for instructions on how to install the kubectl tool.

The code used in this chapter can be found in the book's GitHub repository at https://github.com/PacktPublishing/Cloud-Native-with-Kubernetes/tree/master/Chapter6.

Configuring containerized applications using best practices

By now, we know how to effectively deploy (as covered in *Chapter 4, Scaling and Deploying Your Application*) and expose (as covered in *Chapter 5, Services and Ingress – Communicating with the outside world*) containerized applications on Kubernetes. This is enough to run non-trivial stateless containerized applications on Kubernetes. However, Kubernetes also provides additional tooling for application configuration and Secrets management.

Since Kubernetes runs containers, you could always configure your application to use environment variables baked into your Dockerfile. But this sidesteps some of the real value of an orchestrator like Kubernetes. We want to be able to change our application container without rebuilding a Docker image. For this purpose, Kubernetes gives us two configuration-focused resources: ConfigMaps and Secrets. Let's first look at ConfigMaps.

Understanding ConfigMaps

When running applications in production, developers want the ability to quickly and easily inject application configuration information. There are many patterns for doing this – from using a separate configuration server that is queried, to using environment variables or environment files. These strategies vary in the security and usability they offer.

For containerized applications, environment variables are often the easiest way to go – but injecting these variables in a secure way can require additional tooling or scripts. In Kubernetes, the ConfigMap resource lets us do this in a flexible, easy way. ConfigMaps allow Kubernetes administrators to specify and inject configuration information as either files or environment variables.

For highly sensitive information such as secret keys, Kubernetes gives us another, similar resource – Secrets.

Understanding Secrets

Secrets refer to additional application configuration items that need to be stored in a slightly more secure way – for instance, master keys to restricted APIs, database passwords, and more. Kubernetes provides a resource called a Secret, which stores application configuration information in an encoded fashion. This does not inherently make the Secret more secure, but Kubernetes respects the concept of a secret by not automatically printing secret information in the `kubectl get` or `kubectl describe` commands. This prevents the Secret from being accidentally printed to a log.

To ensure that Secrets are actually secret, encryption at rest must be enabled on your cluster for secret data – we'll review how to do this later in this chapter. Available from Kubernetes 1.13, this functionality lets Kubernetes administrators prevent Secrets from being stored unencrypted in `etcd`, and limits access to `etcd` admins.

Before we do a deep dive into Secrets, let's start by discussing ConfigMaps, which are better for non-sensitive information.

Implementing ConfigMaps

ConfigMaps provide an easy way to store and inject application configuration data for containers running on Kubernetes.

Creating a ConfigMap is simple – and they enable two possibilities for actually injecting the application configuration data:

- Injecting as an environment variable
- Injecting as a file

While the first option operates simply using container environment variables in memory, the latter option touches on some facets of volumes – a Kubernetes storage medium that will be covered in the next chapter. We will keep the review short for now and use it as an introduction to volumes, which will be expanded on in the following chapter, *Chapter 7, Storage on Kubernetes.*

When working with ConfigMaps, it can be easier to create them using an imperative `Kubectl` command. There are a few possible ways to create ConfigMaps, which also result in differences in the way data is stored and accessed from the ConfigMap itself. The first way is to simply create it from a text value, as we will see next.

From text values

Creating a ConfigMap from a text value in a command is done as follows:

```
kubectl create configmap myapp-config --from-
literal=mycategory.mykey=myvalue
```

The previous command creates a `configmap` named `myapp-config` with a single key, called `mycategory.mykey`, that has a value of `myvalue`. You can also create a ConfigMap with multiple keys and values, as follows:

```
kubectl create configmap myapp-config2 --from-
literal=mycategory.mykey=myvalue
--from-literal=mycategory.mykey2=myvalue2
```

The preceding command results in a ConfigMap with two values in the `data` section.

To see what your ConfigMap looks like, run the following command:

```
kubectl get configmap myapp-config2
```

You will see the following output:

configmap-output.yaml

```
apiVersion: v1
kind: ConfigMap
metadata:
  name: myapp-config2
  namespace: default
data:
  mycategory.mykey: myvalue
  mycategory.mykey2: myvalue2
```

When your ConfigMap data is long, it does not make as much sense to create it directly from a text value. For longer configs, we can create our ConfigMap from a file.

From files

In order to make it easier to create a ConfigMap with many different values, or reuse existing environment files you already have, you can create a ConfigMap from a file by following these steps:

1. Let's start by creating our file, which we'll name `env.properties`:

    ```
    myconfigid=1125
    publicapikey=i38ahsjh2
    ```

2. Then, we can create our ConfigMap by running the following command:

    ```
    kubectl create configmap my-config-map --from-file=env.
    properties
    ```

3. To check whether our `kubectl create` command correctly made our ConfigMap, let's describe it using `kubectl describe`:

    ```
    kubectl describe configmaps my-config-map
    ```

This should result in the following output:

```
Name:           my-config-map
Namespace:      default
Labels:         <none>
Annotations:    <none>

Data
====
env.properties:        39 bytes
```

As you can see, this ConfigMap contains our text file (and the number of bytes). Our file in this case could be any text file – but if you know that your file is formatted properly as an environment file, you can let Kubernetes know that, in order to make your ConfigMap a bit easier to read. Let's learn how to do this.

From environment files

If we know that our file is formatted as a normal environment file with key pairs, we can use a slightly different method to create our ConfigMap – the environment file method. This method will make our data more obvious in the ConfigMap object, rather than being hidden inside the file.

Let's use the exact same file as before with our environment-specific creation:

```
kubectl create configmap my-env-config-map --from-env-file=env.
properties
```

Now, let's describe our ConfigMap using the following command:

```
> kubectl describe configmaps my-env-config-map
```

We get the following output:

```
Name:          my-env-config-map
Namespace:     default
Labels:        <none>
Annotations:   <none>

Data
====
myconfigid:
----
1125
publicapikey:
----
i38ahsjh2
Events:  <none>
```

As you can see, by using the -from-env-file method, the data in the env file is easily viewable when you run kubectl describe. This also means we can mount our ConfigMap directly as environment variables – more on that shortly.

Mounting a ConfigMap as a volume

To consume data from a ConfigMap in a Pod, you need to mount it to the Pod in the spec. This mirrors (for good reason, as we'll find out) the way to mount a volume in Kubernetes, which is a resource that provides storage. For now, however, don't worry about volumes.

Let's take a look at our Pod spec, which mounts our my-config-map ConfigMap as a volume on our Pod:

pod-mounting-cm.yaml

```
apiVersion: v1
kind: Pod
metadata:
  name: my-pod-mount-cm
spec:
  containers:
    - name: busybox
      image: busybox
      command:
      - sleep
      - "3600"
      volumeMounts:
      - name: my-config-volume
        mountPath: /app/config
  volumes:
    - name: my-config-volume
      configMap:
        name: my-config-map
  restartPolicy: Never
```

As you can see, our my-config-map ConfigMap is mounted as a volume (my-config-volume) on the /app/config path for our container to access. We'll get to know more about how this works in the next chapter on storage.

In some cases, you may want to mount a ConfigMap as environment variables in your container – we will learn how to do this next.

Mounting a ConfigMap as an environment variable

You can also mount a ConfigMap as an environment variable. This process is pretty similar to mounting a ConfigMap as a volume.

Let's take a look at our Pod spec:

pod-mounting-cm-as-env.yaml

```
apiVersion: v1
kind: Pod
metadata:
  name: my-pod-mount-env
spec:
  containers:
    - name: busybox
      image: busybox
      command:
      - sleep
      - "3600"
      env:
        - name: MY_ENV_VAR
          valueFrom:
            configMapKeyRef:
              name: my-env-config-map
              key: myconfigid
  restartPolicy: Never
```

As you can see, instead of mounting our ConfigMap as a volume, we are simply referencing it in a container environment variable – `MY_ENV_VAR`. To do this, we need to use `configMapRef` in our `valueFrom` key and reference the name of our ConfigMap as well as the key to look at inside the ConfigMap itself.

As we mentioned at the beginning of the chapter in the *Configuring containerized applications using best practices* section, ConfigMaps are not secure by default, and their data is stored as plaintext. For an added layer of security, we can use Secrets instead of ConfigMaps.

Using Secrets

Secrets work very similarly to ConfigMaps, except that they are stored as encoded text (specifically, Base64) instead of plaintext.

Creating a Secret is therefore very similar to creating a ConfigMap, with a few key differences. For starters, creating a Secret imperatively will automatically Base64-encode the data in the Secret. First, let's look at creating a Secret imperatively from a pair of files.

From files

First, let's try creating a Secret from a file (this also works with multiple files). We can do this using the `kubectl create` command:

```
> echo -n 'mysecretpassword' > ./pass.txt
> kubectl create secret generic my-secret --from-file=./pass.txt
```

This should result in the following output:

```
secret "my-secret" created
```

Now, let's see what our Secret looks like using `kubectl describe`:

```
> kubectl describe secrets/db-user-pass
```

This command should result in the following output:

```
Name:           my-secret
Namespace:      default
Labels:         <none>
Annotations:    <none>

Type:           Opaque

Data
====
pass.txt:       16 bytes
```

As you can see, the `describe` command shows the number of bytes contained in the Secret, and its type `Opaque`.

Another way to create a Secret is to manually create it using a declarative approach. Let's look at how to do that next.

Manual declarative approach

When creating a Secret declaratively from a YAML file, you'll need to pre-encode the data to be stored using an encoding utility, such as the `base64` pipe on Linux.

Let's encode our password here using the Linux `base64` command:

```
> echo -n 'myverybadpassword' | base64
bXl2ZXJ5YmFkcGFzc3dvcmQ=
```

Now, we can declaratively create our Secret using a Kubernetes YAML spec, which we can name `secret.yaml`:

```
apiVersion: v1
kind: Secret
metadata:
  name: my-secret
type: Opaque
data:
  dbpass: bXl2ZXJ5YmFkcGFzc3dvcmQ=
```

Our `secret.yaml` spec contains the Base64-encoded string that we created.

To create the Secret, run the following command:

```
kubectl create -f secret.yaml
```

Now you know how to create Secrets. Next, let's learn how to mount a Secret for use by a Pod.

Mounting a Secret as a volume

Mounting Secrets is very similar to mounting ConfigMaps. First, let's take a look at how to mount a Secret to a Pod as a volume (file).

Let's take a look at our Pod spec. In this case, we are running an example application in order to test our Secret. Here is the YAML:

pod-mounting-secret.yaml

```
apiVersion: v1
kind: Pod
metadata:
```

```
    name: my-pod-mount-cm
spec:
  containers:
    - name: busybox
      image: busybox
      command:
        - sleep
        - "3600"
      volumeMounts:
      - name: my-config-volume
        mountPath: /app/config
        readOnly: true
  volumes:
    - name: foo
      secret:
        secretName: my-secret
  restartPolicy: Never
```

The one difference from ConfigMap here is that we specify `readOnly` on the volume to prevent any changes to the Secret while the Pod is running. Everything else is the same as far as how we are mounting the Secret.

Again, we will review volumes in depth in the next chapter, *Chapter 7*, *Storage on Kubernetes*, but for a simple explanation, volumes are a way to add storage to your Pods. In this example, we mounted our volume, which you can consider a filesystem, to our Pod. Our Secret is then created as a file in the filesystem.

Mounting a Secret as an environment variable

Similar to file mounting, we can mount our Secret as an environment variable in much the same way that ConfigMap mounting works.

Let's take a look at another Pod YAML. In this case, we will mount our Secret as an environment variable:

pod-mounting-secret-env.yaml

```
apiVersion: v1
kind: Pod
metadata:
```

```
    name: my-pod-mount-env
spec:
  containers:
    - name: busybox
      image: busybox
      command:
      - sleep
      - "3600"
      env:
        - name: MY_PASSWORD_VARIABLE
          valueFrom:
            secretKeyRef:
              name: my-secret
              key: dbpass
  restartPolicy: Never
```

After creating the preceding Pod with `kubectl apply`, let's run a command to look into our Pod to see if the variable was properly initialized. This works exactly the same way as `docker exec`:

```
> kubectl exec -it my-pod-mount-env -- /bin/bash
> printenv MY_PASSWORD_VARIABLE
myverybadpassword
```

It works! You should now have a good understanding of how to create, mount, and use ConfigMaps and Secrets.

As the final topic concerning Secrets, we will learn how to create secure, encrypted Secrets using the Kubernetes `EncryptionConfig`.

Implementing encrypted Secrets

Several managed Kubernetes services (including Amazon's **Elastic Kubernetes Service (EKS)**) automatically encrypt `etcd` data at rest – so you don't need to do anything in order to implement encrypted Secrets. Cluster provisioners such as Kops have a simple flag (such as `encryptionConfig: true`). But if you're creating your cluster *the hard way*, you'll need to start the Kubernetes API server with a flag, `--encryption-provider-config`, and an `EncryptionConfig` file.

> **Important note**
>
> Creating a cluster completely from scratch is outside the scope of this book (take a look at *Kubernetes The Hard Way* for a great guide on that, at `https://github.com/kelseyhightower/kubernetes-the-hard-way`).

For a quick look at how encryption is handled, take a look at the following `EncryptionConfiguration` YAML, which is passed to `kube-apiserver` on start:

encryption-config.yaml

```yaml
apiVersion: apiserver.config.k8s.io/v1
kind: EncryptionConfiguration
resources:
  - resources:
    - secrets
    providers:
    - aesgcm:
        keys:
        - name: key1
          secret: c2VjcmV0IGlzIHNlY3VyZQ==
        - name: key2
          secret: dGhpcyBpcyBwYXNzd29yZA==
```

The preceding `EncryptionConfiguration` YAML takes a list of the resources that should be encrypted in `etcd`, and one or more providers that can be used to encrypt data. The following providers are allowed as of Kubernetes `1.17`:

- **Identity**: No encryption.

- **Aescbc**: The recommended encryption provider.

- **Secretbox**: Faster than Aescbc, and newer.

- **Aesgcm**: Note that you will need to implement key rotation yourself with Aesgcm.

- **Kms**: Used with a third-party Secrets store, such as Vault or AWS KMS.

To see the full list, see `https://kubernetes.io/docs/tasks/administer-cluster/encrypt-data/#providers`. When multiple providers are added to the list, Kubernetes will use the first configured provider to encrypt objects. When decrypting, Kubernetes will go down the list and attempt decryption with each provider – if none work, it will return an error.

Once we have created a secret (look at any of our previous examples of how to do so), and our `EncryptionConfig` is active, we can check whether our Secrets are actually encrypted.

Checking whether your Secrets are encrypted

The easiest way to check whether your secret is actually encrypted in `etcd` is to fetch the value directly from `etcd` and check the encryption prefix:

1. First, let's go ahead and make a secret key using `base64`:

    ```
    > echo -n 'secrettotest' | base64
    c2VjcmV0dG90ZXN0
    ```

2. Create a file called `secret_to_test.yaml` with the following content:

    ```yaml
    apiVersion: v1
    kind: Secret
    metadata:
      name: secret-to-test
    type: Opaque
    data:
      myencsecret: c2VjcmV0dG90ZXN0
    ```

3. Create the Secret:

    ```
    kubectl apply -f secret_to_test.yaml
    ```

4. With our Secret created, let's check if it is encrypted in etcd by directly querying it. You shouldn't need to directly query etcd very often, but if you have access to the certificates used to bootstrap the cluster, it is an easy process:

```
> export ETCDCTL_API=3
> etcdctl --cacert=/etc/kubernetes/certs/ca.crt
--cert=/etc/kubernetes/certs/etcdclient.crt
--key=/etc/kubernetes/certs/etcdclient.key
get /registry/secrets/default/secret-to-test
```

Depending on your configured encryption provider, your Secret's data will start with a provider tag. For instance, a Secret encrypted with the Azure KMS provider will start with k8s:enc:kms:v1:azurekmsprovider.

5. Now, check to see if the Secret is correctly decrypted (it will still be encoded) via kubectl:

```
> kubectl get secrets secret-to-test -o yaml
```

The output should be myencsecret: c2VjcmV0dG90ZXN0, which is our unencrypted, encoded Secret value:

```
> echo 'c2VjcmV0dG90ZXN0' | base64 --decode
> secrettotest
```

Success!

We now have encryption running on our cluster. Let's find out how to remove it.

Disabling cluster encryption

We can also remove encryption from our Kubernetes resources fairly easily.

First, we need to restart the Kubernetes API server with a blank encryption configuration YAML. If you self-provisioned your cluster, this should be easy, but on EKS or AKS, this isn't possible manually. You'll need to follow the cloud provider-specific documentation on how to disable encryption.

If you've self-provisioned your cluster or used a tool such as Kops or Kubeadm, then you can restart your `kube-apiserver` process on all master nodes with the following `EncryptionConfiguration`:

encryption-reset.yaml

```
apiVersion: apiserver.config.k8s.io/v1
kind: EncryptionConfiguration
resources:
  - resources:
    - secrets
    providers:
    - identity: {}
```

> **Important note**
> Note that the identity provider does not need to be the only provider listed, but it does need to be first, since as we mentioned previously, Kubernetes uses the first provider to encrypt new/updated objects in `etcd`.

Now, we will manually recreate all our Secrets, upon which point they will automatically use the identity provider (unencrypted):

```
kubectl get secrets --all-namespaces -o json | kubectl replace -f -
```

At this point, all of our Secrets are unencrypted!

Summary

In this chapter, we looked at the methods Kubernetes provides for injecting application configuration. First, we looked at some best practices for configuring containerized applications. Then, we reviewed the first method that Kubernetes gives us, ConfigMaps, along with several options for creating and mounting them to Pods. Finally, we looked at Secrets, which when encrypted are a more secure way to handle sensitive configurations. By now, you should have all the tools you need to provide secure and insecure configuration values to your application.

In the next chapter, we'll delve into a topic we already touched on by mounting our Secrets and ConfigMaps – the Kubernetes volume resource and, more generally, storage on Kubernetes.

Questions

1. What are the differences between Secrets and ConfigMaps?

2. How are Secrets encoded?

3. What is the major difference between creating a ConfigMap from a regular file, and creating one from an environment file?

4. How can you make Secrets secure on Kubernetes? Why aren't they secure by default?

Further reading

*   Info on data encryption configuration for Kubernetes can be found in the official documentation at `https://kubernetes.io/docs/tasks/administer-cluster/encrypt-data/`.

7
Storage on Kubernetes

In this chapter, we will learn how to provide application storage on Kubernetes. We'll review two storage resources on Kubernetes, volumes and persistent volumes. Volumes are great for transient data needs, but persistent volumes are necessary for running any serious stateful workload on Kubernetes. With the skills you'll learn in this chapter, you will be able to configure storage for your applications running on Kubernetes in several different ways and environments.

In this chapter, we will cover the following topics:

- Understanding the difference between volumes and persistent volumes
- Using volumes
- Creating persistent volumes
- Persistent volume claims

Technical requirements

In order to run the commands detailed in this chapter, you will need a computer that supports the `kubectl` command-line tool along with a working Kubernetes cluster. See *Chapter 1, Communicating with Kubernetes*, for several methods to get up and running with Kubernetes quickly, and for instructions on how to install the `kubectl` tool.

The code used in this chapter can be found in the book's GitHub repository at `https://github.com/PacktPublishing/Cloud-Native-with-Kubernetes/tree/master/Chapter7`.

Understanding the difference between volumes and persistent volumes

A completely stateless, containerized application may only need disk space for the container files themselves. When running applications of this type, no additional configuration is required on Kubernetes.

However, this is not always true in the real world. Legacy apps that are being moved to containers may need disk space volumes for many possible reasons. In order to hold files for use by containers, you need the Kubernetes volume resource.

There are two main storage resources that can be created in Kubernetes:

- Volumes
- Persistent volumes

The distinction between the two is in the name: while volumes are tied to the lifecycle of a particular Pod, persistent volumes stay alive until deleted and can be shared across different Pods. Volumes can be handy in sharing data across containers within a Pod, while persistent volumes can be used for many possible advanced purposes.

Let's look at how to implement volumes first.

Volumes

Kubernetes supports many different subtypes of volumes. Most can be used for either volumes or persistent volumes, but some are specific to either resource. We'll start with the simplest and review a few types.

> **Important note**
>
> You can see the full current list of volume types at `https://kubernetes.io/docs/concepts/storage/volumes/#types-of-volumes`.

Here is a short list of volume subtypes:

- `awsElasticBlockStore`
- `cephfs`
- `ConfigMap`
- `emptyDir`
- `hostPath`
- `local`
- `nfs`
- `persistentVolumeClaim`
- `rbd`
- `Secret`

As you can see, both ConfigMaps and Secrets are actually implemented as *types* of volume. Additionally, the list includes cloud provider volume types such as `awsElasticBlockStore`.

Unlike persistent volumes, which are created separately from any one Pod, creating a volume is most often done in the context of a Pod.

To create a simple volume, you can use the following Pod YAML:

pod-with-vol.yaml

```yaml
apiVersion: v1
kind: Pod
metadata:
  name: pod-with-vol
spec:
  containers:
  - name: busybox
    image: busybox
    volumeMounts:
```

```
      - name: my-storage-volume
        mountPath: /data
  volumes:
  - name: my-storage-volume
    emptyDir: {}
```

This YAML will create a Pod along with a volume of type emptyDir. Volumes of type emptyDir are provisioned using whatever storage already exists on the node that the Pod is assigned to. As mentioned previously, the volume is tied to the lifecycle of the Pod, not its containers.

This means that in a Pod with multiple containers, all containers will be able to access volume data. Let's take the following example YAML file for a Pod:

pod-with-multiple-containers.yaml

```
apiVersion: v1
kind: Pod
metadata:
  name: my-pod
spec:
  containers:
  - name: busybox
    image: busybox
    volumeMounts:
    - name: config-volume
      mountPath: /shared-config
  - name: busybox2
    image: busybox
    volumeMounts:
    - name: config-volume
      mountPath: /myconfig
  volumes:
  - name: config-volume
    emptyDir: {}
```

In this example, both containers in the Pod can access the volume data, though at different paths. Containers can even communicate via files in the shared volume.

The important parts of the spec are the `volume spec` itself (the list item under `volumes`) and the `mount` for the volume (the list item under `volumeMounts`).

Each mount item contains a name, which corresponds to the name of the volume in the `volumes` section, and a `mountPath`, which will dictate to which file path on the container the volume gets mounted. For instance, in the preceding YAML, the volume `config-volume` will be accessible from within the `busybox` Pod at `/shared-config`, and within the `busybox2` Pod at `/myconfig`.

The volume spec itself takes a name – in this case, `my-storage`, and additional keys/values specific to the volume type, which in this case is `emptyDir` and just takes empty brackets.

Now, let's address the example of a cloud-provisioned volume mounted to a Pod. To mount an AWS **Elastic Block Storage** (**EBS**) volume, for instance, the following YAML can be used:

pod-with-ebs.yaml

```yaml
apiVersion: v1
kind: Pod
metadata:
  name: my-app
spec:
  containers:
  - image: busybox
    name: busybox
    volumeMounts:
    - mountPath: /data
      name: my-ebs-volume
  volumes:
  - name: my-ebs-volume
    awsElasticBlockStore:
      volumeID: [INSERT VOLUME ID HERE]
```

This YAML will, as long as your cluster is set up correctly to authenticate with AWS, attach your existing EBS volume to the Pod. As you can see, we use the `awsElasticBlockStore` key to specifically configure the exact volume ID to be used. In this case, the EBS volume must already exist on your AWS account and region. This is much easier with AWS **Elastic Kubernetes Service** (**EKS**) since it allows us to automatically provision EBS volumes from within Kubernetes.

Kubernetes also includes features within the Kubernetes AWS cloud provider to automatically provision volumes – but these are for use with persistent volumes. We'll look at how to get these automatically provisioned volumes in the *Persistent volumes* section.

Persistent volumes

Persistent volumes hold some key advantages over regular Kubernetes volumes. As mentioned previously, their (persistent volumes) lifecycle is tied to the life of the cluster, not the life of a single Pod. This means that persistent volumes can be shared between Pods and reused as long as the cluster is running. For this reason, the pattern matches much better to external stores such as EBS (a block storage service on AWS) since the storage itself outlasts a single Pod.

Using persistent volumes actually requires two resources: the `PersistentVolume` itself and a `PersistentVolumeClaim`, which is used to mount a `PersistentVolume` to a Pod.

Let's start with the `PersistentVolume` itself – take a look at the basic YAML for creating a `PersistentVolume`:

pv.yaml

```
apiVersion: v1
kind: PersistentVolume
metadata:
  name: my-pv
spec:
  storageClassName: manual
  capacity:
    storage: 5Gi
  accessModes:
    - ReadWriteOnce
  hostPath:
    path: "/mnt/mydata"
```

Now let's pick this apart. Starting with the first line in the spec – `storageClassName`.

This first config, storageClassName, represents the type of storage we want to use. For the hostPath volume type, we simply specify manual, but for AWS EBS, for instance, you could create and use a storage class called gp2Encrypted to match the gp2 storage type in AWS with EBS encryption enabled. Storage classes are therefore combinations of configuration that are available for a particular volume type – which can be referenced in the volume spec.

Moving forward with our AWS StorageClass example, let's provision a new StorageClass for gp2Encrypted:

gp2-storageclass.yaml

```yaml
kind: StorageClass
apiVersion: storage.k8s.io/v1
metadata:
  name: gp2Encrypted
  annotations:
    storageclass.kubernetes.io/is-default-class: "true"
provisioner: kubernetes.io/aws-ebs
parameters:
  type: gp2
  encrypted: "true"
  fsType: ext4
```

Now, we can create our PersistentVolume using the gp2Encrypted storage class. However, there's a shortcut to creating PersistentVolumes using dynamically provisioned EBS (or other cloud) volumes. When using dynamically provisioned volumes, we create the PersistentVolumeClaim first, which then automatically generates the PersistentVolume.

Persistent volume claims

We now know that you can easily create persistent volumes in Kubernetes, however, that does not allow you to bind storage to a Pod. You need to create a PersistentVolumeClaim, which claims a PersistentVolume and allows you to bind that claim to a Pod or multiple Pods.

Building on our new `StorageClass` from the last section, let's make a claim that will automatically result in a new `PersistentVolume` being created since there are no other persistent volumes with our desired `StorageClass`:

pvc.yaml

```
kind: PersistentVolumeClaim
apiVersion: v1
metadata:
  name: my-pv-claim
spec:
  storageClassName: gp2Encrypted
  accessModes:
    - ReadWriteOnce
  resources:
    requests:
      storage: 1Gi
```

Running `kubectl apply -f` on this file should result in a new, autogenerated **Persistent Volume** (**PV**) being created. If your AWS cloud provider is set up correctly, this will result in the creation of a new EBS volume with type GP2 and encryption enabled.

Before we attach our EBS-backed persistent volume to our Pod, let's confirm that the EBS volume was created correctly in AWS.

To do so, we can navigate to our AWS console and ensure we are in the same region that our EKS cluster is running in. Then go to **Services** > **EC2** and click on **Volumes** in the left menu under **Elastic Block Store**. In this section, we should see a line item with an autogenerated volume of the same size (**1 GiB**) as our PVC states. It should have the class of GP2, and it should have encryption enabled. Let's see what this would look like in the AWS console:

Figure 7.1 – AWS console with autocreated EBS volume

As you can see, we have our dynamically generated EBS volume properly created in AWS, with encryption enabled and the **gp2** volume type assigned. Now that we have our volume created, and we've confirmed that it has been created in AWS, we can attach it to our Pod.

Attaching Persistent Volume Claims (PVCs) to Pods

Now we have both a `PersistentVolume` and a `PersistentVolumeClaim`, we can attach them to a Pod for consumption. This process is very similar to attaching a ConfigMap or Secret – which makes sense, because ConfigMaps and Secrets are essentially types of volumes!

Check out the YAML that allows us to attach our encrypted EBS volume to a Pod and name it `pod-with-attachment.yaml`:

Pod-with-attachment.yaml

```
apiVersion: v1
kind: Pod
metadata:
  name: my-pod
spec:
  volumes:
    - name: my-pv
      persistentVolumeClaim:
        claimName: my-pv-claim
  containers:
    - name: my-container
      image: busybox
      volumeMounts:
        - mountPath: "/usr/data"
          name: my-pv
```

Running `kubectl apply -f pod-with-attachment.yaml` will result in the creation of a Pod that has our `PersistentVolume` mounted via our claim to `/usr/data`.

To confirm that the volume has been successfully created, let's exec into our Pod and create a file in the location that our volume has been mounted:

```
> kubectl exec -it shell-demo -- /bin/bash
> cd /usr/data
> touch myfile.txt
```

Now, let's delete the Pod using the following command:

```
> kubectl delete pod my-pod
```

And recreate it again using the following command:

```
> kubectl apply -f my-pod.yaml
```

If we've done our job right, we should be able to see our file when running kubectl exec to get into the Pod again:

```
> kubectl exec -it my-pod -- /bin/bash
> ls /usr/data
> myfile.txt
```

Success!

We now know how to create a cloud-storage-provided persistent volume for Kubernetes. However, you may be running Kubernetes on-premise or on your laptop using minikube. Let's look at some alternate persistent volume subtypes that you can use instead.

Persistent volumes without cloud storage

Our previous examples assume that you are running Kubernetes in a cloud environment and can make use of storage services provided by the cloud platform (AWS EBS and others). This, however, is not always possible. You may be running Kubernetes in a data center environment, or on dedicated hardware.

In this case, there are many potential solutions for providing storage to Kubernetes. A simple one is to change the volume type to hostPath, which works within the node's existing storage devices to create persistent volumes. This is great when running on minikube, for instance, but does not provide as powerful an abstraction as something like AWS EBS. For a tool with on-premise capabilities similar to cloud storage tools like EBS, let's look at using Ceph with Rook. For the full documentation, check out the Rook docs (which will teach you Ceph as well) at https://rook.io/docs/rook/v1.3/ceph-quickstart.html.

Rook is a popular open source Kubernetes storage abstraction layer. It can provide persistent volumes through a variety of providers, such as EdgeFS and NFS. In this case, we'll use Ceph, an open source storage project that provides object, block, and file storage. For simplicity, we'll use block mode.

Installing Rook on Kubernetes is actually pretty simple. We'll take you from installing Rook to setting up a Ceph cluster, to finally provisioning persistent volumes on our cluster.

Installing Rook

We're going to use a typical Rook installation default setup provided by the Rook GitHub repository. This could be highly customized depending on the use case but will allow us to quickly set up block storage for our workloads. Please refer to the following steps to do this:

1. First, let's clone the Rook repository:

    ```
    > git clone --single-branch --branch master https://
    github.com/rook/rook.git
    > cd cluster/examples/kubernetes/ceph
    ```

2. Our next step is to create all the relevant Kubernetes resources, including several **Custom Resource Definitions** (**CRDs**). We'll talk about these in later chapters, but for now, consider them new Kubernetes resources that are specific to Rook, outside of the typical Pods, Services, and so on. To create common resources, run the following command:

    ```
    > kubectl apply -f ./common.yaml
    ```

3. Next, let's start our Rook operator, which will handle provisioning all the necessary resources for a particular Rook provider, which in this case will be Ceph:

    ```
    > kubectl apply -f ./operator.yaml
    ```

4. Before the next step, ensure that the Rook operator Pod is actually running by using the following command:

    ```
    > kubectl -n rook-ceph get pod
    ```

5. Once the Rook Pod is in the `Running` state, we can set up our Ceph cluster! The YAML for this is also in the folder we've cloned from Git. Create it using the following command:

```
> kubectl create -f cluster.yaml
```

This process can take a few minutes. The Ceph cluster is comprised of several different Pod types, including the operator, **Object Storage Devices (OSDs)**, and managers.

To ensure that our Ceph cluster is working properly, Rook provides a toolbox container image that allows you to use the Rook and Ceph command-line tools. To start the toolbox, you can use the toolbox Pod spec provided by the Rook project at `https://rook.io/docs/rook/v0.7/toolbox.html`.

Here is a sample of the spec for the toolbox Pod:

rook-toolbox-pod.yaml

```yaml
apiVersion: v1
kind: Pod
metadata:
  name: rook-tools
  namespace: rook
spec:
  dnsPolicy: ClusterFirstWithHostNet
  containers:
  - name: rook-tools
    image: rook/toolbox:v0.7.1
    imagePullPolicy: IfNotPresent
```

As you can see, this Pod uses a special container image provided by Rook. The image comes with all the tools you need to investigate Rook and Ceph pre-installed.

Once you have the toolbox Pod running, you can use the `rookctl` and `ceph` commands to check on the cluster status (check the Rook docs for specifics).

The rook-ceph-block storage class

Now our cluster is working, we can create our storage class that will be used by our PVs. We will call this storage class `rook-ceph-block`. Here's our YAML file (`ceph-rook-combined.yaml`), which will include our `CephBlockPool` (which will handle our block storage in Ceph – see `https://rook.io/docs/rook/v0.9/ceph-pool-crd.html` for more information) as well as the storage class itself:

ceph-rook-combined.yaml

```yaml
apiVersion: ceph.rook.io/v1
kind: CephBlockPool
metadata:
  name: replicapool
  namespace: rook-ceph
spec:
  failureDomain: host
  replicated:
    size: 3
---
apiVersion: storage.k8s.io/v1
kind: StorageClass
metadata:
    name: rook-ceph-block
provisioner: rook-ceph.rbd.csi.ceph.com
parameters:
    clusterID: rook-ceph
    pool: replicapool
    imageFormat: "2"
currently supports only `layering` feature.
    imageFeatures: layering
    csi.storage.k8s.io/provisioner-secret-name: rook-csi-rbd-provisioner
    csi.storage.k8s.io/provisioner-secret-namespace: rook-ceph
    csi.storage.k8s.io/node-stage-secret-name: rook-csi-rbd-node
    csi.storage.k8s.io/node-stage-secret-namespace: rook-ceph
csi-provisioner
```

```
      csi.storage.k8s.io/fstype: xfs
reclaimPolicy: Delete
```

As you can see, the YAML spec defines both our `StorageClass` and the `CephBlockPool` resource. As we mentioned earlier in this chapter, `StorageClass` is how we tell Kubernetes how to fulfill a `PersistentVolumeClaim`. The `CephBlockPool` resource, on the other hand, tells Ceph how and where to create distributed storage resources – in this case, how much to replicate the storage.

Now we can give some storage to our Pod! Let's create a new PVC with our new storage class:

rook-ceph-pvc.yaml

```
kind: PersistentVolumeClaim
apiVersion: v1
metadata:
  name: rook-pvc
spec:
  storageClassName: rook-ceph-block
  accessModes:
    - ReadWriteOnce
  resources:
    requests:
      storage: 1Gi
```

Our PVC is of storage class `rook-ceph-block`, so it will use the new storage class we just created. Now, let's give the PVC to our Pod in our YAML file:

rook-ceph-pod.yaml

```
apiVersion: v1
kind: Pod
metadata:
  name: my-rook-test-pod
spec:
  volumes:
    - name: my-rook-pv
      persistentVolumeClaim:
```

```
        claimName: rook-pvc
  containers:
    - name: my-container
      image: busybox
      volumeMounts:
        - mountPath: "/usr/rooktest"
          name: my-rook-pv
```

When the Pod is created, Rook should spin up a new persistent volume and attach it to the Pod. Let's peer into the Pod to see if it worked properly:

```
> kubectl exec -it my-rook-test-pod -- /bin/bash
> cd /usr/rooktest
> touch myfile.txt
> ls
```

We get the following output:

```
> myfile.txt
```

Success!

Though we just used Rook's and Ceph's block storage functionality with Ceph, it also has a filesystem mode, which has some benefits – let's discuss why you may want to use it.

The Rook Ceph filesystem

The downside of Rook's Ceph Block provider is that it can only be written to by one Pod at a time. In order to create a `ReadWriteMany` persistent volume with Rook/Ceph, we need to use the filesystem provider, which supports RWX mode. For more information, check out the Rook/Ceph docs at `https://rook.io/docs/rook/v1.3/ceph-quickstart.html`.

Up to creating the Ceph cluster, all the previous steps apply. At this point, we need to create our filesystem. Let's use the following YAML file to create it:

rook-ceph-fs.yaml

```yaml
apiVersion: ceph.rook.io/v1
kind: CephFilesystem
metadata:
  name: ceph-fs
  namespace: rook-ceph
spec:
  metadataPool:
    replicated:
      size: 2
  dataPools:
    - replicated:
        size: 2
  preservePoolsOnDelete: true
  metadataServer:
    activeCount: 1
    activeStandby: true
```

In this case, we're replicating metadata and data to at least two pools for reliability, as configured in the metadataPool and dataPool blocks. We are also preserving the pools on delete using the preservePoolsOnDelete key.

Next, let's create our new storage class specifically for Rook/Ceph filesystem storage. The following YAML does this:

rook-ceph-fs-storageclass.yaml

```yaml
apiVersion: storage.k8s.io/v1
kind: StorageClass
metadata:
  name: rook-cephfs
provisioner: rook-ceph.cephfs.csi.ceph.com
parameters:
  clusterID: rook-ceph
  fsName: ceph-fs
```

```
    pool: ceph-fs-data0
    csi.storage.k8s.io/provisioner-secret-name: rook-csi-cephfs-
provisioner
    csi.storage.k8s.io/provisioner-secret-namespace: rook-ceph
    csi.storage.k8s.io/node-stage-secret-name: rook-csi-cephfs-
node
    csi.storage.k8s.io/node-stage-secret-namespace: rook-ceph
reclaimPolicy: Delete
```

This `rook-cephfs` storage class specifies our previously created pool and describes the reclaim policy of our storage class. Finally, it uses a few annotations that are explained in the Rook/Ceph documentation. Now, we can attach this via a PVC to a deployment, not just a Pod! Take a look at our PV:

rook-cephfs-pvc.yaml

```
kind: PersistentVolumeClaim
apiVersion: v1
metadata:
  name: rook-ceph-pvc
spec:
  storageClassName: rook-cephfs
  accessModes:
    - ReadWriteMany
  resources:
    requests:
      storage: 1Gi
```

This persistent volume references our new `rook-cephfs` storage class in `ReadWriteMany` mode – we're asking for `1 Gi` of this data. Next, we can create our `Deployment`:

rook-cephfs-deployment.yaml

```
apiVersion: v1
kind: Deployment
metadata:
  name: my-rook-fs-test
spec:
```

```
replicas: 3
strategy:
  type: RollingUpdate
  rollingUpdate:
    maxSurge: 25%
    maxUnavailable: 25%
selector:
  matchLabels:
    app: myapp
template:
  spec:
    volumes:
    - name: my-rook-ceph-pv
      persistentVolumeClaim:
        claimName: rook-ceph-pvc
    containers:
    - name: my-container
      image: busybox
      volumeMounts:
      - mountPath: "/usr/rooktest"
        name: my-rook-ceph-pv
```

This `Deployment` references our `ReadWriteMany` persistent volume claim using the `persistentVolumeClaim` block under `volumes`. When deployed, all of our Pods can now read and write to the same persistent volume.

After this, you should have a good understanding of how to create persistent volumes and attach them to Pods.

Summary

In this chapter, we reviewed two methods of providing storage on Kubernetes – volumes and persistent volumes. First, we discussed the difference between these two methods: while volumes are tied to the lifetime of the Pod, persistent volumes last until they or the cluster is deleted. Then, we looked at how to implement volumes and attach them to our Pods. Lastly, we extended our learning on volumes to persistent volumes, and discovered how to use several different types of persistent volumes. These skills will help you assign persistent and non-persistent storage to your applications in many possible environments – from on-premises to the cloud.

In the next chapter, we'll take a detour from application concerns and discuss how to control Pod placement on Kubernetes.

Questions

1. What are the differences between volumes and persistent volumes?

2. What is a `StorageClass`, and how does it relate to a volume?

3. How can you automatically provision cloud resources when creating Kubernetes resources such as a persistent volume?

4. In which use cases do you think that using volumes instead of persistent volumes would be prohibitive?

Further reading

Please refer to the following links for more information:

- Ceph Storage Quickstart for Rook: `https://github.com/rook/rook/blob/master/Documentation/ceph-quickstart.md`

- Rook Toolbox: `https://rook.io/docs/rook/v0.7/toolbox.html`

- Cloud providers: `https://kubernetes.io/docs/tasks/administer-cluster/running-cloud-controller/`

8
Pod Placement Controls

This chapter describes the various ways of controlling Pod placement in Kubernetes, as well as explaining why it may be a good idea to implement these controls in the first place. Pod placement means controlling which node a Pod is scheduled to in Kubernetes. We start with simple controls like node selectors, and then move on to more complex tools like taints and tolerations, and finish with two beta features, node affinity and inter-Pod affinity/anti-affinity.

In past chapters, we've learned how best to run application Pods on Kubernetes – from coordinating and scaling them using deployments, injecting configuration with ConfigMaps and Secrets, to adding storage with persistent volumes.

Throughout all of this, however, we have always relied on the Kubernetes scheduler to put Pods on the optimal node without giving the scheduler much information about the Pods in question. So far, we've added resource limits and requests to our Pods (`resource.requests` and `resource.limits` in the Pod spec). Resource requests specify a minimum level of free resources on a node that the Pod needs in order to be scheduled, while resource limits specify the maximum amount of resources a Pod is allowed to use. However, we have not put any specific requirements on which nodes or set of nodes a Pod must be run.

For many applications and clusters, this is fine. However, as we'll see in the first section, there are many cases where using more granular Pod placement controls is a useful strategy.

In this chapter, we will cover the following topics:

- Identifying use cases for Pod placement
- Using node selectors
- Implementing taints and tolerations
- Controlling Pods with node affinity
- Using inter-Pod affinity and anti-affinity

Technical requirements

In order to run the commands detailed in this chapter, you will need a computer that supports the kubectl command-line tool along with a working Kubernetes cluster. See *Chapter 1*, *Communicating with Kubernetes*, for several methods for getting up and running with Kubernetes quickly, and for instructions on how to install the kubectl tool.

The code used in this chapter can be found in the book's GitHub repository at https://github.com/PacktPublishing/Cloud-Native-with-Kubernetes/tree/master/Chapter8.

Identifying use cases for Pod placement

Pod placement controls are tools that Kubernetes gives us to decide which node to schedule a Pod on, or when to completely prevent Pod scheduling due to a lack of the nodes we want. This can be used in several different patterns, but we'll review a few major ones. To start with, Kubernetes itself implements Pod placement controls completely by default – let's see how.

Kubernetes node health placement controls

Kubernetes uses a few default placement controls to specify which nodes are unhealthy in some way. These are generally defined using taints and tolerations, which we will review in detail later in this chapter.

Some default taints (which we'll discuss in the next section) that Kubernetes uses are as follows:

- `memory-pressure`
- `disk-pressure`
- `unreachable`
- `not-ready`
- `out-of-disk`
- `network-unavailable`
- `unschedulable`
- `uninitialized` (only for cloud-provider-created nodes)

These conditions can mark nodes as unable to receive new Pods, though there is some flexibility in how these taints are handled by the scheduler, as we will see later. The purpose of these system-created placement controls is to prevent unhealthy nodes from receiving workloads that may not function properly.

In addition to system-created placement controls for node health, there are several use cases where you, as a user, may want to implement fine-tuned scheduling, as we will see in the next section.

Applications requiring different node types

In a heterogeneous Kubernetes cluster, every node is not created equal. You may have some more powerful VMs (or bare metal) and some less – or have different specialized sets of nodes.

For instance, in a cluster that runs data science pipelines, you may have nodes with GPU acceleration capabilities to run deep learning algorithms, regular compute nodes to serve applications, nodes with high amounts of memory to do inference based on completed models, and more.

Using Pod placement controls, you can ensure that the various pieces of your platform run on the hardware best suited for the task at hand.

Applications requiring specific data compliance

Similar to the previous example, where application requirements may dictate the need for different types of compute, certain data compliance needs may require specific types of nodes.

For instance, cloud providers such as AWS and Azure often allow you to purchase VMs with dedicated tenancy – which means that no other applications run on the underlying hardware and hypervisor. This is different from other typical cloud-provider VMs, where multiple customers may share a single physical machine.

For certain data regulations, this level of dedicated tenancy is required to maintain compliance. To fulfill this need, you could use Pod placement controls to ensure that the relevant applications only run on nodes with dedicated tenancy, while reducing costs by running the control plane on more typical VMs without it.

Multi-tenant clusters

If you are running a cluster with multiple tenants (separated by namespaces, for instance), you could use Pod placement controls to reserve certain nodes or groups of nodes for a tenant, to physically or otherwise separate them from other tenants in the cluster. This is similar to the concept of dedicated hardware in AWS or Azure.

Multiple failure domains

Though Kubernetes already provides high availability by allowing you to schedule workloads that run on multiple nodes, it is also possible to extend this pattern. We can create our own Pod scheduling strategies that account for failure domains that stretch across multiple nodes. A great way to handle this is via the Pod or node affinity or anti-affinity features, which we will discuss later in this chapter.

For now, let's conceptualize a case where we have our cluster on bare metal with 20 nodes per physical rack. If each rack has its own dedicated power connection and backup, it can be thought of as a failure domain. When the power connections fail, all the machines on the rack fail. Thus, we may want to encourage Kubernetes to run two instances or Pods on separate racks/failure domains. The following figure shows how an application could run across failure domains:

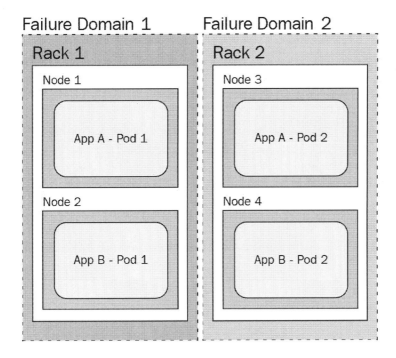

Figure 8.1 – Failure domains

As you can see in the figure, as the application pods are spread across multiple failure domains, not just multiple nodes in the same failure domain, we can maintain uptime even if *Failure Domain 1* goes down. *App A - Pod 1* and *App B - Pod 1* are in the same (red) failure domain. However, if that failure domain (*Rack 1*) goes down, we will still have a replica of each application on *Rack 2*.

We use the word "encourage" here because it is possible to configure some of this functionality as either a hard requirement or on a best effort basis in the Kubernetes scheduler.

These examples should give you a solid understanding of some potential use cases for advanced placement controls.

Let's discuss the actual implementation now, taking each placement toolset one by one. We'll start with the simplest, node selectors.

Using node selectors and node name

Node selectors are a very simple type of placement control in Kubernetes. Each Kubernetes node can be labeled with one or more labels in the metadata block, and Pods can specify a node selector.

To label an existing node, you can use the `kubectl label` command:

```
> kubectl label nodes node1 cpu_speed=fast
```

In this example, we're labeling our `node1` node with the label `cpu_speed` and the value `fast`.

Now, let's assume that we have an application that really needs fast CPU cycles to perform effectively. We can add a `nodeSelector` to our workload to ensure that it is only scheduled on nodes with our fast CPU speed label, as shown in the following code snippet:

pod-with-node-selector.yaml

```yaml
apiVersion: v1
kind: Pod
metadata:
  name: speedy-app
spec:
  containers:
  - name: speedy-app
    image: speedy-app:latest
    imagePullPolicy: IfNotPresent
  nodeSelector:
    cpu_speed: fast
```

When deployed, as part of a Deployment or by itself, our `speedy-app` Pod will only be scheduled on nodes with the `cpu_speed` label.

Keep in mind that unlike some other more advanced Pod placement options that we will review shortly, there is no leeway in node selectors. If there are no nodes that have the required label, the application will not be scheduled at all.

For an even simpler (but far more brittle) selector, you can use `nodeName`, which specifies the exact node that the Pod should be scheduled on. You can use it like this:

pod-with-node-name.yaml

```
apiVersion: v1
kind: Pod
metadata:
  name: speedy-app
spec:
  containers:
  - name: speedy-app
    image: speedy-app:latest
    imagePullPolicy: IfNotPresent
  nodeName: node1
```

As you can see, this selector will only allow the Pod to be scheduled on `node1`, so if it isn't currently accepting Pods for any reason, the Pod will not be scheduled.

For slightly more nuanced placement control, let's move on to taints and tolerations.

Implementing taints and tolerations

Taints and tolerations in Kubernetes work like reverse node selectors. Rather than nodes attracting Pods due to having the proper labels, which are then consumed by a selector, we taint nodes, which repels all Pods from being scheduled on the node, and then mark our Pods with tolerations, which allow them to be scheduled on the tainted nodes.

As mentioned at the beginning of the chapter, Kubernetes uses system-created taints to mark nodes as unhealthy and prevent new workloads from being scheduled on them. For instance, the `out-of-disk` taint will prevent any new pods from being scheduled to a node with that taint.

Let's take the same example use case that we had with node selectors and apply it using taints and tolerations. Since this is basically the reverse of our previous setup, let's first give our node a taint using the `kubectl taint` command:

```
> kubectl taint nodes node2 cpu_speed=slow:NoSchedule
```

Let's pick apart this command. We are giving `node2` a taint called `cpu_speed` and a value, `slow`. We also mark this taint with an effect – in this case, `NoSchedule`.

Once we're done with our example (don't do this quite yet if you're following along with the commands), we can remove the `taint` using the minus operator:

```
> kubectl taint nodes node2 cpu_speed=slow:NoSchedule-
```

The `taint` effect lets us add in some granularity into how the scheduler handles the taints. There are three possible effect values:

- `NoSchedule`
- `NoExecute`
- `PreferNoSchedule`

The first two effects, `NoSchedule` and `NoExecute`, provide hard effects – which is to say that, like node selectors, there are only two possibilities, either the toleration exists on the Pod (as we'll see momentarily) or the Pod is not scheduled. `NoExecute` adds to this base functionality by evicting all Pods on the node that do have the toleration, while `NoSchedule` lets existing pods stay put, while preventing any new Pods without the toleration from joining.

`PreferNoSchedule`, on the other hand, provides the Kubernetes scheduler with some leeway. It tells the scheduler to attempt to find a node for a Pod that doesn't have an untolerated taint, but if none exist, to go ahead and schedule it anyway. It implements a soft effect.

In our case, we have chosen `NoSchedule`, so no new Pods will be assigned to the node – unless, of course, we provide a toleration. Let's do this now. Assume that we have a second application that doesn't care about CPU clock speeds. It is happy to live on our slower node. This is the Pod manifest:

pod-without-speed-requirement.yaml

```yaml
apiVersion: v1
kind: Pod
metadata:
  name: slow-app
spec:
  containers:
  - name: slow-app
    image: slow-app:latest
```

Right now, our `slow-app` Pod will not run on any node with a taint. We need to provide a toleration for this Pod in order for it to be scheduled on a node with a taint – which we can do like this:

pod-with-toleration.yaml

```
apiVersion: v1
kind: Pod
metadata:
  name: slow-app
spec:
  containers:
  - name: slow-app
    image: slow-app:latest
  tolerations:
  - key: "cpu_speed"
    operator: "Equal"
    value: "slow"
    effect: "NoSchedule"
```

Let's pick apart our `tolerations` entry, which is an array of values. Each value has a `key` – which is the same as our taint name. Then there is an `operator` value. This `operator` can be either `Equal` or `Exists`. For `Equal`, you can use the `value` key as in the preceding code to configure a value that the taint must equal in order to be tolerated by the Pod. For `Exists`, the taint name must be on the node, but it does not matter what the value is, as in this Pod spec:

pod-with-toleration2.yaml

```
apiVersion: v1
kind: Pod
metadata:
  name: slow-app
spec:
  containers:
  - name: slow-app
    image: slow-app:latest
  tolerations:
```

```
- key: "cpu_speed"
  operator: "Exists"
  effect: "NoSchedule"
```

As you can see, we have used the `Exists operator` value to allow our Pod to tolerate any `cpu_speed` taint.

Finally, we have our `effect`, which works the same way as the `effect` on the taint itself. It can contain the exact same values as the taint effect – NoSchedule, NoExecute, and PreferNoSchedule.

A Pod with a `NoExecute` toleration will tolerate the taint associated with it indefinitely. However, you can add a field called `tolerationSeconds` in order to have the Pod leave the tainted node after a prescribed time has elapsed. This allows you to specify tolerations that take effect after a period of time. Let's look at an example:

pod-with-toleration3.yaml

```
apiVersion: v1
kind: Pod
metadata:
  name: slow-app
spec:
  containers:
  - name: slow-app
    image: slow-app:latest
  tolerations:
  - key: "cpu_speed"
    operator: "Equal"
    Value: "slow"
    effect: "NoExecute"
    tolerationSeconds: 60
```

In this case, the Pod already running on a node with the taint `slow` when the taint and toleration are executed will remain on the node for 60 seconds before being rescheduled to a different node.

Multiple taints and tolerations

When there are multiple taints or tolerations on a Pod and node, the scheduler will check all of them. There is no OR logic operator here – if any of the taints on the node do not have a matching toleration on the Pod, it will not be scheduled on the node (with the exception of PreferNoSchedule, in which case, as before, the scheduler will try to not schedule on the node if possible). Even if out of six taints on the node, the Pod tolerates five of them, it will still not be scheduled for a NoSchedule taint, and it will still be evicted for a NoExecute taint.

For a tool that gives us a much more subtle way of controlling placement, let's look at node affinity.

Controlling Pods with node affinity

As you can probably tell, taints and tolerations – while much more flexible than node selectors – still leave some use cases unaddressed and in general only allow a *filter* pattern where you can match on a specific taint using Exists or Equals. There may be more advanced use cases where you want more flexible methods of selecting nodes – and *affinities* are a feature of Kubernetes that addresses this.

There are two types of affinity:

- **Node affinity**
- **Inter-Pod affinity**

Node affinity is a similar concept to node selectors except that it allows for a much more robust set of selection characteristics. Let's look at some example YAML and then pick apart the various pieces:

pod-with-node-affinity.yaml

```
apiVersion: v1
kind: Pod
metadata:
  name: affinity-test
spec:
  affinity:
    nodeAffinity:
      requiredDuringSchedulingIgnoredDuringExecution:
        nodeSelectorTerms:
```

```
        - matchExpressions:
          - key: cpu_speed
            operator: In
            values:
            - fast
            - medium_fast
  containers:
  - name: speedy-app
    image: speedy-app:latest
```

As you can see, our `Pod` spec has an `affinity` key, and we've specified a `nodeAffinity` setting. There are two possible node affinity types:

- `requiredDuringSchedulingIgnoredDuringExecution`
- `preferredDuringSchedulingIgnoredDuringExecution`

The functionality of these two types maps directly to how `NoSchedule` and `PreferNoSchedule` work, respectively.

Using requiredDuringSchedulingIgnoredDuringExecution node affinities

For `requiredDuringSchedulingIgnoredDuringExecution`, Kubernetes will never schedule a Pod without a term matching to a node.

For `preferredDuringSchedulingIgnoredDuringExecution`, it will attempt to fulfill the soft requirement but if it cannot, it will still schedule the Pod.

The real capability of node affinity over node selectors and taints and tolerations comes in the actual expressions and logic that you can implement when it comes to the selector.

The functionalities of the `requiredDuringSchedulingIgnoredDuringExecution` and `preferredDuringSchedulingIgnoredDuringExecution` affinities are quite different, so we will review each separately.

For our `required` affinity, we have the ability to specify `nodeSelectorTerms` – which can be one or more blocks containing `matchExpressions`. For each block of `matchExpressions`, there can be multiple expressions.

In the code block we saw in the previous section, we have one single node selector term, a `matchExpressions` block – which itself has only a single expression. This expression looks for `key`, which, just like with node selectors, represents a node label. Next, it has an `operator`, which gives us some flexibility on how we want to identify a match. Here are the possible values for the operator:

- `In`
- `NotIn`
- `Exists`
- `DoesNotExist`
- `Gt` (Note: greater than)
- `Lt` (Note: less than)

In our case, we are using the `In` operator, which will check to see if the value is one of several that we specify. Finally, in our `values` section, we can list one or more values that must match, based on the operator, before the expression is true.

As you can see, this gives us significantly greater granularity in specifying our selector. Let's look at our example of `cpu_speed` using a different operator:

pod-with-node-affinity2.yaml

```yaml
apiVersion: v1
kind: Pod
metadata:
  name: affinity-test
spec:
  affinity:
    nodeAffinity:
      requiredDuringSchedulingIgnoredDuringExecution:
        nodeSelectorTerms:
        - matchExpressions:
          - key: cpu_speed
            operator: Gt
            values:
```

```
           - "5"
  containers:
  - name: speedy-app
      image: speedy-app:latest
```

As you can see, we are using a very granular `matchExpressions` selector. This ability to use more advanced operator matching now allows us to ensure that our `speedy-app` is only scheduled on nodes that have a high enough clock speed (in this case, 5 GHz). Instead of classifying our nodes into broad groups like `slow` and `fast`, we can be much more granular in our specifications.

Next, let's look at the other node affinity type – `preferredDuringSchedulingIgnoredDuringExecution`.

Using preferredDuringSchedulingIgnoredDuringExecution node affinities

The syntax for this is slightly different and gives us even more granularity to affect this `soft` requirement. Let's look at a Pod spec YAML that implements this:

pod-with-node-affinity3.yaml

```
apiVersion: v1
kind: Pod
metadata:
  name: slow-app-affinity
spec:
  affinity:
    nodeAffinity:
      preferredDuringSchedulingIgnoredDuringExecution:
      - weight: 1
        preference:
          matchExpressions:
          - key: cpu_speed
            operator: Lt
            values:
            - "3"
```

```
containers:
- name: slow-app
  image: slow-app:latest
```

This looks a bit different from our `required` syntax.

For `preferredDuringSchedulingIgnoredDuringExecution`, we have the ability to assign a `weight` to each entry, with an associated preference, which can again be a `matchExpressions` block with multiple inner expressions that use the same `key-operator-values` syntax.

The `weight` value is the key difference here. Since `preferredDuringSchedulingIgnoredDuringExecution` is a **soft** requirement, we can list a few different preferences with associated weights, and let the scheduler try its best to satisfy them. The way this works under the hood is that the scheduler will go through all the preferences and compute a score for the node based on the weight of each preference and whether it was satisfied. Assuming all hard requirements are satisfied, the scheduler will select the node with the highest computed score. In the preceding case, we have a single preference with a weight of 1, but weight can be anywhere from 1 to 100 – so let's look at a more complex setup for our `speedy-app` use case:

pod-with-node-affinity4.yaml

```
apiVersion: v1
kind: Pod
metadata:
  name: speedy-app-prefers-affinity
spec:
  affinity:
    nodeAffinity:
      preferredDuringSchedulingIgnoredDuringExecution:
      - weight: 90
        preference:
          matchExpressions:
          - key: cpu_speed
            operator: Gt
            values:
            - "3"
      - weight: 10
        preference:
```

```
        matchExpressions:
        - key: memory_speed
          operator: Gt
          values:
          - "4"
    containers:
    - name: speedy-app
      image: speedy-app:latest
```

In our journey to ensure that our speedy-app runs on the best possible node, we have here decided to only implement soft requirements. If no fast nodes exist, we still want our app to be scheduled and run. To that end, we've specified two preferences – a node with a cpu_speed of over 3 (3 GHz) and a memory speed of over 4 (4 GHz).

Since our app is far more CPU-bound than memory-bound, we've decided to weight our preferences appropriately. In this case, cpu_speed carries a weight of 90, while memory_speed carries a weight of 10.

Thus, any node that satisfies our cpu_speed requirement will have a much higher computed score than one that only satisfies the memory_speed requirement – but still less than one that satisfies both. When we're trying to schedule 10 or 100 new Pods for this app, you can see how this calculation could be valuable.

Multiple node affinities

When we're dealing with multiple node affinities, there are a few key pieces of logic to keep in mind. First off, even with a single node affinity, if it is combined with a node selector on the same Pod spec (which is indeed possible), the node selector must be satisfied before any of the node affinity logic will come into play. This is because node selectors only implement hard requirements, and there is no OR logical operator between the two. An OR logical operator would check both requirements and ensure that at least one of them is true – but node selectors do not let us do this.

Secondly, for a requiredDuringSchedulingIgnoredDuringExecution node affinity, multiple entries under nodeSelectorTerms are handled in an OR logical operator. If one, but not all, is satisfied – the Pod will still be scheduled.

Finally, for any `nodeSelectorTerm` with multiple entries under `matchExpressions`, all must be satisfied – this is an AND logical operator. Let's look at an example YAML of this:

pod-with-node-affinity5.yaml

```yaml
apiVersion: v1
kind: Pod
metadata:
  name: affinity-test
spec:
  affinity:
    nodeAffinity:
      requiredDuringSchedulingIgnoredDuringExecution:
        nodeSelectorTerms:
        - matchExpressions:
          - key: cpu_speed
            operator: Gt
            values:
            - "5"
          - key: memory_speed
            operator: Gt
            values:
            - "4"
  containers:
  - name: speedy-app
    image: speedy-app:latest
```

In this case, if a node has a CPU speed of 5 but does not meet the memory speed requirement (or vice versa), the Pod will not be scheduled.

One final thing to note about node affinity is that, as you've probably already noticed, neither of the two affinity types allows the same `NoExecute` functionality that was available to us in our taints and tolerations settings.

One additional node affinity type – `requiredDuringSchedulingRequiredDuring execution` – will add this functionality in a future version. As of Kubernetes 1.19, this does not yet exist.

Next, we will look at inter-pod affinity and anti-affinity, which provides affinity definitions between Pods, rather than defining rules for nodes.

Using inter-Pod affinity and anti-affinity

Inter-Pod affinity and anti-affinity let you dictate how Pods should run based on which other Pods already exist on a node. Since the number of Pods in a cluster is typically much larger than the number of nodes, and some Pod affinity and anti-affinity rules can be somewhat complex, this feature can put quite a load on your cluster control plane if you are running many pods on many nodes. For this reason, the Kubernetes documentation does not recommend using these features with a large number of nodes in your cluster.

Pod affinities and anti-affinities work fairly differently – let's look at each by itself before discussing how they can be combined.

Pod affinities

As with node affinities, let's dive into the YAML in order to discuss the constituent parts of a Pod affinity spec:

pod-with-pod-affinity.yaml

```
apiVersion: v1
kind: Pod
metadata:
  name: not-hungry-app-affinity
spec:
  affinity:
    podAffinity:
      requiredDuringSchedulingIgnoredDuringExecution:
      - labelSelector:
          matchExpressions:
          - key: hunger
            operator: In
            values:
            - "1"
            - "2"
        topologyKey: rack
  containers:
```

```
    - name: not-hungry-app
      image: not-hungry-app:latest
```

Just like with node affinity, Pod affinity lets us choose between two types:

- `preferredDuringSchedulingIgnoredDuringExecution`
- `requiredDuringSchedulingIgnoredDuringExecution`

Again, similar to node affinity, we can have one or more selectors – which are called `labelSelector` since we are selecting Pods, not nodes. The `matchExpressions` functionality is the same as with node affinity, but Pod affinity adds a brand-new key called `topologyKey`.

`topologyKey` is in essence a selector that limits the scope of where the scheduler should look to see whether other Pods of the same selector are running. That means that Pod affinity doesn't only need to mean other Pods of the same type (selector) on the same node; it can mean groups of multiple nodes.

Let's go back to our failure domain example at the beginning of the chapter. In that example, each rack was its own failure domain with multiple nodes per rack. To extend this concept to `topologyKey`, we could label each node on a rack with `rack=1` or `rack=2`. Then we can use the `topologyKey` rack, as we have in our YAML, to designate that the scheduler should check all of the Pods running on nodes with the same `topologyKey` (which in this case means all of the Pods on `Node 1` and `Node 2` in the same rack) in order to apply Pod affinity or anti-affinity rules.

So, adding this all up, what our example YAML tells the scheduler is this:

- This Pod *MUST* be scheduled on a node with the label `rack`, where the value of the label `rack` separates nodes into groups.
- The Pod will then be scheduled in a group where there already exists a Pod running with the label `hunger` and a value of 1 or 2.

Essentially, we are splitting our cluster into topology domains – in this case, racks – and prescribing to the scheduler to only schedule similar pods together on nodes that share the same topology domain. This is the opposite of our first failure domain example, where we wouldn't want pods to share the same domain if possible – but there are also reasons that you may want to keep like pods on the same domain. For example, in a multitenant setting where tenants want dedicated hardware tenancy over a domain, you could ensure that every Pod that belongs to a certain tenant is scheduled to the exact same topology domain.

You can use `preferredDuringSchedulingIgnoredDuringExecution` in the same way. Before we get to anti-affinities, here's an example with Pod affinities and the `preferred` type:

pod-with-pod-affinity2.yaml

```
apiVersion: v1
kind: Pod
metadata:
  name: not-hungry-app-affinity
spec:
  affinity:
    podAffinity:
      preferredDuringSchedulingIgnoredDuringExecution:
      - weight: 50
        podAffinityTerm:
          labelSelector:
            matchExpressions:
            - key: hunger
              operator: Lt
              values:
              - "3"
          topologyKey: rack
  containers:
  - name: not-hungry-app
    image: not-hungry-app:latest
```

As before, in this code block, we have our `weight` – in this case, `50` – and our expression match – in this case, using a less than (`Lt`) operator. This affinity will induce the scheduler to try its best to schedule the Pod on a node where it is or with another node on the same rack that has a Pod running with a `hunger` of less than 3. The `weight` is used by the scheduler to compare nodes – as discussed in the section on node affinities – *Controlling Pods with Node Affinity* (see `pod-with-node-affinity4.yaml`). In this scenario specifically, the weight of `50` doesn't make any difference because there is only one entry in the affinity list.

Pod anti-affinities extend this paradigm using the same selectors and topologies – let's take a look at them in detail.

Pod anti-affinities

Pod anti-affinities allow you to prevent Pods from running on the same topology domain as pods that match a selector. They implement the opposite logic to Pod affinities. Let's dive into some YAML and explain how this works:

pod-with-pod-anti-affinity.yaml

```
apiVersion: v1
kind: Pod
metadata:
  name: hungry-app
spec:
  affinity:
    podAntiAffinity:
      preferredDuringSchedulingIgnoredDuringExecution:
      - weight: 100
        podAffinityTerm:
          labelSelector:
            matchExpressions:
            - key: hunger
              operator: In
              values:
              - "4"
              - "5"
          topologyKey: rack
  containers:
  - name: hungry-app
    image: hungry-app
```

Similar to Pod affinity, we use the `affinity` key as the location to specify our anti-affinity under `podAntiAffinity`. Also, as with Pod affinity, we have the ability to use either `preferredDuringSchedulingIgnoredDuringExecution` or `requireDuringSchedulingIgnoredDuringExecution`. We even use all the same syntax for the selector as with Pod affinities.

The only actual difference in syntax is the use of `podAntiAffinity` under the `affinity` key.

So, what does this YAML do? In this case, we are recommending to the scheduler (a `soft` requirement) that it should attempt to schedule this Pod on a node where it or any other node with the same value for the `rack` label does not have any Pods running with `hunger` label values of 4 or 5. We're telling the scheduler *try not to colocate this Pod in a domain with any extra hungry Pods*.

This feature gives us a great way to separate pods by failure domain – we can specify each rack as a domain and give it an anti-affinity with a selector of its own kind. This will make the scheduler schedule clones of the Pod (or try to, in a preferred affinity) to nodes that are not in the same failure domain, giving the application greater availability in case of a domain failure.

We even have the option to combine Pod affinities and anti-affinities. Let's look at how this could work.

Combined affinity and anti-affinity

This is one of those situations where you can really put undue load on your cluster control plane. Combining Pod affinities with anti-affinities can allow incredibly nuanced rules that can be passed to the Kubernetes scheduler, which has the Herculean task of working to fulfill them.

Let's look at some YAML for a Deployment spec that combines these two concepts. Remember, affinity and anti-affinity are concepts that are applied to Pods – but we normally do not specify Pods without a controller like a Deployment or a ReplicaSet. Therefore, these rules are applied at the Pod spec level in the Deployment YAML. We are only showing the Pod spec part of this deployment for conciseness, but you can find the full file on the GitHub repository:

pod-with-both-antiaffinity-and-affinity.yaml

```
apiVersion: apps/v1
kind: Deployment
metadata:
  name: hungry-app-deployment
# SECTION REMOVED FOR CONCISENESS
    spec:
      affinity:
        podAntiAffinity:
          preferredDuringSchedulingIgnoredDuringExecution:
          - labelSelector:
```

```
                matchExpressions:
                - key: app
                  operator: In
                  values:
                  - other-hungry-app
                topologyKey: "rack"
          podAffinity:
            requiredDuringSchedulingIgnoredDuringExecution:
            - labelSelector:
                matchExpressions:
                - key: app
                  operator: In
                  values:
                  - hungry-app-cache
                topologyKey: "rack"
      containers:
      - name: hungry-app
        image: hungry-app:latest
```

In this code block, we are telling the scheduler to treat the Pods in our Deployment as such: the Pod must be scheduled onto a node with a `rack` label such that it or any other node with a `rack` label and the same value has a Pod with `app=hungry-label-cache`.

Secondly, the scheduler must attempt to schedule the Pod, if possible, to a node with the `rack` label such that it or any other node with the `rack` label and the same value does not have a Pod with the `app=other-hungry-app` label running.

To boil this down, we want our Pods for `hungry-app` to run in the same topology as the `hungry-app-cache`, and we do not want them to be in the same topology as the `other-hungry-app` if at all possible.

Since with great power comes great responsibility, and our tools for Pod affinity and anti-affinity are equal parts powerful and performance-reducing, Kubernetes ensures that some limits are set on the possible ways you can use both of them in order to prevent strange behavior or significant performance issues.

Pod affinity and anti-affinity limitations

The biggest restriction on affinity and anti-affinity is that you are not allowed to use a blank `topologyKey`. Without restricting what the scheduler treats as a single topology type, some very unintended behavior can happen.

The second limitation is that, by default, if you're using the hard version of anti-affinity – `requiredOnSchedulingIgnoredDuringExecution`, you cannot just use any label as a `topologyKey`.

Kubernetes will only let you use the `kubernetes.io/hostname` label, which essentially means that you can only have one topology per node if you're using `required` anti-affinity. This limitation does not exist for either the `prefer` anti-affinity or either of the affinities, even the `required` one. It is possible to change this functionality, but it requires writing a custom admission controller – which we will discuss in *Chapter 12, Kubernetes Security and Compliance*, and *Chapter 13, Extending Kubernetes with CRDs*.

So far, our work with placement controls has not discussed namespaces. However, with Pod affinities and anti-affinities, they do hold relevance.

Pod affinity and anti-affinity namespaces

Since Pod affinities and anti-affinities cause changes in behavior based on the location of other Pods, namespaces are a relevant piece to decide which Pods count for or against an affinity or anti-affinity.

By default, the scheduler will only look to the namespace in which the Pod with the affinity or anti-affinity was created. For all our previous examples, we haven't specified a namespace so the default namespace will be used.

If you want to add one or more namespaces in which Pods will affect the affinity or anti-affinity, you can do so using the following YAML:

pod-with-anti-affinity-namespace.yaml

```
apiVersion: v1
kind: Pod
metadata:
  name: hungry-app
spec:
  affinity:
    podAntiAffinity:
      preferredDuringSchedulingIgnoredDuringExecution:
```

```
      - weight: 100
        podAffinityTerm:
          labelSelector:
            matchExpressions:
            - key: hunger
              operator: In
              values:
              - "4"
              - "5"
            topologyKey: rack
            namespaces: ["frontend", "backend", "logging"]
  containers:
  - name: hungry-app
    image: hungry-app
```

In this code block, the scheduler will look to the frontend, backend, and logging namespaces when trying to match the anti-affinity (as you can see on the namespaces key in the podAffinityTerm block). This allows us to constrain which namespaces the scheduler operates on when validating its rules.

Summary

In this chapter, we learned about a few different controls that Kubernetes provides in order to enforce certain Pod placement rules via the scheduler. We learned that there are both "hard" requirements and "soft" rules, the latter of which are given the scheduler's best effort but do not necessarily prevent Pods that break the rules from being placed. We also learned a few reasons why you may want to implement scheduling controls – such as real-life failure domains and multitenancy.

We learned that there are simple ways to influence Pod placement, such as node selectors and node names – in addition to more advanced methods like taints and tolerations, which Kubernetes itself also uses by default. Finally, we discovered that there are some advanced tools that Kubernetes provides for node and Pod affinities and anti-affinities, which allow us to create complex rulesets for the scheduler to follow.

In the next chapter, we will discuss observability on Kubernetes. We'll learn how to view application logs and we'll also use some great tools to get a view of what is happening in our cluster in real time.

Questions

1. What is the difference between node selectors and the Node name field?

2. How does Kubernetes use system-provided taints and tolerations? For what reasons?

3. Why should you be careful when using multiple types of Pod affinities or anti-affinities?

4. How could you balance availability across multiple failure zones with colocation for performance reasons for a three-tier web application? Give an example using node or Pod affinities and anti-affinities.

Further reading

- For a more in-depth explanation of the default system taints and tolerations, head to `https://kubernetes.io/docs/concepts/scheduling-eviction/taint-and-toleration/#taint-based-evictions`.

Section 3: Running Kubernetes in Production

In this section, you'll get a glimpse into day 2 operations on Kubernetes, best practices for CI/CD, how to customize and extend Kubernetes, and the basics of the greater cloud-native ecosystem.

This part of the book comprises the following chapters:

- *Chapter 9, Observability on Kubernetes*
- *Chapter 10, Troubleshooting Kubernetes*
- *Chapter 11, Template Code Generation and CI/CD on Kubernetes*
- *Chapter 12, Kubernetes Security and Compliance*

9

Observability on Kubernetes

This chapter dives into capabilities that are highly recommended to implement when running Kubernetes in production. First, we discuss observability in the context of distributed systems such as Kubernetes. Then, we look at the built-in Kubernetes observability stack and what functionality it implements. Finally, we learn how to supplement the built-in observability tooling with additional observability, monitoring, logging, and metrics infrastructure from the ecosystem. The skills you learn in this chapter will help you deploy observability tools to your Kubernetes cluster and enable you to understand how your cluster (and applications running on it) are functioning.

In this chapter, we will cover the following topics:

- Understanding observability on Kubernetes
- Using default observability tooling – metrics, logging, and the dashboard
- Implementing the best of the ecosystem

To start, we will learn the out-of-the-box tools and processes that Kubernetes provides for observability.

Technical requirements

In order to run the commands detailed in this chapter, you will need a computer that supports the `kubectl` command-line tool along with a working Kubernetes cluster. See *Chapter 1, Communicating with Kubernetes*, for several methods for getting up and running with Kubernetes quickly, and for instructions on how to install the kubectl tool.

The code used in this chapter can be found in the book's GitHub repository:

```
https://github.com/PacktPublishing/Cloud-Native-with-
Kubernetes/tree/master/Chapter9
```

Understanding observability on Kubernetes

No production system is complete without a way to monitor it. In software, we define observability as the ability to, at any point in time, understand how our system is performing (and, in the best case, why). Observability grants significant benefits in security, performance, and operational capacity. By knowing how your system is responding at the VM, container, and application level, you can tune it to perform efficiently, react quickly to events, and more easily troubleshoot bugs.

For instance, let's take a scenario where your application is running extremely slowly. In order to find the bottleneck, you may look at the application code itself, the resource specifications of the Pod, the number of Pods in the deployment, the memory and CPU usage at the Pod level or Node level, and externalities such as a MySQL database running outside your cluster.

By adding observability tooling, you would be able to diagnose many of these variables and figure out what issues may be contributing to your application slowdown.

Kubernetes, as a production-ready container orchestration system, gives us some default tools to monitor our applications. For the purposes of this chapter, we will separate observability into four ideas: metrics, logs, traces, and alerts. Let's look at each of them:

- **Metrics** here represents the ability to see numerical representations of the system's current state, with specific attention paid to CPU, memory, network, disk space, and more. These numbers allow us to judge the gap in current state with the system's maximum capacity and ensure that the system remains available to users.

- **Logs** refers to the practice of collecting text logs from applications and systems. Logs will likely be a combination of Kubernetes control plane logs and logs from your application Pods themselves. Logs can help us diagnose the availability of the Kubernetes system, but they also can help with triaging application bugs.

- **Traces** refers to collecting distributed traces. Traces are an observability pattern that delivers end-to-end visibility of a chain of requests – which can be HTTP requests or otherwise. This topic is especially important in a distributed cloud-native setting where microservices are used. If you have many microservices and they call each other, it can be difficult to find bottlenecks or issues when many services are involved in a single end-to-end request. Traces allow you to view requests broken down by each leg of a service-to-service call.

- **Alerts** correspond to the practice of setting automated touch points when certain events happen. Alerts can be set on both *metrics* and *logs*, and delivered through a host of mediums, from text messages to emails to third-party applications and everything in between.

Between these four aspects of observability, we should be able to understand the health of our cluster. However, it is possible to configure many different possible data points for metrics, logs, and even alerting. Therefore, knowing what to look for is important. The next section will discuss the most important observability areas for Kubernetes cluster and application health.

Understanding what matters for Kubernetes cluster and application health

Among the vast number of possible metrics and logs that Kubernetes or third-party observability solutions for Kubernetes can provide, we can narrow down some of the ones that are most likely to cause major issues with your cluster. You should keep these pieces front and center in whichever observability solution you end up using. First, let's look at the connection between CPU usage and cluster health.

Node CPU usage

The state of CPU usage across the Nodes in your Kubernetes cluster is a very important metric to keep an eye on across your observability solution. We've discussed in previous chapters how Pods can define resource requests and limits for CPU usage. However, it is still possible for Nodes to oversubscribe their CPU usage when the limits are set higher than the maximum CPU capacity of the cluster. Additionally, the master Nodes that run our control plane can also encounter CPU capacity issues.

Worker Nodes with maxed-out CPUs may perform poorly or throttle workloads running on Pods. This can easily occur if no limits are set on Pods – or if a Node's total Pod resource limits are greater than its max capacity, even if its total resource requests are lower. Master Nodes with capped-out CPUs may hurt the performance of the scheduler, kube-apiserver, or any of the other control plane components.

In general, CPU usage across worker and master Nodes should be visible in your observability solution. This is best done via a combination of metrics (for instance on a charting solution such as Grafana, which you'll learn about later in this chapter) – and alerts for high CPU usage across the nodes in your cluster.

Memory usage is also an extremely important metric to keep track of, similar to with CPU.

Node memory usage

As with CPU usage, memory usage is an extremely important metric to observe across your cluster. Memory usage can be oversubscribed using Pod Resource Limits – and many of the same issues as with CPU usage can apply for both the master and worker Nodes in the cluster.

Again, a combination of alerting and metrics is important for visibility into cluster memory usage. We will learn some tools for this later in this chapter.

For the next major observability piece, we will look not at metrics but at logs.

Control plane logging

The components of the Kubernetes control plane, when running, output logs that can be used to get an in-depth view of cluster operations. These logs can also significantly help with troubleshooting, as we'll see in *Chapter 10, Troubleshooting Kubernetes*. Logs for the Kubernetes API server, controller manager, scheduler, kube proxy, and kubelet can all be very useful for certain troubleshooting or observability reasons.

Application logging

Application logging can also be incorporated into an observability stack for Kubernetes – being able to view application logs along with other metrics can be very helpful to operators.

Application performance metrics

As with application logging, application performance metrics and monitoring are highly relevant to the performance of your applications on Kubernetes. Memory usage and CPU profiling at the application level can be a valuable piece of the observability stack.

Generally, Kubernetes provides the data infrastructure for application monitoring and logging but stays away from providing higher-level functionality such as charting and searching. With this in mind, let's review the tools that Kubernetes gives us by default to address these concerns.

Using default observability tooling

Kubernetes provides observability tooling even without adding any third-party solutions. These native Kubernetes tools form the basis of many of the more robust solutions, so they are important to discuss. Since observability includes metrics, logs, traces, and alerts, we will discuss each in turn, focusing first on the Kubernetes-native solutions. First, let's discuss metrics.

Metrics on Kubernetes

A lot of information about your applications can be gained by simply running `kubectl describe pod`. We can see information about our Pod's spec, what state it is in, and key issues preventing its functionality.

Let's assume we are having some trouble with our application. Specifically, the Pod is not starting. To investigate, we run `kubectl describe pod`. As a reminder on kubectl aliases mentioned in *Chapter 1*, *Communicating with Kubernetes*, `kubectl describe pod` is the same as `kubectl describe pods`. Here is an example output from the `describe pod` command – we've stripped out everything apart from the `Events` information:

```
Events:
Type      Reason            Age              From             Message
----      ------            ---              ----             -------
Warning   FailedScheduling  35s (x1 over 35s)  default-scheduler  0/3 nodes are available:
                                                                  3 Insufficient memory.
```

Figure 9.1 – Describe Pod Events output

As you can see, this Pod is not being scheduled because our Nodes are all out of memory! That would be a good thing to investigate further.

Let's keep going. By running `kubectl describe nodes`, we can learn a lot about our Kubernetes Nodes. Some of this information can be very relevant to how our system is performing. Here's another example output, this time from the `kubectl describe nodes` command. Rather than putting the entire output here, which can be quite lengthy, let's zero in on two important sections – `Conditions` and `Allocated resources`. First, let's review the `Conditions` section:

```
Conditions:
  Type             Status  LastHeartbeatTime                 LastTransitionTime                Reason                       Message
  ----             ------  -----------------                 ------------------                ------                       -------
  OutOfDisk        False   Wed, 12 Mar 2020 22:45:03 -0400   Tue, 11 Mar 2020 07:10:44 -0400   KubeletHasSufficientDisk     kubelet has sufficient disk space available
  MemoryPressure   True    Wed, 12 Mar 2020 22:45:03 -0400   Tue, 11 Mar 2020 07:10:44 -0400   KubeletHasInsufficientMemory  kubelet has insufficient memory available
  DiskPressure     False   Wed, 12 Mar 2020 22:45:03 -0400   Tue, 11 Mar 2020 07:10:44 -0400   KubeletHasNoDiskPressure     kubelet has no disk pressure
  Ready            True    Wed, 12 Mar 2020 22:45:03 -0400   Tue, 11 Mar 2020 07:10:44 -0400   KubeletReady                 kubelet is posting ready status
```

Figure 9.2 – Describe Node Conditions output

As you can see, we have included the `Conditions` block of the `kubectl describe nodes` command output. It's a great place to look for any issues. As we can see here, our Node is actually experiencing issues. Our `MemoryPressure` condition is true, and the `Kubelet` has insufficient memory. No wonder our Pods won't schedule!

Next, check out the `Allocated resources` block:

```
Allocated resources:
  (Total limits may be over 100 percent, i.e., overcommitted.)
  CPU Requests     CPU Limits      Memory Requests     Memory Limits
  ------------     ----------      ---------------     -------------
  8520m (40%)      4500m (24%)     16328Mi (104%)      16328Mi (104%)
```

Now we're seeing some metrics! It looks like our Pods are requesting too much memory, leading to our Node and Pod issues. As you can tell from this output, Kubernetes is already collecting metrics data about our Nodes, by default. Without that data, the scheduler would not be able to do its job properly, since maintaining Pod resources requests with Node capacity is one of its most important functions.

However, by default, these metrics are not surfaced to the user. They are in fact being collected by each Node's `Kubelet` and delivered to the scheduler for it to do its job. Thankfully, we can easily get these metrics by deploying Metrics Server to our cluster.

Metrics Server is an officially supported Kubernetes application that collects metrics information and surfaces it on an API endpoint for use. Metrics Server is in fact required to make the Horizontal Pod Autoscaler work, but it is not always included by default, depending on the Kubernetes distribution.

Deploying Metrics Server is very quick. As of the writing of this book, the newest version can be installed using the following:

```
kubectl apply -f https://github.com/kubernetes-sigs/metrics-
server/releases/download/v0.3.7/components.yaml
```

> **Important note**
>
> Full documentation on how to use Metrics Server can be found at `https://github.com/kubernetes-sigs/metrics-server`.

Once Metrics Server is running, we can use a brand-new Kubernetes command. The `kubectl top` command can be used with either Pods or Nodes to see granular information about how much memory and CPU capacity is in use.

Let's take a look at some example usage. Run `kubectl top nodes` to see Node-level metrics. Here's the output of the command:

NAME	CPU(cores)	CPU%	MEMORY(bytes)	MEMORY%
ip-10-10-1-231.ec2.internal	22m	2%	355Mi	9%
NAME	CPU(cores)	CPU%	MEMORY(bytes)	MEMORY%
ip-10-10-1-109.ec2.internal	24m	2%	355Mi	9%
NAME	CPU(cores)	CPU%	MEMORY(bytes)	MEMORY%
ip-10-10-1-266.ec2.internal	29m	3%	354Mi	9%

Figure 9.3 – Node Metrics output

As you can see, we are able to see both absolute and relative CPU and memory usage.

> **Important note**
>
> CPU cores are measured in `millcpu` or `millicores`. 1,000 `millicores` is equivalent to one virtual CPU. Memory is measured in bytes.

Next, let's take a look at the `kubectl top pods` command. Run it with the `--namespace kube-system` flag to see Pods in the `kube-system` namespace.

To do this, we run the following command:

```
Kubectl top pods -n kube-system
```

And we get the following output:

NAMESPACE	NAME	CPU(cores)	MEMORY(bytes)
default	my-hungry-pod	8m	50Mi
default	my-lightweight-pod	2m	10Mi

As you can see, this command uses the same absolute units as `kubectl top nodes` – millicores and bytes. There are no relative percentages when looking at Pod-level metrics.

Next, we'll look at how Kubernetes handles logging.

Logging on Kubernetes

We can split up logging on Kubernetes into two areas – *application logs* and *control plane logs*. Let's start with control plane logs.

Control plane logs

Control plane logs refers to the logs created by the Kubernetes control plane components, such as the scheduler, API server, and others. For a vanilla Kubernetes install, control plane logs can be found on the Nodes themselves and require direct access to the Nodes in order to see. For clusters with components set up to use `systemd`, logs are found using the `journalctl` CLI tool (refer to the following link for more information: `https://manpages.debian.org/stretch/systemd/journalctl.1.en.html`).

On master Nodes, you can find logs in the following locations on the filesystem:

- At `/var/log/kube-scheduler.log`, you can find the Kubernetes scheduler logs.
- At `/var/log/kube-controller-manager.log`, you can find the controller manager logs (for instance, to see scaling events).
- At `/var/log/kube-apiserver.log`, you can find the Kubernetes API server logs.

On worker Nodes, logs are available in two locations on the filesystem:

- At `/var/log/kubelet.log`, you can find the kubelet logs.
- At `/var/log/kube-proxy.log`, you can find the kube proxy logs.

Although, generally, cluster health is influenced by the health of the Kubernetes master and worker Node components, it is of course also important to keep track of your application's logs.

Application logs

It's very easy to find application logs on Kubernetes. Before we explain how it works, let's look at an example.

To check logs for a specific Pod, you can use the `kubectl logs <pod_name>` command. The output of the command will display any text written to the container's `stdout` or `stderr`. If a Pod has multiple containers, you must include the container name in the command:

```
kubectl logs <pod_name> <container_name>
```

Under the hood, Kubernetes handles Pod logs by using the container engine's logging driver. Typically, any logs to `stdout` or `stderr` are persisted to each Node's disk in the `/var/logs` folder. Depending on the Kubernetes distribution, log rotations may be set up to prevent overuse of Node disk space by logs. In addition, Kubernetes components such as the scheduler, kubelet, and kube-apiserver also persist logs to Node disk space, usually within the `/var/logs` folder. It is important to note how limited this default logging capability is – a robust observability stack for Kubernetes would certainly include a third-party solution for log forwarding, as we'll see shortly.

Next, for general Kubernetes observability, we can use Kubernetes Dashboard.

Installing Kubernetes Dashboard

Kubernetes Dashboard provides all of the functionality of kubectl – including viewing logs and editing resources – in a GUI. It's very easy to get the dashboard set up – let's see how.

The dashboard can be installed in a single `kubectl apply` command. For customizations, check out the Kubernetes Dashboard GitHub page at `https://github.com/kubernetes/dashboard`.

To install a version of Kubernetes Dashboard, run the following `kubectl` command, replacing the `<VERSION>` tag with your desired version, based on the version of Kubernetes you are using (again, check the Dashboard GitHub page for version compatibility):

```
kubectl apply -f https://raw.githubusercontent.com/kubernetes/
dashboard/<VERSION> /aio/deploy/recommended.yaml
```

In our case, as of the writing of this book, we will use v2.0.4 – the final command looks like this:

```
kubectl apply -f https://raw.githubusercontent.com/kubernetes/
dashboard/v2.0.4/aio/deploy/recommended.yaml
```

Once Kubernetes Dashboard has been installed, there are a few methods to access it.

> **Important note**
>
> It is not usually recommended to use Ingress or a public load balancer service, because Kubernetes Dashboard allows users to update cluster objects. If for some reason your login methods for the dashboard are compromised or easy to figure out, you could be looking at a large security risk.

With that in mind, we can use either `kubectl port-forward` or `kubectl proxy` in order to view our dashboard from our local machine.

For this example, we will use the `kubectl proxy` command, because we haven't used it in an example yet.

The `kubectl proxy` command, unlike the `kubectl port-forward` command, requires only one command to proxy to every service running on your cluster. It does this by proxying the Kubernetes API directly to a port on your local machine, which is by default `8081`. For a full discussion of the `Kubectl proxy` command, check the docs at `https://kubernetes.io/docs/reference/generated/kubectl/kubectl-commands#proxy`.

In order to access a specific Kubernetes service using `kubectl proxy`, you just need to have the right path. The path to access Kubernetes Dashboard after running `kubectl proxy` will be the following:

```
http://localhost:8001/api/v1/namespaces/kubernetes-dashboard/
services/https:kubernetes-dashboard:/proxy/
```

As you can see, the `kubectl proxy` path we put in our browser is on localhost port `8001`, and mentions the namespace (`kubernetes-dashboard`), the service name and selector (`https:kubernetes-dashboard`), and a proxy path.

Let's put our Kubernetes Dashboard URL in a browser and see the result:

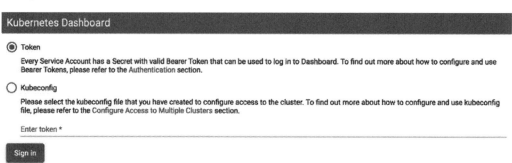

Figure 9.4 – Kubernetes Dashboard login

When we deploy and access Kubernetes Dashboard, we are met with a login screen. We can either create a Service Account (or use our own) to log in to the dashboard, or simply link our local `Kubeconfig` file. By logging in to Kubernetes Dashboard with a specific Service Account's token, the dashboard user will inherit that Service Account's permissions. This allows you to specify what type of actions a user will be able to take using Kubernetes Dashboard – for instance, read-only permissions.

Let's go ahead and create a brand-new Service Account for our Kubernetes Dashboard. You could customize this Service Account and limit its permissions, but for now we will give it admin permissions. To do this, follow these steps:

1. We can create a Service Account imperatively using the following Kubectl command:

    ```
    kubectl create serviceaccount dashboard-user
    ```

    This results in the following output, confirming the creation of our Service Account:

    ```
    serviceaccount/dashboard-user created
    ```

2. Now, we need to link our Service Account to a ClusterRole. You could also use a Role, but we want our dashboard user to be able to access all namespaces. To link a Service Account to the `cluster-admin` default ClusterRole using a single command, we can run the following:

    ```
    kubectl create clusterrolebinding dashboard-user \
    --clusterrole=cluster-admin
    --serviceaccount=default:dashboard-user
    ```

    This command will result in the following output:

    ```
    clusterrolebinding.rbac.authorization.k8s.io/dashboard-
    user created
    ```

3. After this command is run, we should be able to log in to our dashboard! First, we just need to find the token that we will use to log in. A Service Account's token is stored as a Kubernetes secret, so let's see what it looks like. Run the following command to see which secret our token is stored in:

    ```
    kubectl get secrets
    ```

In the output, you should see a secret that looks like the following:

```
NAME                                    TYPE
DATA    AGE
dashboard-user-token-dcn2g    kubernetes.io/service-
account-token    3        112s
```

4. Now, to get our token for signing in to the dashboard, we only need to describe the secret contents using the following:

```
kubectl describe secret dashboard-user-token-dcn2g
```

The resulting output will look like the following:

```
Name:           dashboard-user-token-dcn2g
Namespace:      default
Labels:         <none>
Annotations:    kubernetes.io/service-account.name:
dashboard-user
                kubernetes.io/service-account.uid:
9dd255sd-426c-43f4-88c7-66ss91h44215


Type:   kubernetes.io/service-account-token

Data
====
ca.crt:         1025 bytes
namespace:      7 bytes
token: < LONG TOKEN HERE >
```

5. To log in to the dashboard, copy the string next to `token`, copy it into the token input on the Kubernetes Dashboard login screen, and click **Sign In**. You should be greeted with the Kubernetes Dashboard overview page!

6. Go ahead and click around the dashboard – you should be able to see all the same resources you would be able to using kubectl, and you can filter by namespace in the left-hand sidebar. For instance, here's a view of the **Namespaces** page:

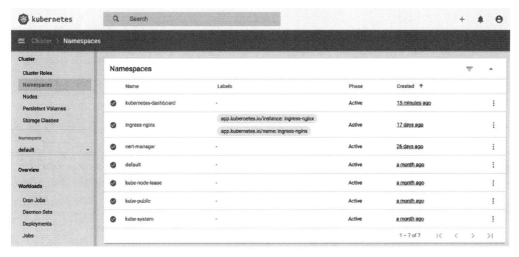

Figure 9.5 – Kubernetes Dashboard detail

7. You can also click on individual resources, and even edit those resources using
    the dashboard as long as the Service Account you used to log in has the proper
    permissions.

Here's a view of editing a Deployment resource from the deployment detail page:

Edit a resource

```
    YAML    JSON
 1  kind: Deployment
 2  apiVersion: apps/v1
 3  metadata:
 4    name: external-dns
 5    namespace: default
 6    selfLink: /apis/apps/v1/namespaces/default/deployments/external-dns
 7    uid: 3ffdb53c-4363-4aa9-8239-af2a5b40a174
 8    resourceVersion: '6346014'
 9    generation: 1
10    creationTimestamp: '2020-09-02T01:25:26Z'
11    annotations:
12      deployment.kubernetes.io/revision: '1'
13      kubectl.kubernetes.io/last-applied-configuration: >
14        {"apiVersion":"apps/v1","kind":"Deployment","metadata":{"annotations":{},"name"
          :"external-dns","namespace":"default"},"spec":{"selector":{"matchLabels":{"app"
          :"external-dns"}},"strategy":{"type":"Recreate"},"template":{"metadata":{"labels"
          :{"app":"external-dns"}},"spec":{"containers":[{"args":["--source=service","--source
          =ingress","--domain-filter=dakotamarketplace.net","--provider=aws","--policy=upsert
          -only","--aws-zone-type=public","--registry=txt","--txt-owner-id=my-identifier"]
          ,"image":"registry.opensource.zalan.do/teapot/external-dns:v0.5.9","name":"external
          -dns"}],"serviceAccountName":"external-dns"}}}}
15  spec:
16    replicas: 1
17    selector:
18      matchLabels:
```

ℹ This action is equivalent to: `kubectl apply -f <spec.yaml>`

Update   Cancel

Figure 9.6 – Kubernetes Dashboard edit view

Kubernetes Dashboard also lets you view Pod logs and dive into many other resource types in your cluster. To understand the full capabilities of the dashboard, check the docs at the previously mentioned GitHub page.

Finally, to round out our discussion of default observability on Kubernetes, let's take a look at alerting.

Alerts and traces on Kubernetes

Unfortunately, the last two pieces of the observability puzzle – *alerts* and *traces* – are not yet native pieces of functionality on Kubernetes. In order to create this type of functionality, let's move on to our next section – incorporating open source tooling from the Kubernetes ecosystem.

Enhancing Kubernetes observability using the best of the ecosystem

As we've discussed, though Kubernetes provides the basis for powerful visibility functionality, it is generally up to the community and vendor ecosystem to create higher-level tooling for metrics, logging, traces, and alerting. For the purposes of this book, we will focus on fully open source, self-hosted solutions. Since many of these solutions fulfill multiple visibility pillars between metrics, logs, traces, and alerting, instead of categorizing solutions into each visibility pillar during our review, we will review each solution separately.

Let's start with an often-used combination of technologies for metrics and alerts: **Prometheus** and **Grafana**.

Introducing Prometheus and Grafana

Prometheus and Grafana are a typical combination of visibility technologies on Kubernetes. Prometheus is a time series database, query layer, and alerting system with many integrations, while Grafana is a sophisticated graphing and visualization layer that integrates with Prometheus. We'll walk you through the installation and usage of these tools, starting with Prometheus.

Installing Prometheus and Grafana

There are many ways to install Prometheus on Kubernetes, but most use Deployments in order to scale the service. For our purposes, we will be using the `kube-prometheus` project (`https://github.com/coreos/kube-prometheus`). This project includes an `operator` as well as several **custom resource definitions** (**CRDs**). It will also automatically install Grafana for us!

An operator is essentially an application controller on Kubernetes (deployed like other applications in a Pod) that happens to make commands to the Kubernetes API in order to correctly run or operate its application.

A CRD, on the other hand, allows us to model custom functionality inside of the Kubernetes API. We'll learn a lot more about operators and CRDs in *Chapter 13*, *Extending Kubernetes with CRDs*, but for now just think of operators as a way to create *smart deployments* where the application can control itself properly and spin up other Pods and Deployments as necessary – and think of CRDs as a way to use Kubernetes to store application-specific concerns.

To install Prometheus, first we need to download a release, which may be different depending on the newest version of Prometheus or your intended version of Kubernetes:

```
curl -LO https://github.com/coreos/kube-prometheus/archive/
v0.5.0.zip
```

Next, unzip the file using any tool. First, we're going to need to install the CRDs. In general, most Kubernetes tooling installation instructions will have you create the CRDs on Kubernetes first, since any additional setup that uses the CRD will fail if the underlying CRD has not already been created on Kubernetes.

Let's install them using the following command:

```
kubectl apply -f manifests/setup
```

We'll need to wait a few seconds while the CRDs are created. This command will also create a `monitoring` namespace for our resources to live in. Once everything is ready, let's spin up the rest of the Prometheus and Grafana resources using the following:

```
kubectl apply -f manifests/
```

Let's talk about what this command will actually create. The entire stack consists of the following:

- **Prometheus Deployment**: Pods of the Prometheus application
- **Prometheus Operator**: Controls and operates the Prometheus app Pods
- **Alertmanager Deployment**: A Prometheus component to specify and trigger alerts
- **Grafana**: A powerful visualization dashboard
- **Kube-state-metrics agent**: Generates metrics from the Kubernetes API state
- **Prometheus Node Exporter**: Exports Node hardware- and OS-level metrics to Prometheus
- **Prometheus Adapter for Kubernetes Metrics**: Adapter for Kubernetes Resource Metrics API and Custom Metrics API for ingest into Prometheus

Together, all these components will provide sophisticated visibility into our cluster, from the command plane down to the application containers themselves.

Once the stack has been created (check by using the `kubectl get po -n monitoring` command), we can start using our components. Let's dive into usage, starting with plain Prometheus.

Using Prometheus

Though the real power of Prometheus is in its data store, query, and alert layer, it does provide a simple UI to developers. As you'll see later, Grafana provides many more features and customizations, but it is worth it to get acquainted with the Prometheus UI.

By default, `kube-prometheus` will only create ClusterIP services for Prometheus, Grafana, and Alertmanager. It's up to us to expose them outside the cluster. For the purposes of this tutorial, we're simply going to port forward the service to our local machine. For production, you may want to use Ingress to route requests to the three services.

In order to `port-forward` to the Prometheus UI service, use the `port-forward` kubectl command:

```
Kubectl -n monitoring port-forward svc/prometheus-k8s 3000:9090
```

We need to use port `9090` for the Prometheus UI. Access the service on your machine at `http://localhost:3000`.

You should see something like the following screenshot:

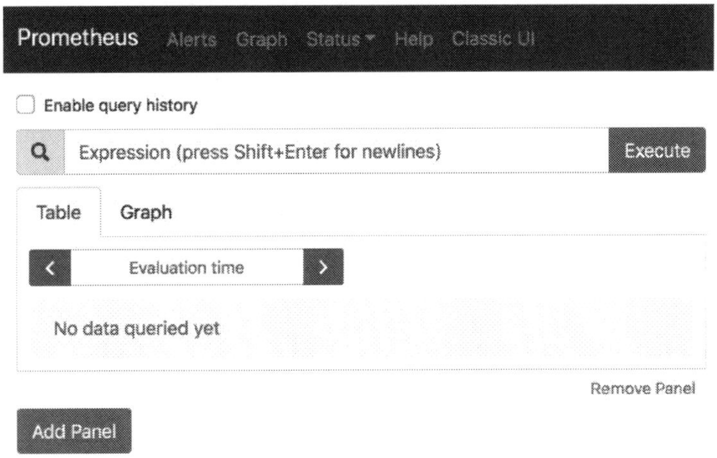

Figure 9.7 – Prometheus UI

As you can see, the Prometheus UI has a **Graph** page, which is what you can see in *Figure 9.4*. It also has its own UI for seeing configured alerts – but it doesn't allow you to create alerts via the UI. Grafana and Alertmanager will help us for that task.

To perform a query, navigate to the **Graph** page and enter the query command into the **Expression** bar, then click **Execute**. Prometheus uses a query language called `PromQL` – we won't present it fully to you in this book, but the Prometheus docs are a great way to learn. You can refer to it using the following link: `https://prometheus.io/docs/prometheus/latest/querying/basics/`.

To show how this works, let's enter a basic query, as follows:

```
kubelet_http_requests_total
```

This query will list the total number of HTTP requests made to the kubelet on each Node, for each request category, as shown in the following screenshot:

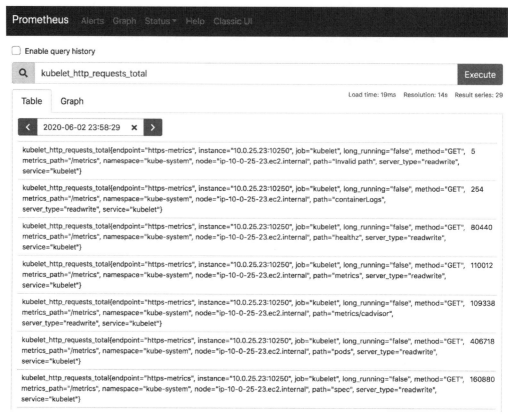

Figure 9.8 – HTTP requests query

You can also see the requests in graph form by clicking the **Graph** tab next to **Table** as shown in the following screenshot:

Figure 9.9 – HTTP requests query – graph view

This provides a time series graph view of the data from the preceding screenshot. As you can see, the graphing capability is fairly simple.

Prometheus also provides an **Alerts** tab for configuring Prometheus alerts. Typically, these alerts are configured via code instead of using the **Alerts** tab UI, so we will skip that page in our review. For more information, you can check the official Prometheus documentation at `https://prometheus.io/docs/alerting/latest/overview/`.

Let's move on to Grafana, where we can extend Prometheus powerful data tooling with visualizations.

Using Grafana

Grafana provides powerful tools for visualizing metrics, with many supported charting types that can update in real time. We can connect Grafana to Prometheus in order to see our cluster metrics charted on the Grafana UI.

To get started with Grafana, do the following:

1. We will end our current port forwarding (*CTRL + C* will do the trick) and set up a new port forward listener to the Grafana UI:

```
Kubectl -n monitoring port-forward svc/grafana 3000:3000
```

2. Again, navigate to localhost:3000 to see the Grafana UI. You should be able to log in with **Username**: admin and **Password**: admin, at which point you should be able to change the initial password as shown in the following screenshot:

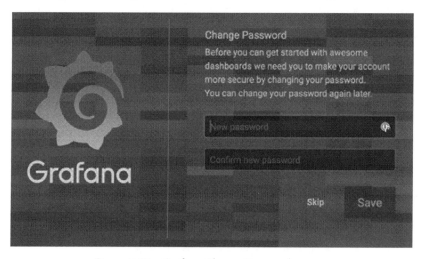

Figure 9.10 – Grafana Change Password screen

3. Upon login, you will see the following screen. Grafana does not come preconfigured with any dashboards, but we can add them easily by clicking the + sign as shown in the following screenshot:

Figure 9.11 – Grafana main page

4. Each Grafana dashboard includes one or more graphs for different sets of metrics. To add a preconfigured dashboard (instead of creating one yourself), click the plus sign (+) on the left-hand menu bar and click **Import**. You should see a page like the following screenshot:

Figure 9.12 – Grafana Dashboard Import

We can add a dashboard via this page either using the JSON configuration or by pasting in a public dashboard ID.

5. You can find public dashboards and their associated IDs at `https://grafana.com/grafana/dashboards/315`. Dashboard #315 is a great starter dashboard for Kubernetes – let's add it to the textbox labeled **Grafana.com Dashboard** and click **Load**.

6. Then, on the next page, select the **Prometheus** data source from the **Prometheus** option dropdown, which is used to pick between multiple data sources if available. Click **Import**, and the dashboard should be loaded, which will look like the following screenshot:

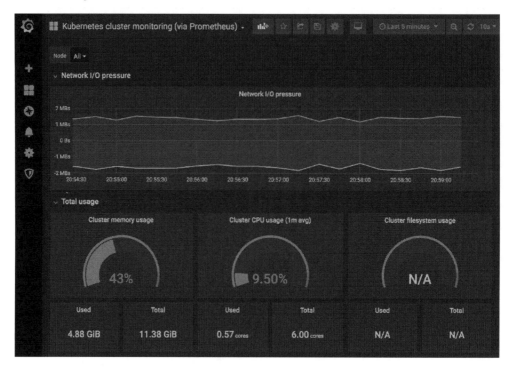

Figure 9.13 – Grafana dashboard

This particular Grafana dashboard provides a good high-level overview of network, memory, CPU, and filesystem utilization across the cluster, and it is broken down per Pod and container. It is configured with real-time graphs for **Network I/O pressure**, **Cluster memory usage**, **Cluster CPU usage**, and **Cluster filesystem usage** – though this last option may not be enabled depending on how you have installed Prometheus.

Finally, let's look at the Alertmanager UI.

Using Alertmanager

Alertmanager is an open source solution for managing alerts generated from Prometheus alerts. We installed Alertmanager previously as part of our stack – let's take a look at what it can do:

1. First, let's `port-forward` the Alertmanager service using the following command:

```
Kubectl -n monitoring port-forward svc/alertmanager-main
3000:9093
```

2. As usual, navigate to `localhost:3000` to see the UI as shown in the following screenshot. It looks similar to the Prometheus UI:

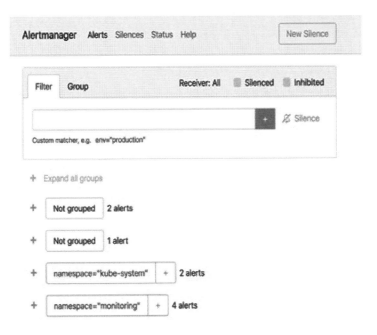

Figure 9.14 – Alertmanager UI

Alertmanager works together with Prometheus alerts. You can use the Prometheus server to specify alert rules, and then use Alertmanager to group similar alerts into single notifications, perform deduplications, and create *silences*, which are essentially a way to mute alerts if they match specific rules.

Next, we will review a popular logging stack for Kubernetes – Elasticsearch, FluentD, and Kibana.

Implementing the EFK stack on Kubernetes

Similar to the popular ELK stack (Elasticsearch, Logstash, and Kibana), the EFK stack swaps out Logstash for the FluentD log forwarder, which is well supported on Kubernetes. Implementing this stack is easy and allows us to get started with log aggregation and search functionalities using purely open source tooling on Kubernetes.

Installing the EFK stack

There are many ways to install the EFK Stack on Kubernetes, but the Kubernetes GitHub repository itself has some supported YAML, so let's just use that:

1. First, clone or download the Kubernetes repository using the following command:

```
git clone https://github.com/kubernetes/kubernetes
```

2. The manifests are located in the `kubernetes/cluster/addons` folder, specifically under `fluentd-elasticsearch`:

```
cd kubernetes/cluster/addons
```

   For a production workload, we would likely make some changes to these manifests in order to properly customize the configuration for our cluster, but for the purposes of this tutorial we will leave everything as default. Let's start the process of bootstrapping our EFK stack.

3. First, let's create the Elasticsearch cluster itself. This runs as a StatefulSet on Kubernetes, and also provides a Service. To create the cluster, we need to run two `kubectl` commands:

```
kubectl apply -f ./fluentd-elasticsearch/es-statefulset.
yaml
```
```
kubectl apply -f ./fluentd-elasticsearch/es-service.yaml
```

> **Important note**
>
> A word of warning for the Elasticsearch StatefulSet – by default, the resource request for each Pod is 3 GB of memory, so if none of your Nodes have that available, you will not be able to deploy it as configured by default.

4. Next, let's deploy the FluentD logging agents. These will run as a DaemonSet – one per Node – and forward logs from the Nodes to Elasticsearch. We also need to create the ConfigMap YAML, which contains the base FluentD agent configuration. This can be further customized to add things such as log filters and new sources.

5. To install the DaemonSet for the agents and their configuration, run the following two `kubectl` commands:

```
kubectl apply -f ./fluentd-elasticsearch/fluentd-es-
configmap.yaml
kubectl apply -f ./fluentd-elasticsearch/fluentd-es-ds.
yaml
```

6. Now that we've created the ConfigMap and the FluentD DaemonSet, we can create our Kibana application, which is a GUI for interacting with Elasticsearch. This piece runs as a Deployment, with a Service. To deploy Kibana to our cluster, run the final two `kubectl` commands:

```
kubectl apply -f ./fluentd-elasticsearch/kibana-
deployment.yaml
kubectl apply -f ./fluentd-elasticsearch/kibana-service.
yaml
```

7. Once everything has been initiated, which may take several minutes, we can access the Kibana UI in the same way that we did Prometheus and Grafana. To check the status of the resources we just created, we can run the following:

```
kubectl get po -A
```

8. Once all Pods for FluentD, Elasticsearch, and Kibana are in the **Ready** state, we can move on. If any of your Pods are in the **Error** or **CrashLoopBackoff** stage, consult the Kubernetes GitHub documentation in the `addons` folder for more information.

9. Once we've confirmed that our components are working properly, let's use the `port-forward` command to access the Kibana UI. By the way, our EFK stack pieces will live in the `kube-system` namespace – so our command needs to reflect that. So, let's use the following command:

```
kubectl port-forward -n kube-system svc/kibana-logging
8080:5601
```

This command will start a `port-forward` to your local machine's port `8080` from the Kibana UI.

10. Let's check out the Kibana UI at `localhost:8080`. It should look something like the following, depending on your exact version and configuration:

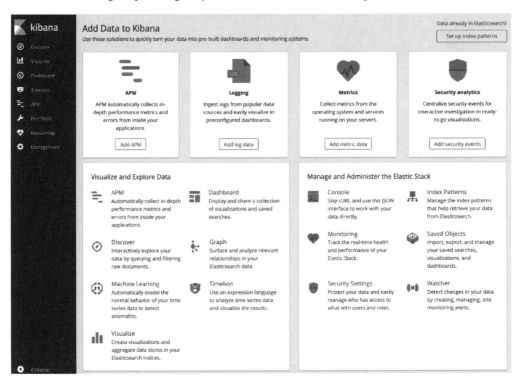

Figure 9.15 – Basic Kibana UI

Kibana provides several different features for searching and visualizing logs, metrics, and more. The most important section of the dashboard for our purposes is **Logging**, since we are using Kibana solely as a log search UI in our example.

However, Kibana has many other functions, some of which are comparable to Grafana. For instance, it includes a full visualization engine, **application performance monitoring** (**APM**) capabilities, and Timelion, an expression engine for time series data very similar to what is found in Prometheus's PromQL. Kibana's metrics functionality is similar to Prometheus and Grafana.

11. In order to get Kibana working, we will first need to specify an index pattern. To do this, click on the **Visualize** button, then click **Add an Index Pattern**. Select an option from the list of patterns and choose the index with the current date on it, then create the index pattern.

Now that we're set up, the **Discover** page will provide you with search functionality. This uses the Apache Lucene query syntax (`https://www.elastic.co/guide/en/elasticsearch/reference/6.7/query-dsl-query-string-query.html#query-string-syntax`) and can handle everything from simple string matching expressions to extremely complex queries. In the following screenshot, we are doing a simple string match for the letter `h`:

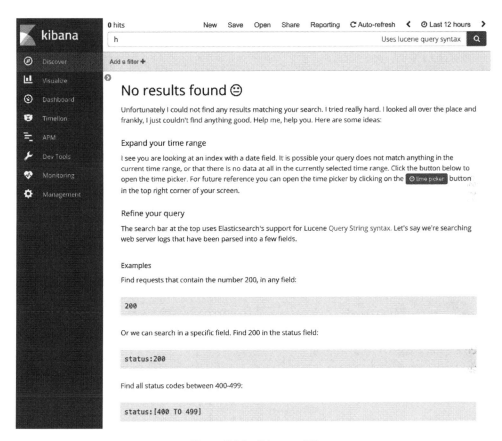

Figure 9.16 – Discover UI

When Kibana cannot find any results, it gives you a handy set of possible solutions including query examples, as you can see in *Figure 9.13*.

Now that you know how to create search queries, you can create visualizations from queries on the **Visualize** page. These can be chosen from a selection of visualization types including graphs, charts, and more, and then customized with specific queries as shown in the following screenshot:

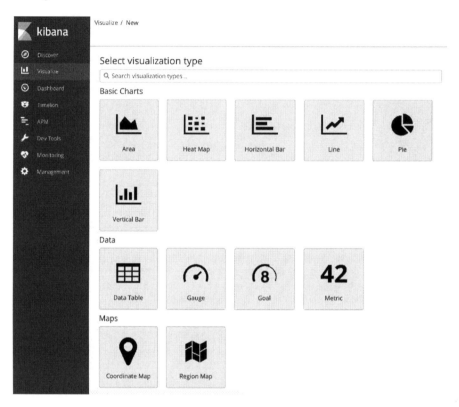

Figure 9.17 – New visualization

Next, these visualizations can be combined into dashboards. This works similarly to Grafana where multiple visualizations can be added to a dashboard, which can then be saved and reused.

You can also use the search bar to further filter your dashboard visualizations – pretty nifty! The following screenshot shows how a dashboard can be tied to a specific query:

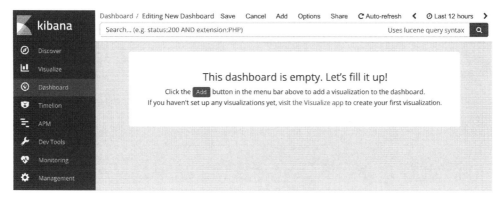

Figure 9.18 – Dashboard UI

As you can see, a dashboard can be created for a specific query using the **Add** button.

Next, Kibana provides a tool called *Timelion*, which is a time series visualization synthesis tool. Essentially, it allows you to combine separate data sources into a single visualization. Timelion is very powerful, but a full discussion of its feature set is outside the scope of this book. The following screenshot shows the Timelion UI – you may notice some similarities to Grafana, as these two sets of tools offer very similar capabilities:

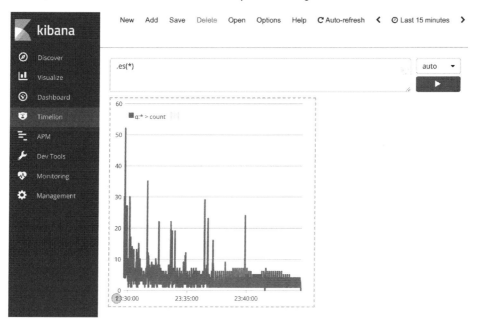

Figure 9.19 – Timelion UI

As you can see, in Timelion a query can be used to drive a real-time updating graph, just like in Grafana.

Additionally, though less relevant to this book, Kibana provides APM functionality, which requires some further setup, especially with Kubernetes. In this book we lean on Prometheus for this type of information while using the EFK stack to search logs from our applications.

Now that we've covered Prometheus and Grafana for metrics and alerting, and the EFK stack for logging, only one piece of the observability puzzle is left. To solve this, we will use another excellent piece of open source software – Jaeger.

Implementing distributed tracing with Jaeger

Jaeger is an open source distributed tracing solution compatible with Kubernetes. Jaeger implements the OpenTracing specification, which is a set of standards for defining distributed traces.

Jaeger exposes a UI for viewing traces and integrates with Prometheus. The official Jaeger documentation can be found at `https://www.jaegertracing.io/docs/`. Always check the docs for new information, since things may have changed since the publishing of this book.

Installing Jaeger using the Jaeger Operator

To install Jaeger, we are going to use the Jaeger Operator, which is the first operator that we've come across in this book. An *operator* in Kubernetes is simply a pattern for creating custom application controllers that speak Kubernetes's language. This means that instead of having to deploy all the various Kubernetes resources for an application, you can deploy a single Pod (or usually, single Deployment) and that application will talk to Kubernetes and spin up all the other required resources for you. It can even go further and self-operate the application, making resource changes when necessary. Operators can be highly complex, but they make it easier for us as end users to deploy commercial or open source software on our Kubernetes clusters.

To get started with the Jaeger Operator, we need to create a few initial resources for Jaeger, and then the operator will do the rest. A prerequisite for this installation of Jaeger is that the `nginx-ingress` controller is installed on our cluster, since that is how we will access the Jaeger UI.

First, we need to create a namespace for Jaeger to live in. We can get this via the `kubectl create namespace` command:

```
kubectl create namespace observability
```

Now that our namespace is created, we need to create some **CRDs** that Jaeger and the operator will use. We will discuss CRDs in depth in our chapter on extending Kubernetes, but for now, think of them as a way to co-opt the Kubernetes API to build custom functionality for applications. Using the following steps, let's install Jaeger:

1. To create the Jaeger CRDs, run the following command:

```
kubectl create -f https://raw.githubusercontent.com/
jaegertracing/jaeger-operator/master/deploy/crds/
jaegertracing.io_jaegers_crd.yaml
```

    With our CRDs created, the operator needs a few Roles and Bindings to be created in order to do its work.

2. We want Jaeger to have cluster-wide permission in our cluster, so we will create some optional ClusterRoles and ClusterRoleBindings as well. To accomplish this, we run the following commands:

```
kubectl create -n observability -f https://raw.
githubusercontent.com/jaegertracing/jaeger-operator/
master/deploy/service_account.yaml
```

```
kubectl create -n observability -f https://raw.
githubusercontent.com/jaegertracing/jaeger-operator/
master/deploy/role.yaml
```

```
kubectl create -n observability -f https://raw.
githubusercontent.com/jaegertracing/jaeger-operator/
master/deploy/role_binding.yaml
```

```
kubectl create -f https://raw.githubusercontent.com/
jaegertracing/jaeger-operator/master/deploy/cluster_role.
yaml
```

```
kubectl create -f https://raw.githubusercontent.com/
jaegertracing/jaeger-operator/master/deploy/cluster_role_
binding.yaml
```

3. Now, we finally have all the pieces necessary for our operator to work. Let's install the operator with one last `kubectl` command:

```
kubectl create -n observability -f https://raw.
githubusercontent.com/jaegertracing/jaeger-operator/
master/deploy/operator.yaml
```

4. Finally, check to see if the operator is running, using the following command:

```
kubectl get deploy -n observability
```

If the operator is running correctly, you will see something similar to the following output, with one available Pod for the deployment:

Figure 9.20 – Jaeger Operator Pod output

We now have our Jaeger Operator up and running – but Jaeger itself isn't running. Why is this the case? Jaeger is a highly complex system and can run in different configurations, and the operator makes it easier to deploy these configurations.

The Jaeger Operator uses a CRD called `Jaeger` to read a configuration for your Jaeger instance, at which time the operator will deploy all the necessary Pods and other resources on Kubernetes.

Jaeger can run in three main configurations: *AllInOne*, *Production*, and *Streaming*. A full discussion of these configurations is outside the scope of this book (check the Jaeger docs link shared previously), but we will be using the AllInOne configuration. This configuration combines the Jaeger UI, Collector, Agent, and Ingestor into a single Pod, without any persistent storage included. This is perfect for demo purposes – to see production-ready configurations, check the Jaeger docs.

In order to create our Jaeger deployment, we need to tell the Jaeger Operator about our chosen configuration. We do that using the CRD that we created earlier – the Jaeger CRD. Create a new file for this CRD instance:

Jaeger-allinone.yaml

```
apiVersion: jaegertracing.io/v1
kind: Jaeger
metadata:
  name: all-in-one
  namespace: observability
spec:
  strategy: allInOne
```

We are just using a small subset of the possible Jaeger type configurations – again, check the docs for the full story.

Now, we can create our Jaeger instance by running the following:

```
Kubectl apply -f jaeger-allinone.yaml
```

This command creates an instance of the Jaeger CRD we installed previously. At this point, the Jaeger Operator should realize that the CRD has been created. In less than a minute, our actual Jaeger Pod should be running. We can check for it by listing all the Pods in the observability namespace, with the following command:

```
Kubectl get po -n observability
```

As an output, you should see the newly created Jaeger Pod for our all-in-one instance:

NAME	READY	STATUS	RESTARTS	AGE
all-in-one-12t6bc95sr-aog4s	1/1	Running	0	5m

The Jaeger Operator creates an Ingress record when we also have an Ingress controller running on our cluster. This means that we can simply list our Ingress entries using kubectl to see where to access the Jaeger UI.

You can list ingresses using this command:

```
Kubectl get ingress -n observability
```

The output should show your new Ingress for the Jaeger UI as shown:

NAMESPACE	NAME	HOSTS	ADDRESS	PORTS	AGE
observability	all-in-one-query	*	10.200.208.231	80	46s

Figure 9.21 – Jaeger UI Service output

Now you can navigate to the address listed in your cluster's Ingress record to see the Jaeger UI. It should look like the following:

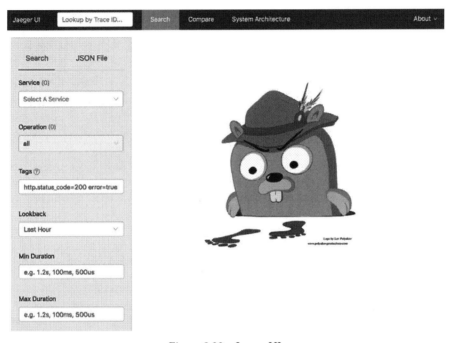

Figure 9.22 – Jaeger UI

As you can see, the Jaeger UI is pretty simple. There are three tabs at the top – **Search**, **Compare**, and **System Architecture**. We will focus on the **Search** tab, but for more information about the other two, check the Jaeger docs at `https://www.jaegertracing.io`.

The Jaeger **Search** page lets us search for traces based on many inputs. We can search based on which Service is included in the trace, or based on tags, duration, or more. However, right now there's nothing in our Jaeger system.

The reason for this is that even though we have Jaeger up and running, our apps still need to be configured to send traces to Jaeger. This usually needs to be done at the code or framework level and is out of the scope of this book. If you want to play around with Jaeger's tracing capabilities, a sample app is available to install – see the Jaeger docs page at `https://www.jaegertracing.io/docs/1.18/getting-started/#sample-app-hotrod`.

With services sending traces to Jaeger, it is possible to see traces. A trace in Jaeger looks like the following. We've cropped out some of the later parts of the trace for readability, but this should give you a good idea of what a trace can look like:

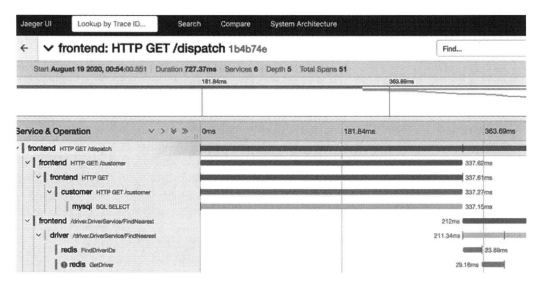

Figure 9.23 – Trace view in Jaeger

As you can see, the Jaeger UI view for a trace splits up service traces into constituent parts. Each service-to-service call, as well as any specific calls within the services themselves, have their own line in the trace. The horizontal bar chart you see moves from left to right with time, and each individual call in the trace has its own line. In this trace, you can see we have HTTP calls, SQL calls, as well as some Redis statements.

You should be able to see how Jaeger and tracing in general can help developers make sense of a web of service-to-service calls and can help find bottlenecks.

With that review of Jaeger, we have a fully open source solution to every problem in the observability bucket. However, that does not mean that there is no use case where a commercial solution makes sense – in many cases it does.

Third-party tooling

In addition to many open source libraries, there are many commercially available products for metrics, logging, and alerting on Kubernetes. Some of these can be much more powerful than the open source options.

Generally, most tooling in metrics and logging will require you to provision resources on your cluster to forward metrics and logs to your service of choice. In the examples we've used in this chapter, these services are running in the cluster, though in commercial products these can often be separate SaaS applications where you log on to analyze your logs and see your metrics. For instance, with the EFK stack we provisioned in this chapter, you can pay Elastic for a hosted solution where the Elasticsearch and Kibana pieces of the solution would be hosted on Elastic's infrastructure, reducing complexity in the solution. There are also many other solutions in this space, from vendors including Sumo Logic, Logz.io, New Relic, DataDog, and AppDynamics.

For a production environment, it is common to use separate compute (either a separate cluster, service, or SaaS tool) to perform log and metric analytics. This ensures that the cluster running your actual software can be dedicated to the application alone, and any costly log searching or querying functionality can be handled separately. It also means that if our application cluster goes down, we can still view logs and metrics up until the point of the failure.

Summary

In this chapter, we learned about observability on Kubernetes. We first learned about the four major tenets of observability: metrics, logging, traces, and alerts. Then we discovered how Kubernetes itself provides tooling for observability, including how it manages logs and resource metrics and how to deploy Kubernetes Dashboard. Finally, we learned how to implement and use some key open source tools to provide visualization, searching, and alerting for the four pillars. This knowledge will help you build robust observability infrastructure for your future Kubernetes clusters and help you decide what is most important to observe in your cluster.

In the next chapter, we will use what we learned about observability to help us troubleshoot applications on Kubernetes.

Questions

1. Explain the difference between metrics and logs.

2. Why would you use Grafana instead of simply using the Prometheus UI?

3. When running an EFK stack in production (so as to keep as much compute off the production app cluster as possible), which piece(s) of the stack would run on the production app cluster? And which piece(s) would run off the cluster?

Further reading

- In-depth review of Kibana Timelion: `https://www.elastic.co/guide/en/kibana/7.10/timelion-tutorial-create-time-series-visualizations.html`

10
Troubleshooting Kubernetes

This chapter reviews the best-practice methods for effectively troubleshooting Kubernetes clusters and the applications that run on them. This includes a discussion of common Kubernetes issues, as well as how to debug the masters and workers separately. The common Kubernetes issues will be discussed and taught in a case study format, split into cluster issues and application issues.

We will start with a discussion of some common Kubernetes failure modes, before moving on to how to best troubleshoot clusters and applications.

In this chapter, we will cover the following topics:

- Understanding failure modes for distributed applications
- Troubleshooting Kubernetes clusters
- Troubleshooting applications on Kubernetes

Technical requirements

In order to run the commands detailed in this chapter, you will need a computer that supports the `kubectl` command-line tool along with a working Kubernetes cluster. See *Chapter 1, Communicating with Kubernetes*, for several methods for getting up and running with Kubernetes quickly, and for instructions on how to install the `kubectl` tool.

The code used in this chapter can be found in the book's GitHub repository at `https://github.com/PacktPublishing/Cloud-Native-with-Kubernetes/tree/master/Chapter10`.

Understanding failure modes for distributed applications

Kubernetes components (and applications running on Kubernetes) are distributed by default if they run more than one replica. This can result in some interesting failure modes, which can be hard to debug.

For this reason, applications on Kubernetes are less prone to failure if they are stateless – in which case, the state is offloaded to a cache or database running outside of Kubernetes. Kubernetes primitives such as StatefulSets and PersistentVolumes can make it much easier to run stateful applications on Kubernetes – and with every release, the experience of running stateful applications on Kubernetes improves. Still, deciding to run fully stateful applications on Kubernetes introduces complexity and therefore the potential for failure.

Failure in distributed applications can be introduced by many different factors. Things as simple as network reliability and bandwidth constraints can cause major issues. These are so varied that *Peter Deutsch* at *Sun Microsystems* helped pen the *Fallacies of distributed computing* (along with *James Gosling*, who added the 8th point), which are commonly agreed-upon factors for failures in distributed applications. In the paper *Fallacies of distributed computing explained*, *Arnon Rotem-Gal-Oz* discusses the source of these fallacies (`https://www.rgoarchitects.com/Files/fallacies.pdf`).

The fallacies are as follows, in numerical order:

1. The network is reliable.
2. Latency is zero.

3. Bandwidth is infinite.

4. The network is secure.

5. The topology doesn't change.

6. There is one administrator.

7. Transport cost is zero.

8. The network is homogeneous.

Kubernetes has been engineered and developed with these fallacies in mind and is therefore more tolerant. It also helps address these issues for applications running on Kubernetes – but not perfectly. It is therefore very possible that your applications, when containerized and running on Kubernetes, will exhibit problems when faced with any of these issues. Each fallacy, when assumed to be untrue and taken to its logical conclusion, can introduce failure modes in distributed applications. Let's go through each of the fallacies as applied to Kubernetes and applications running on Kubernetes.

The network is reliable

Applications running on multiple logical machines must communicate over the internet – so any reliability problems in the network can introduce issues. On Kubernetes specifically, the control plane itself can be distributed in a highly available setup (which means a setup with multiple master Nodes – see *Chapter 1, Communicating with Kubernetes*), which means that failure modes can be introduced at the controller level. If the network is unreliable, then kubelets may not be able to communicate with the control plane, leading to Pod placement issues.

Similarly, the Nodes of the control plane may not be able to communicate with each other – though `etcd` is of course built with a consensus protocol that can tolerate communication failures.

Finally, the worker Nodes may not be able to communicate with each other – which, in a microservices scenario, could cause problems depending on Pod placement. In some cases, the workers may all be able to communicate with the control plane while still not being able to communicate with each other, which can cause issues with the Kubernetes overlay network.

As with general unreliability, latency can also cause many of the same problems.

Latency is zero

If network latency is significant, many of the same failures as with network unreliability will also apply. For instance, calls between kubelets and the control plane may fail, leading to periods of inaccuracy in `etcd` because the control plane may not be able to contact the kubelets – or properly update `etcd`. Similarly, requests could be lost between applications running on worker Nodes that would otherwise work perfectly if the applications were collocated on the same Node.

Bandwidth is infinite

Bandwidth limitations can expose similar issues as with the previous two fallacies. Kubernetes does not currently have a fully supported method to place Pods based on bandwidth subscription. This means that Nodes that are hitting their network bandwidth limits can still have new Pods scheduled to them, causing increased failure rates and latency issues for requests. There have been requests to add this as a core Kubernetes scheduling feature (basically, a way to schedule on Node bandwidth consumption as with CPU and memory), but for now, the solutions are mostly restricted to **Container Network Interface** (**CNI**) plugins.

> **Important note**
>
> For instance, the CNI bandwidth plugin supports traffic shaping at the Pod level – see `https://kubernetes.io/docs/concepts/extend-kubernetes/compute-storage-net/network-plugins/#support-traffic-shaping`.

Third-party Kubernetes networking implementations may also provide additional features around bandwidth – and many are compatible with the CNI bandwidth plugin.

The network is secure

Network security has effects that reach far beyond Kubernetes – as any insecure network is privy to a whole class of attacks. Attackers may be able to gain SSH access to the master or worker Nodes in a Kubernetes cluster, which can cause significant breaches. Since so much of Kubernetes' magic happens over the network rather than in a single machine, access to the network is doubly problematic in an attack situation.

The topology doesn't change

This fallacy is extra relevant in the context of Kubernetes, since not only can the meta network topology change with new Nodes being added and removed – the overlay network topology is also altered directly by the Kubernetes control plane and CNI.

For this reason, an application that is running in one logical location at one moment may be running in a completely different spot in the network. For this reason, the use of Pod IPs to identify logical applications is a bad idea – this is one of the purposes of the Service abstraction (see *Chapter 5, Service and Ingress – Communicating with the outside world*). Any application concerns that do not assume an indefinite topology (at least concerning IPs) within the cluster may have issues. As an example, routing applications to a specific Pod IP only works until something happens to that Pod. If that Pod shuts down, the Deployment (for instance) controlling it will start a new Pod to replace it, but the IP will be completely different. A cluster DNS (and by extension, Services) offers a much better way to make requests between applications in a cluster, unless your application has the capability to adjust on the fly to cluster changes such as Pod placements.

There is only one administrator

Multiple administrators and conflicting rules can cause issues in the base network, and multiple Kubernetes administrators can cause further issues by changing resource configurations such as Pod resource limits, leading to unintended behavior. Use of Kubernetes **Role-Based Access Control** (**RBAC**) capabilities can help address this by giving Kubernetes users only the permissions they need (read-only, for instance).

Transport cost is zero

There are two common ways this fallacy is interpreted. Firstly, that the latency cost of transport is zero – which is obviously untrue, as the speed of data transfer over wires is not infinite, and lower-level networking concerns add latency. This is essentially identical to the effects stemming from the *latency is zero* fallacy.

Secondly, this statement can be interpreted to mean that the cost of creating and operating a network for the purposes of transport is zero – as in zero dollars and zero cents. While also being patently untrue (just look at your cloud provider's data transfer fees for proof of this), this does not specifically correspond to application troubleshooting on Kubernetes, so we will focus on the first interpretation.

The network is homogeneous

This final fallacy has less to do with Kubernetes' components, and more to do with applications running on Kubernetes. However, the fact is that developers operating in today's environment are well aware that application networking may have different implementations across applications – from HTTP 1 and 2 to protocols such as *gRPC*.

Now that we've reviewed some major reasons for application failure on Kubernetes, we can dive into the actual process of troubleshooting both Kubernetes and applications that run on Kubernetes.

Troubleshooting Kubernetes clusters

Since Kubernetes is a distributed system that has been designed to tolerate failure where applications are run, most (but not all) issues tend to be centered on the control plane and API. A worker Node failing, in most scenarios, will just result in the Pods being rescheduled to another Node – though compounding factors can introduce issues.

In order to walk through common Kubernetes cluster issue scenarios, we will use a case study methodology. This should give you all the tools you need to investigate real-world cluster issues. Our first case study is centered on the failure of the API server itself.

> **Important note**
>
> For the purposes of this tutorial, we will assume a self-managed cluster. Managed Kubernetes services such as EKS, AKS, and GKE generally remove some of the failure domains (by autoscaling and managing master Nodes, for instance). A good rule is to check your managed service documentation first, as any issues may be specific to the implementation.

Case study – Kubernetes Pod placement failure

Let's set the scene. Your cluster is up and running, but you are experiencing a problem with Pod scheduling. Pods stay stuck in the Pending state indefinitely. Let's confirm this with the command:

```
kubectl get pods
```

The output of the command is the following:

NAME AGE	READY	STATUS	RESTARTS
app-1-pod-2821252345-tj8ks	0/1	Pending	0

2d				
app-1-pod-2821252345-9fj2k	0/1	Pending	0	
2d				
app-1-pod-2821252345-06hdj	0/1	Pending	0	
2d				

As we can see, none of our Pods are running. Furthermore, we're running three replicas of the application and none of them are getting scheduled. A great next step would be to check the Node state and see if there are any issues there. Run the following command to get the output:

```
kubectl get nodes
```

We get the following output:

NAME	STATUS	ROLES	AGE	VERSION
node-01	NotReady	<none>	5m	v1.15.6

This output gives us some good information – we only have one worker Node, and it isn't available for scheduling. When a get command doesn't give us enough information to go by, describe is usually a good next step.

Let's run kubectl describe node node-01 and check the conditions key. We've dropped a column in order to fit everything neatly on the page, but the most important columns are there:

```
Conditions:
  Type              Status    LastTransitionTime                    Reason                        Message
  ----              ------    ------------------                    ------                        -------
  OutOfDisk         Unknown   Fri, 22 May 2020 04:19:00 +0000       NodeStatusUnknown             kubelet stopped posting node status.
  MemoryPressure    False     Thu, 21 May 2020 14:42:51 +0000       KubeletHasSufficientMemory    kubelet has sufficient memory available
  DiskPressure      False     Thu, 21 May 2020 14:42:51 +0000       KubeletHasNoDiskPressure      kubelet has no disk pressure
  Ready             Unknown   Fri, 22 May 2020 04:19:00 +0000       NodeStatusUnknown             kubelet stopped posting node status.
```

Figure 10.1 – Describe Node Conditions output

What we have here is an interesting split: both MemoryPressure and DiskPressure are fine, while the OutOfDisk and Ready conditions are unknown with the message kubelet stopped posting node status. At a first glance this seems nonsensical – how can MemoryPressure and DiskPressure be fine while the kubelet stopped working?

The important part is in the LastTransitionTime column. The kubelet's most recent memory- and disk-specific communication sent positive statuses. Then, at a later time, the kubelet stopped posting its Node status, leading to Unknown statuses for the OutOfDisk and Ready conditions.

At this point, we're certain that our Node is the problem – the kubelet is no longer sending the Node status to the control plane. However, we don't know why this occurred. It could be a network error, a problem with the machine itself, or something more specific. We'll need to dig further to figure it out.

A good next step here is to get closer to our malfunctioning Node, as we can reasonably assume that it is encountering some sort of issue. If you have access to the node-01 VM or machine, now is a great time to SSH into it. Once we are in the machine, let's start troubleshooting further.

First, let's check whether the Node can access the control plane over the network. If not, this is an obvious reason why the kubelet wouldn't be able to post statuses. Let's assume a scenario where our cluster control plane (for instance an on-premise load balancer) is available at 10.231.0.1. In order to check whether our Node can access the Kubernetes API server, we can ping the control plane as follows:

```
ping 10.231.0.1
```

> **Important note**
> In order to find the control plane IP or DNS, please check your cluster configuration. In a managed Kubernetes service such as AWS Elastic Kubernetes Service or Azure AKS, this will likely be available to view in the console. If you bootstrapped your own cluster using kubeadm, for instance, this is a value that you provided during the setup as part of the installation.

Let's check the results:

```
Reply from 10.231.0.1: bytes=1500 time=28ms TTL=54
Reply from 10.231.0.1: bytes=1500 time=26ms TTL=54
Reply from 10.231.0.1: bytes=1500 time=27ms TTL=54
```

That confirms it – our Node can indeed talk to the Kubernetes control plane. So, the network isn't the issue. Next, let's check the actual kubelet service. The Node itself seems to be operational, and the network is fine, so logically, the kubelet is the next thing to check.

Kubernetes components run as system services on Linux Nodes.

> **Important note**
>
> On Windows Nodes, the troubleshooting instructions will be slightly different – see the Kubernetes documentation for more information (`https://kubernetes.io/docs/setup/production-environment/windows/intro-windows-in-kubernetes/`).

In order to find out the status of our `kubelet` service, we can run the following command:

```
systemctl status kubelet -l
```

This gives us the following output:

```
• kubelet.service - kubelet: The Kubernetes Node Agent
    Loaded: loaded (/lib/systemd/system/kubelet.service;
enabled)
   Drop-In: /etc/systemd/system/kubelet.service.d
            └─10-kubeadm.conf
    Active: activating (auto-restart) (Result: exit-code) since
Fri 2020-05-22 05:44:25 UTC; 3s ago
      Docs: http://kubernetes.io/docs/
   Process: 32315 ExecStart=/usr/bin/kubelet $KUBELET_
KUBECONFIG_ARGS $KUBELET_SYSTEM_PODS_ARGS $KUBELET_NETWORK_ARGS
$KUBELET_DNS_ARGS $KUBELET_AUTHZ_ARGS $KUBELET_CADVISOR_ARGS
$KUBELET_CERTIFICATE_ARGS $KUBELET_EXTRA_ARGS (code=exited,
status=1/FAILURE)
  Main PID: 32315 (code=exited, status=1/FAILURE)
```

Looks like our kubelet is currently not running – it exited with a failure. This explains everything we've seen as far as cluster status and Pod issues.

To actually fix the issue, we can first try to restart the `kubelet` using the command:

```
systemctl start kubelet
```

Now, let's re-check the status of our `kubelet` with our status command:

```
• kubelet.service - kubelet: The Kubernetes Node Agent
    Loaded: loaded (/lib/systemd/system/kubelet.service;
enabled)
   Drop-In: /etc/systemd/system/kubelet.service.d
            └─10-kubeadm.conf
```

```
    Active: activating (auto-restart) (Result: exit-code) since
Fri 2020-05-22 06:13:48 UTC; 10s ago
      Docs: http://kubernetes.io/docs/
   Process: 32007 ExecStart=/usr/bin/kubelet $KUBELET_
KUBECONFIG_ARGS $KUBELET_SYSTEM_PODS_ARGS $KUBELET_NETWORK_ARGS
$KUBELET_DNS_ARGS $KUBELET_AUTHZ_ARGS $KUBELET_CADVISOR_ARGS
$KUBELET_CERTIFICATE_ARGS $KUBELET_EXTRA_ARGS (code=exited,
status=1/FAILURE)
  Main PID: 32007 (code=exited, status=1/FAILURE)
```

It looks like the kubelet failed again. We're going to need to source some additional information about the failure mode in order to find out what happened.

Let's use the journalctl command to find out if there are any relevant logs:

```
sudo journalctl -u kubelet.service | grep "failed"
```

The output should show us logs of the kubelet service where a failure occurred:

```
May 22 04:19:16 nixos kubelet[1391]: F0522 04:19:16.83719
1287 server.go:262] failed to run Kubelet: Running with swap
on is not supported, please disable swap! or set --fail-
swap-on flag to false. /proc/swaps contained: [Filename
Type            Size        Used         Priority /dev/sda1
partition       6198732      0           -1]
```

Looks like we've found the cause – Kubernetes does not support running on Linux machines with swap set to on by default. Our only choices here are either disabling swap or restarting the kubelet with the --fail-swap-on flag set to false.

In our case, we'll just change the swap setting by using the following command:

```
sudo swapoff -a
```

Now, restart the kubelet service:

```
sudo systemctl restart kubelet
```

Finally, let's check to see if our fix worked. Check the Nodes using the following command:

```
kubectl get nodes
```

This should show output similar to the following:

NAME	STATUS	ROLES	AGE	VERSION
node-01	Ready	\<none>	54m	v1.15.6

Our Node is finally posting a `Ready` status!

Let's check on our Pod with the following command:

```
kubectl get pods
```

This should show output like this:

NAME AGE	READY	STATUS	RESTARTS
app-1-pod-2821252345-tj8ks 1m	1/1	Running	0
app-1-pod-2821252345-9fj2k 1m	1/1	Running	0
app-1-pod-2821252345-06hdj 1m	1/1	Running	0

Success! Our cluster is healthy, and our Pods are running.

Next, let's look at how to troubleshoot applications on Kubernetes once any cluster issues are sorted out.

Troubleshooting applications on Kubernetes

A perfectly running Kubernetes cluster may still have application issues to debug. These could be due to bugs in the application itself, or due to misconfigurations in the Kubernetes resources that make up the application. As with troubleshooting the cluster, we will dive into these concepts by using a case study.

Case study 1 – Service not responding

We're going to break this section down into troubleshooting at various levels of the Kubernetes stack, starting with higher-level components, then ending with a deep dive into Pod and container debugging.

Let's assume that we have configured our application `app-1` to respond to requests via a `NodePort` Service, on port `32688`. The application listens on port `80`.

We can try to access our application via a `curl` request on one of our Nodes. The command will look as follows:

```
curl http://10.213.2.1:32688
```

The output of the `curl` command if it fails will look like the following:

```
curl: (7) Failed to connect to 10.231.2.1 port 32688:
Connection refused
```

At this point, our `NodePort` Service isn't routing requests to any Pod. Following our typical debug path, let's first see which resources are running in the cluster with the following command:

```
kubectl get services
```

Add the `-o wide` flag to see additional information. Next, run the following command:

```
kubectl get services -o wide
```

This gives us the following output:

```
NAME TYPE CLUSTER-IP EXTERNAL-IP PORT(S) AGE SELECTOR
app-1-svc NodePort 10.101.212.57 <none> 80:32688/TCP 3m01s
app=app-1
```

It is clear that our Service exists with a proper Node port – but our requests are not being routed to the Pods, as is obvious from the failed `curl` command.

To see which routes our Service has set up, let's use the `get endpoints` command. This will list the Pod IPs, if any, for the Service as configured:

```
kubectl get endpoints app-1-svc
```

Let's check the resulting output of the command:

```
NAME          ENDPOINTS
app-1-svc     <none>
```

Well, something is definitely wrong here.

Our Service isn't pointing to any Pods. This likely means that there aren't any Pods matching our Service selector available. This could be because there are no Pods available at all – or because those Pods don't properly match the Service selector.

To check on our Service selector, let's take the next step in the debug path and use the `describe` command as follows:

```
kubectl describe service app-1-svc
```

This gives us an output like the following:

Name:	app-1-svc
Namespace:	default
Labels:	app=app-11
Annotations:	<none>
Selector:	app=app-11
Type:	NodePort
IP:	10.57.0.15
Port:	<unset> 80/TCP
TargetPort:	80/TCP
NodePort:	<unset> 32688/TCP
Endpoints:	<none>
Session Affinity:	None
Events:	<none>

As you can see, our Service is configured to talk to the correct port on our application. However, the selector is looking for Pods that match the label `app = app-11`. Since we know our application is named `app-1`, this could be the cause of our issue.

Let's edit our Service to look for the correct Pod label, `app-1`, running another `describe` command to be sure:

```
kubectl describe service app-1-svc
```

This gives the following output:

Name:	app-1-svc
Namespace:	default
Labels:	app=app-1
Annotations:	<none>
Selector:	app=app-1
Type:	NodePort
IP:	10.57.0.15
Port:	<unset> 80/TCP

TargetPort:	80/TCP
NodePort:	<unset> 32688/TCP
Endpoints:	<none>
Session Affinity:	None
Events:	<none>

Now, you can see in the output that our Service is looking for the proper Pod selector, but we still do not have any endpoints. Let's check to see what is going on with our Pods by using the following command:

```
kubectl get pods
```

This shows the following output:

NAME AGE	READY	STATUS	RESTARTS
app-1-pod-2821252345-tj8ks -	0/1	Pending	0
app-1-pod-2821252345-9fj2k -	0/1	Pending	0
app-1-pod-2821252345-06hdj -	0/1	Pending	0

Our Pods are still waiting to be scheduled. This explains why, even with the proper selector, our Service isn't functioning. To get some granularity on why our Pods aren't being scheduled, let's use the describe command:

```
kubectl describe pod app-1-pod-2821252345-tj8ks
```

The following is the output. Let's focus on the Events section:

```
Events:
Type      Reason      Age               From                Message
----      ------      ---               ----                -------
Normal    Scheduled   5m                default-scheduler   Successfully assigned app-1-pod-2821252345-tj8ks to node-01
Normal    BackOff     4m (x2 over 5m)   kubelet, node-01    Back-off pulling image "myappimage:lates"
Normal    Pulling     3m (x2 over 5m)   kubelet, node-01    pulling image "myappimage:lates"
Warning   Failed      4m (x2 over 5m)   kubelet, node-01    Error: ErrImagePull
Warning   Failed      4m (x2 over 5m)   kubelet, node-01    Failed to pull image "myappimage:lates": rpc error: code = Unknown desc =
                                                            Error response from daemon: manifest for myappimage:lates not found
```

Figure 10.2 – Describe Pod Events output

From the Events section, it looks like our Pod is failing to be scheduled due to container image pull failure. There are many possible reasons for this – our cluster may not have the necessary authentication mechanisms to pull from a private repository, for instance – but that would present a different error message.

From the context and the `Events` output, we can probably assume that the issue is that our Pod definition is looking for a container named `myappimage:lates` instead of `myappimage:latest`.

Let's update our Deployment spec with the proper image name and roll out the update.

Use the following command to get confirmation:

```
kubectl get pods
```

The output looks like this:

NAME AGE	READY	STATUS	RESTARTS
app-1-pod-2821252345-152sf 1m	1/1	Running	0
app-1-pod-2821252345-9gg9s 1m	1/1	Running	0
app-1-pod-2821252345-pfo92 1m	1/1	Running	0

Our Pods are now running – let's check to see that our Service has registered the proper endpoints. Use the following command to do this:

```
kubectl describe services app-1-svc
```

The output should look like this:

Name:	app-1-svc
Namespace:	default
Labels:	app=app-1
Annotations:	<none>
Selector:	app=app-1
Type:	NodePort
IP:	10.57.0.15
Port:	<unset> 80/TCP
TargetPort:	80/TCP
NodePort:	<unset> 32688/TCP
Endpoints: :80	10.214.1.3:80,10.214.2.3:80,10.214.4.2
Session Affinity:	None
Events:	<none>

Success! Our Service is properly pointing to our application Pods.

In the next case study, we'll dig a bit deeper by troubleshooting a Pod with incorrect startup parameters.

Case study 2 – Incorrect Pod startup command

Let's assume we have our Service properly configured and our Pods running and passing health checks. However, our Pod is not responding to requests as we would expect. We are sure that this is less of a Kubernetes problem and more of an application or configuration problem.

Our application container works as follows: it takes a startup command with a flag for `color` and combines it with a variable for `version number` based on the container's `image` tag, and echoes that back to the requester. We are expecting our application to return `green 3`.

Thankfully, Kubernetes gives us some good tools to debug applications, which we can use to delve into our specific containers.

First, let's `curl` the application to see what response we get:

```
curl http://10.231.2.1:32688
red 2
```

We expected `green 3` but got `red 2`, so it looks like something is wrong with the input, and the version number variable. Let's start with the former.

As usual, we begin with checking our Pods with the following command:

```
kubectl get pods
```

The output should look like the following:

NAME AGE	READY	STATUS	RESTARTS
app-1-pod-2821252345-152sf 5m	1/1	Running	0
app-1-pod-2821252345-9gg9s 5m	1/1	Running	0
app-1-pod-2821252345-pfo92 5m	1/1	Running	0

Everything looks good in this output. It seems that our app is running as part of a Deployment (and therefore, a ReplicaSet) – we can make sure by running the following command:

```
kubectl get deployments
```

The output should look like the following:

NAME	DESIRED	CURRENT	UP-TO-DATE	AVAILABLE	AGE
app-1-pod	3	3	3	3	5m

Let's look a bit closer at our Deployment to see how our Pods are configured using the following command:

```
kubectl describe deployment app-1-pod -o yaml
```

The output looks like the following:

Broken-deployment-output.yaml

```yaml
apiVersion: apps/v1
kind: Deployment
metadata:
  name: app-1-pod
spec:
  selector:
    matchLabels:
      app: app-1
  replicas: 3
  template:
    metadata:
      labels:
        app: app-1
    spec:
      containers:
      - name: app-1
        image: mycustomrepository/app-1:2
        command: [ "start", "-color", "red" ]
        ports:
        - containerPort: 80
```

Let's see if we can fix our issue, which is really quite simple. We're using the wrong version of our application, and our startup command is wrong. In this case, let's assume we don't have a file with our Deployment spec – so let's just edit it in place.

Let's use `kubectl edit deployment app-1-pod`, and edit the Pod spec to the following:

fixed-deployment-output.yaml

```
apiVersion: apps/v1
kind: Deployment
metadata:
  name: app-1-pod
spec:
  selector:
    matchLabels:
      app: app-1
  replicas: 3
  template:
    metadata:
      labels:
        app: app-1
    spec:
      containers:
      - name: app-1
        image: mycustomrepository/app-1:3
        command: [ "start", "-color", "green" ]
        ports:
        - containerPort: 80
```

Once the Deployment is saved, you should start seeing your new Pods come up. Let's double-check by using the following command:

```
kubectl get pods
```

The output should look like the following:

NAME AGE	READY	STATUS	RESTARTS
app-1-pod-2821252345-f928a	1/1	Running	0

```
1m
app-1-pod-2821252345-jjsa8         1/1        Running     0
1m
app-1-pod-2821252345-92jhd         1/1        Running     0
1m
```

And finally – let's make a `curl` request to check that everything is working:

```
curl http://10.231.2.1:32688
```

The output of the command is as follows:

```
green 3
```

Success!

Case study 3 – Pod application malfunction with logs

After spending the previous chapter, *Chapter 9*, *Observability on Kubernetes*, implementing observability to our applications, let's take a look at a case where those tools can really come in handy. We will use manual `kubectl` commands for the purposes of this case study – but know that by aggregating logs (for instance, in our EFK stack implementation), we could make the process of debugging this application significantly easier.

In this case study, we once again have a deployment of Pods – to check it, let's run the following command:

```
kubectl get pods
```

The output of the command is as follows:

NAME	READY	STATUS	RESTARTS	AGE
app-2-ss-0	1/1	Running	0	10m
app-2-ss-1	1/1	Running	0	10m
app-2-ss-2	1/1	Running	0	10m

It looks like, in this case, we are working with a StatefulSet instead of a Deployment – a key characteristic here is the incrementing Pod IDs starting from 0.

We can confirm this by checking for StatefulSets using the following command:

```
kubectl get statefulset
```

The output of the command is as follows:

NAME	DESIRED	CURRENT	UP-TO-DATE	AVAILABLE	AGE
app-2-ss	3	3	3	3	10m

Let's take a closer look at our StatefulSet with `kubectl get statefulset -o yaml app-2-ss`. By using the `get` command along with `-o yaml` we can get our `describe` output in the same format as the typical Kubernetes resource YAML.

The output of the preceding command is as follows. We've removed the Pod spec section to keep it shorter:

statefulset-output.yaml

```
apiVersion: apps/v1
kind: StatefulSet
metadata:
  name: app-2-ss
spec:
  selector:
    matchLabels:
      app: app-2
  replicas: 3
  template:
    metadata:
      labels:
        app: app-2
```

We know that our app is using a service. Let's see which one it is!

Run `kubectl get services -o wide`. The output should be something like the following:

```
NAME TYPE CLUSTER-IP EXTERNAL-IP PORT(S) AGE SELECTOR
app-2-svc NodePort 10.100.213.13 <none> 80:32714/TCP 3m01s
app=app-2
```

It's clear that our service is called `app-2-svc`. Let's see our exact service definition using the following command:

```
kubectl describe services app-2-svc
```

The output is as follows:

Name:	app-2-svc
Namespace:	default
Labels:	app=app-2
Annotations:	<none>
Selector:	app=app-2
Type:	NodePort
IP:	10.57.0.12
Port:	<unset> 80/TCP
TargetPort:	80/TCP
NodePort:	<unset> 32714/TCP
Endpoints: :80	10.214.1.1:80,10.214.2.3:80,10.214.4.4
Session Affinity:	None
Events:	<none>

To see exactly what our application is returning for a given input, we can use `curl` on our `NodePort` Service:

```
> curl http://10.231.2.1:32714?equation=1plus1
3
```

Based on our existing knowledge of the application, we would assume that this call should return 2, not 3. The application developer on our team has asked us to investigate any logging output that would help them figure out what the issue is.

We know from previous chapters that you can investigate the logging output with `kubectl logs <pod name>`. In our case, we have three replicas of our application, so we may not be able to find our logs in a single iteration of this command. Let's pick a Pod at random and see if it was the one that served our request:

```
> kubectl logs app-2-ss-1
>
```

It looks like this was not the Pod that served our request, as our application developer has told us that the application definitely logs to `stdout` when a `GET` request is made to the server.

Instead of checking through the other two Pods individually, we can use a joint command to get logs from all three Pods. The command will be as follows:

```
> kubectl logs statefulset/app-2-ss
```

And the output is as follows:

```
> Input = 1plus1
> Operator = plus
> First Number = 1
> Second Number = 2
```

That did the trick – and what's more, we can see some good insight into our issue.

Everything seems as we would expect, other than the log line reading Second Number. Our request clearly used 1plus1 as the query string, which would make both the first number and the second number (split by the operator value) equal to one.

This will take some additional digging. We could triage this issue by sending additional requests and checking the output in order to guess what is happening, but in this case it may be better to just get bash access to the Pod and figure out what is going on.

First, let's check our Pod spec, which was removed from the preceding StatefulSet YAML. To see the full StatefulSet spec, check the GitHub repository:

Statefulset-output.yaml

```
spec:
  containers:
  - name: app-2
    image: mycustomrepository/app-2:latest
    volumeMounts:
    - name: scratch
      mountPath: /scratch
  - name: sidecar
    image: mycustomrepository/tracing-sidecar
  volumes:
  - name: scratch-volume
    emptyDir: {}
```

It looks like our Pod is mounting an empty volume as a scratch disk. It also has two containers in each Pod – a sidecar used for application tracing, and our app itself. We'll need this information to ssh into one of the Pods (it doesn't matter which one for this exercise) using the kubectl exec command.

We can do it using the following command:

```
kubectl exec -it app-2-ss-1 app2 -- sh.
```

This command should give you a bash terminal as the output:

```
> kubectl exec -it app-2-ss-1 app2 -- sh
#
```

Now, using the terminal we just created, we should be able to investigate our application code. For the purposes of this tutorial, we are using a highly simplified Node.js application.

Let's check our Pod filesystem to see what we're working with using the following command:

```
# ls
# app.js calculate.js scratch
```

Looks like we have two JavaScript files, and our previously mentioned scratch folder. It's probably a good bet to assume that app.js contains the logic for bootstrapping and serving the application, and calculate.js contains our controller code for doing the calculations.

We can confirm by printing the contents of the calculate.js file:

Broken-calculate.js

```
# cat calculate.js
export const calculate(first, second, operator)
{
  second++;
  if(operator === "plus")
  {
    return first + second;
  }
}
```

Even with little to no knowledge of JavaScript, it's pretty obvious what the issue is here. The code is incrementing the `second` variable before performing the calculation.

Since we're inside of the Pod, and we're using a non-compiled language, we can actually edit this file inline! Let's use `vi` (or any text editor) to correct this file:

```
# vi calculate.js
```

And edit the file to read as follows:

fixed-calculate.js

```
export const calculate(first, second, operator)
{
    if (operator === "plus")
    {
      return first + second;
    }
}
```

Now, our code should run properly. It's important to state that this fix is only temporary. As soon as our Pod shuts down or gets replaced by another Pod, it will revert to the code that was originally included in the container image. However, this pattern does allow us to try out quick fixes.

After exiting the `exec` session using the `exit` bash command, let's try our URL again:

```
> curl http://10.231.2.1:32714?equation=1plus1
2
```

As you can see, our hotfixed container shows the right result! Now, we can update our code and Docker image in a more permanent way with our fix. Using `exec` is a great way to troubleshoot and debug running containers.

Summary

In this chapter, we learned about troubleshooting applications on Kubernetes. First, we covered some common failure modes of distributed applications. Then, we learned how to triage issues with Kubernetes components. Finally, we reviewed several scenarios where Kubernetes configuration and application debugging were performed. The Kubernetes debugging and troubleshooting techniques you learned in this chapter will help you when triaging issues with any Kubernetes clusters and applications you may work on.

In the next chapter, *Chapter 11, Template Code Generation and CI/CD on Kubernetes*, we will look into some ecosystem extensions for templating Kubernetes resource manifests and continuous integration/continuous deployment with Kubernetes.

Questions

1. How does the distributed systems fallacy, "*the topology doesn't change*," apply to applications on Kubernetes?

2. How are the Kubernetes control plane components (and kubelet) implemented at the OS level?

3. How would you go about debugging an issue where Pods are stuck in the `Pending` status? What would be your first step? And your second?

Further reading

- The CNI plugin for traffic shaping: `https://kubernetes.io/docs/concepts/extend-kubernetes/compute-storage-net/network-plugins/#support-traffic-shaping`

11

Template Code Generation and CI/ CD on Kubernetes

This chapter discusses some easier ways to template and configure large Kubernetes deployments with many resources. It also details a number of methods for implementing **Continuous Integration/Continuous Deployment (CI/CD)** on Kubernetes, as well as the pros and cons associated with each possible method. Specifically, we talk about in-cluster CI/CD, where some or all of the CI/CD steps are performed in our Kubernetes cluster, and out-of-cluster CI/CD, where all the steps take place outside our cluster.

The case study in this chapter will include creating a Helm chart from scratch, along with an explanation of each piece of a Helm chart and how it works.

To begin, we will cover the landscape of Kubernetes resource template generation, and the reasons why a template generation tool should be used at all. Then, we will cover implementing CI/CD to Kubernetes, first with AWS CodeBuild, and next with FluxCD.

In this chapter, we will cover the following topics:

- Understanding options for template code generation on Kubernetes
- Implementing templates on Kubernetes with Helm and Kustomize

- Understanding CI/CD paradigms on Kubernetes – in-cluster and out-of-cluster
- Implementing in-cluster and out-of-cluster CI/CD with Kubernetes

Technical requirements

In order to run the commands detailed in this chapter, you will need a computer that supports the kubectl command-line tool along with a working Kubernetes cluster. Refer to *Chapter 1, Communicating with Kubernetes*, for several methods for getting up and running with Kubernetes quickly, and for instructions on how to install the kubectl tool. Additionally, you will need a machine that supports the Helm CLI tool, which typically has the same prerequisites as kubectl – for details, check out the Helm documentation at https://helm.sh/docs/intro/install/.

The code used in this chapter can be found in the book's GitHub repository at

https://github.com/PacktPublishing/Cloud-Native-with-Kubernetes/tree/master/Chapter11.

Understanding options for template code generation on Kubernetes

As discussed in *Chapter 1, Communicating with Kubernetes*, one of the greatest strengths of Kubernetes is that its API can communicate in terms of declarative resource files. This allows us to run commands such as kubectl apply and have the control plane ensure that whatever resources are running in the cluster match our YAML or JSON file.

However, this capability introduces some unwieldiness. Since we want to have all our workloads declared in configuration files, any large or complex applications, especially if they include many microservices, could result in a large number of configuration files to write and maintain.

This issue is further compounded with multiple environments. Say we want development, staging, UAT, and production environments, this would require four separate YAML files per Kubernetes resource, assuming we wanted to maintain one resource per file for cleanliness.

One way to fix these issues is to work with templating systems that support variables, allowing a single template file to work for multiple applications or multiple environments by injecting different sets of variables.

There are several popular community-supported open source options for this purpose. In this book, we will focus on two of the most popular ones:

- Helm
- Kustomize

There are many other options available, including Kapitan, Ksonnet, Jsonnet, and more, but a full review of all of them is not within the scope of this book. Let's start by reviewing Helm, which is, in many ways, the most popular templating tool.

Helm

Helm actually plays double duty as a templating/code generation tool and a CI/CD tool. It allows you to create YAML-based templates that can be hydrated with variables, allowing for code and template reuse across applications and environments. It also comes with a Helm CLI tool to roll out changes to applications based on the templates themselves.

For this reason, you are likely to see Helm all over the Kubernetes ecosystem as the default way to install tools or applications. We'll be using Helm for both of its purposes in this chapter.

Now, let's move on to Kustomize, which is quite different to Helm.

Kustomize

Unlike Helm, Kustomize is officially supported by the Kubernetes project, and support is integrated directly into `kubectl`. Unlike Helm, Kustomize operates using vanilla YAML without variables, and instead recommends a *fork and patch* workflow where sections of YAML are replaced with new YAML depending on the patch chosen.

Now that we have a basic understanding of how the tools differ, we can use them in practice.

Implementing templates on Kubernetes with Helm and Kustomize

Now that we know our options, we can implement each of them with an example application. This will allow us to understand the specifics of how each tool handles variables and the process of templating. Let's start with Helm.

Using Helm with Kubernetes

As mentioned previously, Helm is an open source project that makes it easy to template and deploy applications on Kubernetes. For the purposes of this book, we will be focused on the newest version (as of the time of writing), Helm V3. A previous version, Helm V2, had more moving parts, including a controller, called *Tiller*, that would run on the cluster. Helm V3 is simplified and only contains the Helm CLI tool. It does, however, use custom resource definitions on the cluster to track releases, as we will see shortly.

Let's start by installing Helm.

Installing Helm

If you want to use a specific version of Helm, you can install it by following the specific version docs at `https://helm.sh/docs/intro/install/`. For our use case, we will simply use the `get helm` script, which will install the newest version.

You can fetch and run the script as follows:

```
curl -fsSL -o get_helm.sh https://raw.githubusercontent.com/
helm/helm/master/scripts/get-helm-3
chmod 700 get_helm.sh
./get_helm.sh
```

Now, we should be able to run `helm` commands. By default, Helm will automatically use your existing `kubeconfig` cluster and context, so in order to switch clusters for Helm, you just need to use `kubectl` to change your `kubeconfig` file, as you would normally do.

To install an application using Helm, run the `helm install` command. But how does Helm decide what and how to install? We'll need to discuss the concepts of Helm charts, Helm repositories, and Helm releases.

Helm charts, repositories, and releases

Helm provides a way to template and deploy applications on Kubernetes with variables. In order to do this, we specify workloads via a set of templates, which is called a *Helm chart*.

A Helm chart consists of one or more templates, some chart metadata, and a `values` file that fills in the template variables with final values. In practice, you would then have one `values` file per environment (or app, if you are reusing your template for multiple apps), which would hydrate the shared template with a new configuration. This combination of template and values would then be used to install or deploy an application to your cluster.

So, where can you store Helm charts? You can put them in a Git repository as you would with any other Kubernetes YAML (which works for most use cases), but Helm also supports the concept of repositories. A Helm repository is represented by a URL and can contain multiple Helm charts. For instance, Helm has its own official repository at `https://hub.helm.sh/charts`. Again, each Helm chart consists of a folder with a metadata file, a `Chart.yaml` file, one or more template files, and optionally a values file.

In order to install a local Helm chart with a local values file, you can pass a path for each to `helm install`, as shown in the following command:

```
helm install -f values.yaml /path/to/chart/root
```

However, for commonly installed charts, you can also install the chart directly from a chart repository, and you can optionally add a custom repository to your local Helm in order to be able to install charts easily from non-official sources.

For instance, in order to install Drupal via the official Helm chart, you can run the following command:

```
helm install -f values.yaml stable/drupal
```

This code installs charts out of the official Helm chart repository. To use a custom repository, you just need to add it to Helm first. For instance, to install `cert-manager`, which is hosted on the `jetstack` Helm repository, we can do the following:

```
helm repo add jetstack https://charts.jetstack.io
helm install certmanager --namespace cert-manager jetstack/
cert-manager
```

This code adds the `jetstack` Helm repository to your local Helm CLI tool, and then installs `cert-manager` via the charts hosted there. We also name the release as `cert-manager`. A Helm release is a concept implemented using Kubernetes secrets in Helm V3. When we create a Release in Helm, it will be stored as a secret in the same namespace.

To illustrate this, we can create a Helm release using the preceding `install` command. Let's do it now:

```
helm install certmanager --namespace cert-manager jetstack/
cert-manager
```

This command should result in the following output, which may be slightly different depending on the current version of Cert Manager. We'll split the output into two sections for readability.

First, the output of the command gives us a status of the Helm release:

```
NAME: certmanager
LAST DEPLOYED: Sun May 23 19:07:04 2020
NAMESPACE: cert-manager
STATUS: deployed
REVISION: 1
TEST SUITE: None
```

As you can see, this section contains a timestamp for the deployment, namespace information, a revision, and a status. Next, we'll see the notes section of the output:

```
NOTES:
cert-manager has been deployed successfully!

In order to begin issuing certificates, you will need to set up
a ClusterIssuer
or Issuer resource (for example, by creating a 'letsencrypt-
staging' issuer).

More information on the different types of issuers and how to
configure them
can be found in our documentation:

https://cert-manager.io/docs/configuration/

For information on how to configure cert-manager to
automatically provision
Certificates for Ingress resources, take a look at the
`ingress-shim`
```

```
documentation:
```

```
https://cert-manager.io/docs/usage/ingress/
```

As you can see, our Helm `install` command has resulted in a success message, which also gives us some information from `cert-manager` about how to use it. This output can be helpful to look at when installing Helm packages, as they sometimes include documentation such as the previous snippet. Now, to see how our release object looks in Kubernetes, we can run the following command:

```
Kubectl get secret -n cert-manager
```

This results in the following output:

```
certmanager-cert-manager-cainjector-token-829kk    kubernetes.io/service-account-token    3    24m
certmanager-cert-manager-token-hh6gn               kubernetes.io/service-account-token    3    24m
certmanager-cert-manager-webhook-ca                Opaque                                 3    24m
certmanager-cert-manager-webhook-token-cstp8       kubernetes.io/service-account-token    3    24m
default-token-d6hgh                                 kubernetes.io/service-account-token    3    24m
sh.helm.release.v1.certmanager.v1                  helm.sh/release.v1                     1    24m
```

Figure 11.1 – Secrets List output from kubectl

As you can see, one of the secrets has its type as `helm.sh/release.v1`. This is the secret that Helm is using to track the Cert Manager release.

Finally, to see the release listed in the Helm CLI, we can run the following command:

```
helm ls -A
```

This command will list Helm releases in all namespaces (just like `kubectl get pods -A` would list pods in all namespaces). The output will be as follows:

```
NAME         NAMESPACE     REVISION  UPDATED                                STATUS    CHART                  APP VERSION
certmanager  cert-manager  1         2020-05-23 19:07:04.798578 -0400 EDT   deployed  cert-manager-v0.16.1   v0.16.1
```

Figure 11.2 – Helm Release List output

Now, Helm has more moving parts, including `upgrades`, `rollbacks` and more, and we'll review these in the next section. In order to show off what Helm can do, we will create and install a chart from scratch.

Creating a Helm chart

So, we want to create a Helm chart for our application. Let's set the stage. Our goal is to deploy a simple Node.js application easily to multiple environments. To this end, we will create a chart with the component pieces of our application, and then combine it with three separate values files (dev, staging, and production) in order to deploy our application to our three environments.

Let's start with the folder structure of our Helm chart. As we mentioned previously, a Helm chart consists of templates, a metadata file, and optional values. We're going to inject the values when we actually install our chart, but we can structure our folder like this:

```
Chart.yaml
charts/
templates/
dev-values.yaml
staging-values.yaml
production-values.yaml
```

One thing we haven't yet mentioned is that you can actually have a folder of Helm charts inside an existing chart! These subcharts can make it easy to split up complex applications into components. For the purpose of this book, we will not be using subcharts, but if your application is getting too complex or modular for a singular chart, this is a valuable feature.

Also, you can see that we have a different environment file for each environment, which we will use during our installation command.

So, what does a Chart.yaml file look like? This file will contain some basic metadata about your chart, and typically looks something like this as a minimum:

```
apiVersion: v2
name: mynodeapp
version: 1.0.0
```

The Chart.yaml file supports many optional fields, which you can see at https://helm.sh/docs/topics/charts/, but for the purposes of this tutorial, we will keep it simple. The mandatory fields are apiVersion, name, and version.

In our `Chart.yaml` file, `apiVersion` corresponds to the version of Helm that the chart corresponds to. Somewhat confusingly, the current release of Helm, Helm V3, uses `apiVersion v2`, while older versions of Helm, including Helm V2, also use `apiVersion v2`.

Next, the `name` field corresponds to the name of our chart. This is pretty self-explanatory, although remember that we have the ability to name a specific release of a chart – something that comes in handy for multiple environments.

Finally, we have the `version` field, which corresponds to the version of the chart. This field supports **SemVer** (semantic versioning).

So, what do our templates actually look like? Helm charts use the Go templates library under the hood (see `https://golang.org/pkg/text/template/` for more information) and support all sorts of powerful manipulations, helper functions, and much, much more. For now, we will keep things extremely simple to give you an idea of the basics. A full discussion of Helm chart creation could be a book on its own!

To start, we can use a Helm CLI command to autogenerate our `Chart` folder, with all the previous files and folders, minus subcharts and values files, generated for you. Let's try it – first create a new Helm chart with the following command:

```
helm create myfakenodeapp
```

This command will create an autogenerated chart in a folder named `myfakenodeapp`. Let's check the contents of our `templates` folder with the following command:

```
Ls myfakenodeapp/templates
```

This command will result in the following output:

```
helpers.tpl
deployment.yaml
NOTES.txt
service.yaml
```

This autogenerated chart can help a lot as a starting point, but for the purposes of this tutorial, we will make these from scratch.

Create a new folder called `mynodeapp` and put the `Chart.yaml` file we showed you earlier in it. Then, create a folder inside called `templates`.

One thing to keep in mind: a Kubernetes resource YAML is, by itself, a valid Helm template. There is no requirement to use any variables in your templates. You can just write regular YAML, and Helm installs will still work.

To show this, let's get started by adding a single template file to our templates folder. Call it `deployment.yaml` and include the following non-variable YAML:

deployment.yaml:

```yaml
apiVersion: apps/v1
kind: Deployment
metadata:
  name: frontend-myapp
  labels:
    app: frontend-myapp
spec:
  replicas: 2
  selector:
    matchLabels:
      app: frontend-myapp
  template:
    metadata:
      labels:
        app: frontend-myapp
    spec:
      containers:
      - name: frontend-myapp
        image: myrepo/myapp:1.0.0
        ports:
        - containerPort: 80
```

As you can see, this YAML is just a regular Kubernetes resource YAML. We aren't using any variables in our template.

Now, we have enough to actually install our chart. Let's do that next.

Installing and uninstalling a Helm chart

To install a chart with Helm V3, you run a `helm install` command from the `root` directory of the chart:

```
helm install myapp .
```

This installation command creates a Helm release called `frontend-app` and installs our chart. Right now, our chart only consists of a single deployment with two pods, and we should be able to see it running in our cluster with the following command:

```
kubectl get deployment
```

This should result in the following output:

NAMESPACE	NAME	READY	UP-TO-DATE	AVAILABLE	AGE
default	frontend-myapp	2/2	2	2	2m

As you can see from the output, our Helm `install` command has successfully created a deployment object in Kubernetes.

Uninstalling our chart is just as easy. We can install all the Kubernetes resources installed via our chart by running the following command:

```
helm uninstall myapp
```

This `uninstall` command (`delete` in Helm V2) just takes the name of our Helm release.

Now, so far, we have not used any of the real power of Helm – we've been using it as a `kubectl` alternative without any added features. Let's change this by implementing some variables in our chart.

Using template variables

Adding variables to our Helm chart templates is as simple as using double bracket – {{ }} – syntax. What we put in the double brackets will be taken directly from the values that we use when installing our chart using dot notation.

Let's look at a quick example. So far, we have our app name (and container image name/version) hardcoded into our YAML file. This constrains us significantly if we want to use our Helm chart to deploy different applications or different application versions.

In order to address this, we're going to add template variables to our chart. Take a look at this resulting template:

Templated-deployment.yaml:

```
apiVersion: apps/v1
kind: Deployment
metadata:
  name: frontend-{{ .Release.Name }}
  labels:
    app: frontend-{{ .Release.Name }}
    chartVersion: {{ .Chart.version }}
spec:
  replicas: 2
  selector:
    matchLabels:
      app: frontend-{{ .Release.Name }}
  template:
    metadata:
      labels:
        app: frontend-{{ .Release.Name }}
    spec:
      containers:
      - name: frontend-{{ .Release.Name }}
        image: myrepo/{{ .Values.image.name }}
:{{ .Values.image.tag }}
        ports:
        - containerPort: 80
```

Let's go over this YAML file and review our variables. We're using a few different types of variables in this file, but they all use the same dot notation.

Helm actually supports a few different top-level objects. These are the main objects you can reference in your templates:

- `.Chart`: Used to reference metadata values in the `Chart.yaml` file

- `.Values`: Used to reference values passed into the chart from a `values` file at install time

- `.Template`: Used to reference some info about the current template file
- `.Release`: Used to reference information about the Helm release
- `.Files`: Used to reference files in the chart that are not YAML templates (for instance, `config` files)
- `.Capabilities`: Used to reference information about the target Kubernetes cluster (in other words, version)

In our YAML file, we're using several of these. Firstly, we're referencing the `name` of our release (contained within the `.Release` object) in several places. Next, we are leveraging the `Chart` object to inject metadata into the `chartVersion` key. Finally, we are using the `Values` object to reference both the container image `name` and `tag`.

Now, the last thing we're missing is the actual values that we will inject via `values.yaml`, or in the CLI command. Everything else will be created using `Chart.yaml`, or values that we will inject at runtime via the `helm` command itself.

With that in mind, let's create our values file from our template that we will be passing in our image `name` and `tag`. So, let's include those in the proper format:

```
image:
  name: myapp
  tag: 2.0.1
```

Now we can install our app via our Helm chart! Do this with the following command:

```
helm install myrelease -f values.yaml .
```

As you can see, we are passing in our values with the `-f` key (you can also use `--values`). This command will install the release of our application.

Once we have a release, we can upgrade to a new version or roll back to an old one using the Helm CLI – we'll cover this in the next section.

Upgrades and rollbacks

Now that we have an active Helm release, we can upgrade it. Let's make a small change to our `values.yaml`:

```
image:
  name: myapp
  tag: 2.0.2
```

To make this a new version of our release, we also need to change our chart YAML:

```
apiVersion: v2
name: mynodeapp
version: 1.0.1
```

Now, we can upgrade our release using the following command:

```
helm upgrade myrelease -f values.yaml .
```

If, for any reason, we wanted to roll back to an earlier version, we can do so with the following command:

```
helm rollback myrelease 1.0.0
```

As you can see, Helm allows for seamless templating, releases, upgrades, and rollbacks of applications. As we mentioned previously, Kustomize hits many of the same points but does it in a much different way – let's see how.

Using Kustomize with Kubernetes

While Helm charts can get quite complex, Kustomize uses YAML without any variables, and instead uses a patch and override-based method of applying different configurations to a base set of Kubernetes resources.

Using Kustomize is extremely simple, and as we mentioned earlier in the chapter, there's no prerequisite CLI tool. Everything works by using the kubectl apply -k /path/ kustomize.yaml command without installing anything new. However, we will also demonstrate the flow using the Kustomize CLI tool.

> **Important note**
> In order to install the Kustomize CLI tool, you can check the installation instructions at https://kubernetes-sigs.github.io/ kustomize/installation.

Currently, the installation uses the following command:

```
curl -s "https://raw.githubusercontent.com/\
kubernetes-sigs/kustomize/master/hack/install_kustomize.sh" |
bash
```

Now that we have Kustomize installed, let's apply Kustomize to our existing use case. We're going to start from our plain Kubernetes YAML (before we started adding Helm variables):

plain-deployment.yaml:

```
apiVersion: apps/v1
kind: Deployment
metadata:
  name: frontend-myapp
  labels:
    app: frontend-myapp
spec:
  replicas: 2
  selector:
    matchLabels:
      app: frontend-myapp
  template:
    metadata:
      labels:
        app: frontend-myapp
    spec:
      containers:
      - name: frontend-myapp
        image: myrepo/myapp:1.0.0
        ports:
        - containerPort: 80
```

With our initial `deployment.yaml` created, we can now create a Kustomization file, which we call `kustomize.yaml`.

When we later call a `kubectl` command with the `-k` parameter, `kubectl` will look for this `kustomize` YAML file and use it to determine which patches to apply to all the other YAML files passed to the `kubectl` command.

Kustomize lets us patch individual values or set common values to be automatically set. In general, Kustomize will create new lines, or update old lines if the key already exists in the YAML. There are three ways to apply these changes:

- Specify changes directly in a Kustomization file.
- Use the `PatchStrategicMerge` strategy with a `patch.yaml` file along with a Kustomization file.
- Use the `JSONPatch` strategy with a `patch.yaml` file along with a Kustomization file.

Let's start with using a Kustomization file specifically to patch the YAML.

Specifying changes directly in a Kustomization file

If we want to directly specify changes within the Kustomization file, we can do so, but our options are somewhat limited. The types of keys we can use for a Kustomization file are as follows:

- `resources` – Specifies which files are to be customized when patches are applied
- `transformers` – Ways to directly apply patches from within the Kustomization file
- `generators` – Ways to create new resources from the Kustomization file
- `meta` – Sets metadata fields that can influence generators, transformers, and resources

If we want to specify direct patches in our Kustomization file, we need to use transformers. The aforementioned `PatchStrategicMerge` and `JSONPatch` merge strategies are two types of transformers. However, to directly apply changes to the Kustomization file, we can use one of several transformers, which include `commonLabels`, `images`, `namePrefix`, and `nameSuffix`.

In the following Kustomization file, we are applying changes to our initial deployment YAML using both `commonLabels` and `images` transformers.

Deployment-kustomization-1.yaml:

```
apiVersion: kustomize.config.k8s.io/v1beta1
kind: Kustomization
resources:
- deployment.yaml
```

```
namespace: default
commonLabels:
  app: frontend-app
images:
  - name: frontend-myapp
    newTag: 2.0.0
    newName: frontend-app-1
```

This particular `Kustomization.yaml` file updates the image tag from `1.0.0` to `2.0.0`, updates the name of the app from `frontend-myapp` to `frontend-app`, and updates the name of the container from `frontend-myapp` to `frontend-app-1`.

For a full rundown of the specifics of each of these transformers, you can check the Kustomize docs at `https://kubernetes-sigs.github.io/kustomize/`. The Kustomize file assumes that `deployment.yaml` is in the same folder as itself.

To see the result when our Kustomize file is applied to our deployment, we can use the Kustomize CLI tool. We will use the following command to generate the kustomized output:

```
kustomize build deployment-kustomization1.yaml
```

This command will give the following output:

```
apiVersion: apps/v1
kind: Deployment
metadata:
  name: frontend-myapp
  labels:
    app: frontend-app
spec:
  replicas: 2
  selector:
    matchLabels:
      app: frontend-app
  template:
    metadata:
      labels:
        app: frontend-app
    spec:
```

```
      containers:
      - name: frontend-app-1
        image: myrepo/myapp:2.0.0
        ports:
        - containerPort: 80
```

As you can see, the customizations from our Kustomization file have been applied. Because a `kustomize build` command outputs Kubernetes YAML, we can easily deploy the output to Kubernetes as follows:

```
kustomize build deployment-kustomization.yaml | kubectl apply
-f -
```

Next, let's see how we can patch our deployment using a YAML file with `PatchStrategicMerge`.

Specifying changes using PatchStrategicMerge

To illustrate a `PatchStrategicMerge` strategy, we once again start with our same `deployment.yaml` file. This time, we will issue our changes via a combination of the `kustomization.yaml` file and a `patch.yaml` file.

First, let's create our `kustomization.yaml` file, which looks like this:

Deployment-kustomization-2.yaml:

```
apiVersion: kustomize.config.k8s.io/v1beta1
kind: Kustomization
resources:
- deployment.yaml
namespace: default
patchesStrategicMerge:
  - deployment-patch-1.yaml
```

As you can see, our Kustomization file references a new file, `deployment-patch-1.yaml`, in the `patchesStrategicMerge` section. Any number of patch YAML files can be added here.

Then, our `deployment-patch-1.yaml` file is a simple file that mirrors our deployment with the changes we intend to make. Here is what it looks like:

Deployment-patch-1.yaml:

```
apiVersion: apps/v1
kind: Deployment
metadata:
  name: frontend-myapp
  labels:
    app: frontend-myapp
spec:
  replicas: 4
```

This patch file is a subset of the fields in the original deployment. In this case, it simply updates the `replicas` from 2 to 4. Once again, to apply the changes, we can use the following command:

```
kustomize build deployment-kustomization2.yaml
```

However, we can also use the `-k` flag in a `kubectl` command! This is how it looks:

```
Kubectl apply -k deployment-kustomization2.yaml
```

This command is the equivalent of the following:

```
kustomize build deployment-kustomization2.yaml | kubectl apply
-f -
```

Similar to `PatchStrategicMerge`, we can also specify JSON-based patches in our Kustomization – let's look at that now.

Specifying changes using JSONPatch

To specify changes with a JSON patch file, the process is very similar to that involving a YAML patch.

First, we need our Kustomization file. It looks like this:

Deployment-kustomization-3.yaml:

```
apiVersion: kustomize.config.k8s.io/v1beta1
kind: Kustomization
resources:
- deployment.yaml
namespace: default
patches:
- path: deployment-patch-2.json
  target:
    group: apps
    version: v1
    kind: Deployment
    name: frontend-myapp
```

As you can see, our Kustomize file has a section, `patches`, which references a JSON patch file along with a target. You can reference as many JSON patches as you want in this section. `target` is used to determine which Kubernetes resource specified in the resources section will receive the patch.

Finally, we need our patch JSON itself, which looks like this:

Deployment-patch-2.json:

```
[
  {
    "op": "replace",
    "path": "/spec/template/spec/containers/0/name",
    "value": "frontend-myreplacedapp"
  }
]
```

This patch, when applied will perform the `replace` operation on the name of our first container. You can follow the path along with our original `deployment.yaml` file to see that it references the name of that first container. It will replace this name with the new value, `frontend-myreplacedapp`.

Now that we have a solid foundation in Kubernetes resource templating and releases with Kustomize and Helm, we can move on to the automation of deployments to Kubernetes. In the next section, we'll look at two patterns to accomplishing CI/CD with Kubernetes.

Understanding CI/CD paradigms on Kubernetes – in-cluster and out-of-cluster

Continuous integration and deployment to Kubernetes can take many forms.

Most DevOps engineers will be familiar with tools such as Jenkins, TravisCI, and others. These tools are fairly similar in that they provide an execution environment to build applications, perform tests, and call arbitrary Bash scripts in a controlled environment. Some of these tools run commands inside containers, while others don't.

When it comes to Kubernetes, there are multiple schools of thought in how and where to use these tools. There is also a newer breed of CI/CD platforms that are much more tightly coupled to Kubernetes primitives, and many that are architected to run on the cluster itself.

To thoroughly discuss how tooling can pertain to Kubernetes, we will split our pipelines into two logical steps:

1. **Build**: Compiling, testing applications, building container images, and sending to image repositories
2. **Deploy**: Updating Kubernetes resources via kubectl, Helm, or a different tool

For the purposes of this book, we are going to focus mostly on the second deploy-focused step. Though many of the options available handle both build and deploy steps, the build step can happen just about anywhere, and is not worth our focus in a book relating to the specifics of Kubernetes.

With this in mind, to discuss our tooling options, we will split our set of tools into two categories as far as the Deploy part of our pipelines:

- Out-of-cluster CI/CD
- In-cluster CI/CD

Out-of-cluster CI/CD

In the first pattern, our CI/CD tool runs outside of our target Kubernetes cluster. We call this out-of-cluster CI/CD. There is a gray area where the tool may run in a separate Kubernetes cluster that is focused on CI/CD, but we will ignore that option for now as the difference between the two categories is still mostly valid.

You'll often find industry standard tooling such as Jenkins used with this pattern, but any CI tool that has the ability to run scripts and retain secret keys in a secure way can work here. A few examples are **GitLab CI** , **CircleCI**, **TravisCI**, **GitHub Actions**, and **AWS CodeBuild**. Helm is also a big part of this pattern, as out-of-cluster CI scripts can call Helm commands in lieu of kubectl.

Some of the strengths of this pattern are to be found in its simplicity and extensibility. This is a `push`-based pattern where changes to code synchronously trigger changes in Kubernetes workloads.

Some of the weaknesses of out-of-cluster CI/CD are scalability when pushing to many clusters, and the need to keep cluster credentials in the CI/CD pipeline so it has the ability to call kubectl or Helm commands.

In-cluster CI/CD

In the second pattern, our tool runs on the same cluster that our applications run on, which means that CI/CD happens within the same Kubernetes context as our applications, as pods. We call this in-cluster CI/CD. This in-cluster pattern can still have the "build" steps occur outside the cluster, but the deploy step happens from within the cluster.

These types of tools have been gaining popularity since Kubernetes was released, and many use custom resource definitions and custom controllers to do their jobs. Some examples are **FluxCD**, **Argo CD**, **JenkinsX**, and **Tekton Pipelines**. The **GitOps** pattern, where a Git repository is used as the source of truth for what applications should be running on a cluster, is popular in these tools.

Some of the strengths of the in-cluster CI/CD pattern are scalability and security. By having the cluster "pull" changes from GitHub via a GitOps operating model, the solution can be scaled to many clusters. Additionally, it removes the need to keep powerful cluster credentials in the CI/CD system, instead having GitHub credentials on the cluster itself, which can be much better from a security standpoint.

The weaknesses of the in-cluster CI/CD pattern include complexity, since this pull-based operation is slightly asynchronous (as `git pull` usually occurs on a loop, not always occurring exactly when changes are pushed).

Implementing in-cluster and out-of-cluster CI/CD with Kubernetes

Since there are so many options for CI/CD with Kubernetes, we will choose two options and implement them one by one so you can compare their feature sets. First, we'll implement CI/CD to Kubernetes on AWS CodeBuild, which is a great example implementation that can be reused with any external CI system that can run Bash scripts, including Bitbucket Pipelines, Jenkins, and others. Then, we'll move on to FluxCD, an in-cluster GitOps-based CI option that is Kubernetes-native. Let's start with the external option.

Implementing Kubernetes CI with AWS Codebuild

As mentioned earlier, our AWS CodeBuild CI implementation will be easy to duplicate in any script- based CI system. In many cases, the pipeline YAML definition we'll use is near identical. Also, as we discussed earlier, we are going to skip the actual building of the container image. We will instead focus on the actual deployment piece.

To quickly introduce AWS CodeBuild, it is a script-based CI tool that runs Bash scripts, like many other similar tools. In the context of AWS CodePipeline, a higher-level tool, multiple separate AWS CodeBuild steps can be combined into larger pipelines.

In our example, we will be using both AWS CodeBuild and AWS CodePipeline. We will not be discussing in depth how to use these two tools, but instead will keep our discussion tied specifically to how to use them for deployment to Kubernetes.

> **Important note**
>
> We highly recommend that you read and review the documentation for both CodePipeline and CodeBuild, since we will not be covering all of the basics in this chapter. You can find the documentation at `https://docs.aws.amazon.com/codebuild/latest/userguide/welcome.html` for CodeBuild, and `https://docs.aws.amazon.com/codepipeline/latest/userguide/welcome.html` for CodePipeline.

In practice, you would have two CodePipelines, each with one or more CodeBuild steps. The first CodePipeline is triggered on a code change in either AWS CodeCommit or another Git repository (such as GitHub).

The first CodeBuild step for this pipeline runs tests and builds the container image, pushing the image to AWS **Elastic Container Repository** (**ECR**). The second CodeBuild step for the first pipeline deploys the new image to Kubernetes.

The second CodePipeline is triggered anytime we commit a change to our secondary Git repository with Kubernetes resource files (infrastructure repository). It will update the Kubernetes resources using the same process.

Let's start with the first CodePipeline. As mentioned earlier, it contains two CodeBuild steps:

1. First, to test and build the container image and push it to the ECR

2. Second, to deploy the updated container to Kubernetes

As we mentioned earlier in this section, we will not be spending much time on the code-to-container-image pipeline, but here is an example (not production ready) codebuild YAML for implementing this first step:

Pipeline-1-codebuild-1.yaml:

```
version: 0.2
phases:
  build:
    commands:
        - npm run build
  test:
    commands:
        - npm test
  containerbuild:
    commands:
        - docker build -t $ECR_REPOSITORY/$IMAGE_NAME:$IMAGE_TAG
  push:
    commands:
        - docker push $ECR_REPOSITORY/$IMAGE_NAME:$IMAGE_TAG
```

This CodeBuild pipeline consists of four phases. CodeBuild pipeline specs are written in YAML, and contain a version tag that corresponds to the version of the CodeBuild spec. Then, we have a phases section, which is executed in order. This CodeBuild first runs a build command, and then runs a test command in the test phase. Finally, the containerbuild phase creates the container image, and the push phase pushes the image to our container repository.

One thing to keep in mind is that every value with a $ in front of it in CodeBuild is an environment variable. These can be customized via the AWS Console or the AWS CLI, and some can come directly from the Git repository.

Let's now take a look at the YAML for the second CodeBuild step of our first CodePipeline:

Pipeline-1-codebuild-2.yaml:

```
version: 0.2
phases:
  install:
    commands:
      - curl -o kubectl https://amazon-eks.s3.us-west-2.
amazonaws.com/1.16.8/2020-04-16/bin/darwin/amd64/kubectl
      - chmod +x ./kubectl
      - mkdir -p $HOME/bin && cp ./kubectl $HOME/bin/kubectl &&
export PATH=$PATH:$HOME/bin
      - echo 'export PATH=$PATH:$HOME/bin' >> ~/.bashrc
      - source ~/.bashrc
  pre_deploy:
    commands:
      - aws eks --region $AWS_DEFAULT_REGION update-kubeconfig
--name $K8S_CLUSTER
  deploy:
    commands:
      - cd $CODEBUILD_SRC_DIR
      - kubectl set image deployment/$KUBERNETES-DEPLOY-NAME
myrepo:"$IMAGE_TAG"
```

Let's break this file down. Our CodeBuild setup is broken down into three phases: install, pre_deploy, and deploy. In the install phase, we install the kubectl CLI tool.

Then, in the `pre_deploy` phase, we use an AWS CLI command and a couple of environment variables to update our `kubeconfig` file for communicating with our EKS cluster. In any other CI tool (or when not using EKS) you could use a different method for giving cluster credentials to your CI tool. It is important to use a safe option here, as including the `kubeconfig` file directly in your Git repository is not secure. Typically, some combination of environment variables would be great here. Jenkins, CodeBuild, CircleCI, and more have their own systems for this.

Finally, in the `deploy` phase, we use `kubectl` to update our deployment (also contained in an environment variable) with the new image tag specified in the first CodeBuild step. This `kubectl rollout restart` command will ensure that new pods are started for our deployment. In combination with using the `imagePullPolicy` of `Always`, this will result in our new application version being deployed.

In this case, we are patching our deployment with a specific image tag name in the ECR. The `$IMAGE_TAG` environment variable will be auto populated with the newest tag from GitHub so we can use that to automatically roll out the new container image to our deployment.

Next, let's take a look at our second CodePipeline. This one contains only one step – it listens to changes from a separate GitHub repository, our "infrastructure repository". This repository does not contain code for our applications themselves, but instead Kubernetes resource YAMLs. Thus, we can change a Kubernetes resource YAML value – for instance, the number of replicas in a deployment, and see it updated in Kubernetes after the CodePipeline runs. This pattern can be extended to use Helm or Kustomize very easily.

Let's take a look at the first, and only, step of our second CodePipeline:

Pipeline-2-codebuild-1.yaml:

```yaml
version: 0.2
phases:
  install:
    commands:
      - curl -o kubectl https://amazon-eks.s3.us-west-2.
amazonaws.com/1.16.8/2020-04-16/bin/darwin/amd64/kubectl
      - chmod +x ./kubectl
      - mkdir -p $HOME/bin && cp ./kubectl $HOME/bin/kubectl &&
export PATH=$PATH:$HOME/bin
      - echo 'export PATH=$PATH:$HOME/bin' >> ~/.bashrc
      - source ~/.bashrc
  pre_deploy:
```

```
    commands:
        - aws eks --region $AWS_DEFAULT_REGION update-kubeconfig
--name $K8S_CLUSTER
  deploy:
    commands:
        - cd $CODEBUILD_SRC_DIR
        - kubectl apply -f .
```

As you can see, this CodeBuild spec is quite similar to our previous one. As before, we install kubectl and prep it for use with our Kubernetes cluster. Since we are running on AWS, we do it using the AWS CLI, but this could be done any number of ways, including by just adding a Kubeconfig file to our CodeBuild environment.

The difference here is that instead of patching a specific deployment with a new version of an application, we are running an across-the-board kubectl apply command while piping in our entire infrastructure folder. This could then make any changes performed in Git be applied to the resources in our cluster. For instance, if we scaled our deployment from 2 replicas to 20 replicas by changing the value in the deployment.yaml file, it would be deployed to Kubernetes in this CodePipeline step and the deployment would scale up.

Now that we've covered the basics of using an out-of-cluster CI/CD environment to make changes to Kubernetes resources, let's take a look at a completely different CI paradigm, where the pipeline runs on our cluster.

Implementing Kubernetes CI with FluxCD

For our in-cluster CI tool, we will be using **FluxCD**. There are several options for in-cluster CI, including **ArgoCD** and **JenkinsX**, but we like **FluxCD** for its relative simplicity, and for the fact that it automatically updates pods with new container versions without any additional configuration. As an added twist, we will use FluxCD's Helm integration for managing deployments. Let's start with the installation of FluxCD (we'll assume you already have Helm installed from the previous parts of the chapter). These installations follow the official FluxCD installation instructions for Helm compatibility, as of the time of writing of this book.

The official FluxCD docs can be found at https://docs.fluxcd.io/, and we highly recommend you give them a look! FluxCD is a very complex tool, and we are only scratching the surface in this book. A full review is not in scope – we are simply trying to introduce you to the in-cluster CI/CD pattern and relevant tooling.

Let's start our review by installing FluxCD on our cluster.

Installing FluxCD (H3)

FluxCD can easily be installed using Helm in a few steps:

1. First, we need to add the Flux Helm chart repository:

    ```
    helm repo add fluxcd https://charts.fluxcd.io
    ```

2. Next, we need to add a custom resource definition that FluxCD requires in order to be able to work with Helm releases:

    ```
    kubectl apply -f https://raw.githubusercontent.com/
    fluxcd/helm-operator/master/deploy/crds.yaml
    ```

3. Before we can install the FluxCD Operator (which is the core of FluxCD functionality on Kubernetes) and the FluxCD Helm Operator, we need to create a namespace for FluxCD to live in:

    ```
    kubectl create namespace flux
    ```

    Now we can install the main pieces of FluxCD, but we'll need to give FluxCD some additional information about our Git repository.

    Why? Because FluxCD uses a GitOps pattern for updates and deployments. This means that FluxCD will actively reach out to our Git repository every few minutes, instead of responding to Git hooks such as CodeBuild, for instance.

    FluxCD will also respond to new ECR images via a pull-based strategy, but we'll get to that in a bit.

4. To install the main pieces of FluxCD, run the following two commands and replace GITHUB_USERNAME and REPOSITORY_NAME with the GitHub user and repository that you will be storing your workload specs (Kubernetes YAML or Helm charts) in.

This instruction set assumes that the Git repository is public, which it likely isn't. Since most organizations use private repositories, FluxCD has specific configurations to handle this case – just check the docs at `https://docs.fluxcd.io/en/latest/tutorials/get-started-helm/`. In fact, to see the real power of FluxCD, you'll need to give it advanced access to your Git repository in any case, since FluxCD can write to your Git repository and automatically update manifests as new container images are created. However, we won't be getting into that functionality in this book. The FluxCD docs are definitely worth a close read as this is a complex piece of technology with many features. To tell FluxCD which GitHub repository to look at, you can set variables when installing using Helm, as in the following command:

```
helm upgrade -i flux fluxcd/flux \
--set git.url=git@github.com:GITHUB_USERNAME/REPOSITORY_
NAME \
--namespace flux


helm upgrade -i helm-operator fluxcd/helm-operator \
--set git.ssh.secretName=flux-git-deploy \
--namespace flux
```

As you can see, we need to pass our GitHub username, the name of our repository, and a name that will be used for our GitHub secret in Kubernetes.

At this point, FluxCD is fully installed in our cluster and pointed at our infrastructure repository on Git! As mentioned before, this GitHub repository will contain Kubernetes YAML or Helm charts on the basis of which FluxCD will update workloads running in the cluster.

5. To actually give Flux something to do, we need to create the actual manifest for Flux. We do so using a `HelmRelease` YAML file, which looks like the following:

helmrelease-1.yaml:

```
apiVersion: helm.fluxcd.io/v1
kind: HelmRelease
metadata:
  name: myapp
  annotations:
    fluxcd.io/automated: "true"
    fluxcd.io/tag.chart-image: glob:myapp-v*
```

```
spec:
  releaseName: myapp
  chart:
    git: ssh://git@github.
com/<myuser>/<myinfrastructurerepository>/myhelmchart
    ref: master
    path: charts/myapp
  values:
    image:
      repository: myrepo/myapp
      tag: myapp-v2
```

Let's pick this file apart. We are specifying the Git repository where Flux will find the Helm chart for our application. We are also marking the `HelmRelease` with an `automated` annotation, which tells Flux to go and poll the container image repository every few minutes and see whether there is a new version to deploy. To aid this, we include a `chart-image` filter pattern, which the tagged container image must match in order to trigger a redeploy. Finally, in the values section, we have Helm values that will be used for the initial installation of the Helm chart.

To give FluxCD this information, we simply need to add this file to the root of our GitHub repository and push up a change.

Once we add this release file, `helmrelease-1.yaml`, to our Git repository, Flux will pick it up within a few minutes, and then look for the specified Helm chart in the `chart` value. There's just one problem – we haven't made it yet!

Currently, our infrastructure repository on GitHub only contains our single Helm release file. The folder contents look like this:

```
helmrelease1.yaml
```

To close the loop and allow Flux to actually deploy our Helm chart, we need to add it to this infrastructure repository. Let's do so, making the final folder contents in our GitHub repository look like this:

```
helmrelease1.yaml
myhelmchart/
   Chart.yaml
   Values.yaml
   Templates/
      ... chart templates
```

Now, when FluxCD next checks the infrastructure repository on GitHub, it will first find the Helm release YAML file, which will then point it to our new Helm chart.

FluxCD, with a new release and a Helm chart, will then deploy our Helm chart to Kubernetes!

Then, any time a change is made to either the Helm release YAML or any file in our Helm chart, FluxCD will pick it up and, within a few minutes (on its next loop), will deploy the change.

In addition, any time a new container image with a matching tag to the filter pattern is pushed to the image repository, a new version of the app will automatically be deployed – it's that easy. This means that FluxCD is listening to two locations – the infrastructure GitHub repository and the container repository, and will deploy any changes to either location.

You can see how this maps to our out-of-cluster CI/CD implementation where we had one CodePipeline to deploy new versions of our App container, and another CodePipeline to deploy any changes to our infrastructure repository. FluxCD does the same thing in a pull-based way.

Summary

In this chapter, we learned about template code generation on Kubernetes. We reviewed how to create flexible resource templates using both Helm and Kustomize. With this knowledge, you will be able to template your complex applications using either solution, create, or deploy releases. Then, we reviewed two types of CI/CD on Kubernetes; first, external CI/CD deployment to Kubernetes via kubectl, and then in-cluster CI paradigms using FluxCD. With these tools and techniques, you will be able to set up CI/CD to Kubernetes for production applications.

In the next chapter, we will review security and compliance on Kubernetes, an important topic in today's software environment.

Questions

1. What are two differences between Helm and Kustomize templating?

2. How should Kubernetes API credentials be handled when using an external CI/CD setup?

3. What are some of the reasons as to why an in-cluster CI setup may be preferable to an out-of-cluster setup? And vice versa?

Further reading

- Kustomize docs: `https:https://kubernetes-sigs.github.io/kustomize/`

- Helm docs `https://docs.fluxcd.io/en/latest/tutorials/get-started-helm/`

12

Kubernetes Security and Compliance

In this chapter, you will learn about some of the key pieces of Kubernetes security. We'll discuss some recent Kubernetes security issues, and the finding of a recent audit that was performed on Kubernetes. Then, we'll look at implementing security at each level of our cluster, starting with the security of Kubernetes resources and their configurations, moving on to container security, and then finally, runtime security with intrusion detection. To start, we will discuss some key security concepts as they relate to Kubernetes.

In this chapter, we will cover the following topics:

- Understanding security on Kubernetes

- Reviewing CVEs and security audits for Kubernetes

- Implementing tools for cluster configuration and container security

- Handling intrusion detection, runtime security, and compliance on Kubernetes

Technical requirements

In order to run the commands detailed in this chapter, you will need a computer that supports the `kubectl` command-line tool, along with a working Kubernetes cluster. See *Chapter 1, Communicating with Kubernetes*, for several methods for getting up and running with Kubernetes quickly, and for instructions on how to install the `kubectl` tool.

Additionally, you will need a machine that supports the Helm CLI tool, which typically has the same prerequisites as `kubectl` – for details, check the Helm documentation at `https://helm.sh/docs/intro/install/`.

The code used in this chapter can be found in the book's GitHub repository at `https://github.com/PacktPublishing/Cloud-Native-with-Kubernetes/tree/master/Chapter12`.

Understanding security on Kubernetes

When discussing security on Kubernetes, it is very important to note security boundaries and shared responsibility. The *Shared Responsibility Model* is a common term used to describe how security is handled in public cloud services. It states that the customer is responsible for the security of their applications, and the security of their configuration of public cloud components and services. The public cloud provider, on the other hand, is responsible for the security of the services themselves as well as the infrastructure they run on, all the way to the data center and physical layer.

Similarly, security on Kubernetes is shared. Though upstream Kubernetes is not a commercial product, the thousands of Kubernetes contributors and significant organizational heft from large tech companies ensure that the security of Kubernetes components is maintained. Additionally, the large ecosystem of individual contributors and companies using the technology ensures that it gets better as CVEs are reported and handled. Unfortunately, as we will discuss in the next section, the complexity of Kubernetes means that there are many possible attack vectors.

Applying the shared responsibility model then, as a developer you are responsible for the security of how you configure Kubernetes components, the security of the applications that you run on Kubernetes, and access-level security in your cluster configuration. While the security of your applications and containers themselves are not quite in scope for this book, they are definitely important to Kubernetes security. We will spend most of our time discussing configuration-level security, access security, and runtime security.

Either Kubernetes itself or the Kubernetes ecosystem provides tooling, libraries, and full-blown products to handle security at each of these levels – and we'll be reviewing some of these options in this chapter.

Now, before we discuss these solutions, it's best to start with a base understanding of why they may be needed in the first place. Let's move on to the next section, where we'll detail some issues that Kubernetes has encountered in the realm of security.

Reviewing CVEs and security audits for Kubernetes

Kubernetes has encountered several **Common Vulnerabilities and Exposures** (**CVEs**) in its storied history. The MITRE CVE database, at the time of writing, lists 73 CVE announcements from 2015 to 2020 when searching for `kubernetes`. Each one of these is related either directly to Kubernetes, or to a common open source solution that runs on Kubernetes (like the NGINX ingress controller, for instance).

Several of these were critical enough to require hotfixes to the Kubernetes source, and thus they list the affected versions in the CVE description. A full list of all CVEs related to Kubernetes can be found at `https://cve.mitre.org/cgi-bin/cvekey.cgi?keyword=kubernetes`. To give you an idea of some of the issues that have been found, let's review a few of these CVEs in chronological order.

Understanding CVE-2016-1905 – Improper admission control

This CVE was one of the first major security issues with production Kubernetes. The National Vulnerability Database (a NIST website) gives this issue a base score of 7.7, putting it in the high-impact category.

With this issue, a Kubernetes admission controller would not ensure that a `kubectl patch` command followed admission rules, allowing users to completely work around the admission controller – a nightmare in a multitenant scenario.

Understanding CVE-2018-1002105 – Connection upgrading to the backend

This CVE was likely the most critical to date in the Kubernetes project. In fact, NVD gives it a 9.8 criticality score! In this CVE, it was found that it was possible in some versions of Kubernetes to piggyback on an error response from the Kubernetes API server and then upgrade the connection. Once the connection was upgraded, it was possible to send authenticated requests to any backend server in the cluster. This allowed a malicious user to essentially emulate a perfectly authenticated TLS request without proper credentials.

In addition to these CVEs (and likely partially driven by them), the CNCF sponsored a third-party security audit of Kubernetes in 2019. The results of the audit are open source and publicly available and are worth a review.

Understanding the 2019 security audit results

As we mentioned in the previous section, the 2019 Kubernetes security audit was performed by a third party, and the results of the audit are completely open source. The full audit report with all sections can be found at `https://www.cncf.io/blog/2019/08/06/open-sourcing-the-kubernetes-security-audit/`.

In general, this audit focused on the following pieces of Kubernetes functionality:

- `kube-apiserver`
- `etcd`
- `kube-scheduler`
- `kube-controller-manager`
- `cloud-controller-manager`
- `kubelet`
- `kube-proxy`
- The Container Runtime

The intent was to focus on the most important and relevant pieces of Kubernetes when it came to security. The results of the audit included not just a full security report, but also a threat model and a penetration test, as well as a whitepaper.

Diving deep into the audit results is not in the scope of this book, but there are some major takeaways that are great windows into the crux of many of the biggest Kubernetes security issues.

In short, the audit found that since Kubernetes is a complex, highly networked system with many different settings, there are many possible configurations that inexperienced engineers may perform and in doing so, open their cluster to outside attackers.

This idea of Kubernetes being complex enough that an insecure configuration could happen easily is important to note and take to heart.

The entire audit is worth a read – for those with significant knowledge of network security and containers, it is an excellent view of some of the security decisions that were made as part of the development of Kubernetes as a platform.

Now that we have discussed where Kubernetes security issues have been found, we can start looking into ways to increase the security posture of your clusters. Let's start with some default Kubernetes functionality for security.

Implementing tools for cluster configuration and container security

Kubernetes gives us many inbuilt options for the security of cluster configurations and container permissions. Since we've already talked about RBAC, TLS Ingress, and encrypted Kubernetes Secrets, let's discuss a few concepts that we haven't had time to review yet: admission controllers, Pod security policies, and network policies.

Using admission controllers

Admission controllers are an often overlooked but extremely important Kubernetes feature. Many of Kubernetes' advanced features use admission controllers under the hood. In addition, you can create new admission controller rules in order to add custom functionality to your cluster.

There are two general types of admission controllers:

- Mutating admission controllers
- Validating admission controllers

Mutating admission controllers take in Kubernetes resource specifications and return an updated resource specification. They also perform side-effect calculations or make external calls (in the case of custom admission controllers).

On the other hand, validating admission controllers simply accept or deny Kubernetes resource API requests. It is important to know that both types of controllers only act on create, update, delete, or proxy requests. These controllers cannot mutate or change requests to list resources.

When a request of one of those types comes into the Kubernetes API server, it will first run the request through all the relevant mutating admission controllers. Then, the output, which may be mutated, will pass through the validating admission controllers, before finally being acted upon (or not, if the call is denied by an admission controller) in the API server.

Structurally, the Kubernetes-provided admission controllers are functions or "plugins," which run as part of the Kubernetes API server. They rely on two webhook controllers (which are admission controllers themselves, just special ones): **MutatingAdmissionWebhook** and **ValidatingAdmissionWebhook**. All other admission controllers use either one of these webhooks under the hood, depending on their type. In addition, any custom admission controllers you write can be attached to either one of these webhooks.

Before we look at the process of creating a custom admission controller, let's review a few of the default admission controllers that Kubernetes provides. For a full list, check the Kubernetes official documentation at `https://kubernetes.io/docs/reference/access-authn-authz/admission-controllers/#what-does-each-admission-controller-do`.

Understanding default admission controllers

There are quite a few default admission controllers present in a typical Kubernetes setup – many of which are required for some fairly important basic functionality. Here are some examples of default admission controllers.

The NamespaceExists admission controller

The **NamespaceExists** admission controller checks any incoming Kubernetes resource (other than namespaces themselves). This is to check whether the namespace attached to the resource exists. If not, it denies the resource request at the admission controller level.

The PodSecurityPolicy admission controller

The **PodSecurityPolicy** admission controller supports Kubernetes Pod security policies, which we will learn about momentarily. This controller prevents resources that do not follow Pod security policies from being created.

In addition to the default admission controllers, we can create custom admission controllers.

Creating custom admission controllers

Creating a custom admission controller can be done dynamically using one of the two webhook controllers. The way this works is as follows:

1. You must write your own server or script that runs separately to the Kubernetes API server.

2. Then, you configure one of the two previously mentioned webhook triggers to make a request with resource data to your custom server controller.

3. Based on the result, the webhook controller will then tell the API server whether or not to proceed.

Let's start with the first step: writing a quick admission server.

Writing a server for a custom admission controller

To create our custom admission controller server (which will accept webhooks from the Kubernetes control plane), we can use any programming language. As with most extensions to Kubernetes, Go has the best support and libraries that make the task of writing a custom admission controller easier. For now, we will use some pseudocode.

The control flow for our server will look something like this:

Admission-controller-server.pseudo

```
// This function is called when a request hits the
// "/mutate" endpoint
function acceptAdmissionWebhookRequest(req)
{
   // First, we need to validate the incoming req
   // This function will check if the request is formatted
properly
   // and will add a "valid" attribute If so
   // The webhook will be a POST request from Kubernetes in the
   // "AdmissionReviewRequest" schema
   req = validateRequest(req);
   // If the request isn't valid, return an Error
```

```
    if(!req.valid) return Error;


    // Next, we need to decide whether to accept or deny the
Admission
    // Request. This function will add the "accepted" attribute
    req = decideAcceptOrDeny(req);
    if(!req.accepted) return Error;


    // Now that we know we want to allow this resource, we need
to
    // decide if any "patches" or changes are necessary
    patch = patchResourceFromWebhook(req);


    // Finally, we create an AdmissionReviewResponse and pass it
back
    // to Kubernetes in the response
    // This AdmissionReviewResponse includes the patches and
    // whether the resource is accepted.
    admitReviewResp = createAdmitReviewResp(req, patch);


    return admitReviewResp;
}
```

Now that we have a simple server for our custom admission controller, we can configure a Kubernetes admission webhook to call it.

Configuring Kubernetes to call a custom admission controller server

In order to tell Kubernetes to call our custom admission server, it needs a place to call. We can run our custom admission controller anywhere – it doesn't need to be on Kubernetes.

That being said, it's easy for the purposes of this chapter to run it on Kubernetes. We won't go through the full manifest, but let's assume we have a Service and a Deployment that it is pointed at, running a container that is our server. The Service would look something like this:

Service-webhook.yaml

```
apiVersion: v1
kind: Service
metadata:
  name: my-custom-webhook-server
spec:
  selector:
    app: my-custom-webhook-server
  ports:
    - port: 443
      targetPort: 8443
```

It's important to note that our server needs to use HTTPS in order for Kubernetes to accept webhook responses. There are many ways to configure this, and we won't get into it in this book. The certificate can be self-signed, but the common name of the certificate and CA needs to match the one used when setting up the Kubernetes cluster.

Now that we have our server running and accepting HTTPS requests, let's tell Kubernetes where to find it. To do this, we use `MutatingWebhookConfiguration`.

An example of `MutatingWebhookConfiguration` is shown in the following code block:

Mutating-webhook-config-service.yaml

```
apiVersion: admissionregistration.k8s.io/v1beta1
kind: MutatingWebhookConfiguration
metadata:
  name: my-service-webhook
webhooks:
  - name: my-custom-webhook-server.default.svc
    rules:
      - operations: [ "CREATE" ]
        apiGroups: [""]
        apiVersions: ["v1"]
        resources: ["pods", "deployments", "configmaps"]
    clientConfig:
      service:
```

```
        name: my-custom-webhook-server
        namespace: default
        path: "/mutate"
     caBundle: ${CA_PEM_B64}
```

Let's pick apart the YAML for our `MutatingWebhookConfiguration`. As you can see, we can configure more than one webhook in this configuration – though we've only done one in this example.

For each webhook, we set `name`, `rules`, and a `configuration`. The `name` is simply the identifier for the webhook. The `rules` allow us to configure exactly in which cases Kubernetes should make a request to our admission controller. In this case, we have configured our webhook to fire whenever a `CREATE` event for resources of the types `pods`, `deployments`, and `configmaps` occurs.

Finally, we have the `clientConfig`, where we specify exactly where and how Kubernetes should make the webhook request. Since we're running our custom server on Kubernetes, we specify the Service name as in the previous YAML, in addition to the path on our server to hit (`"/mutate"` is a best practice here), and the CA of the cluster to compare to the certificate of the HTTPS termination. If your custom admission server is running somewhere else, there are other possible configuration fields – check the docs if you need them (`https://kubernetes.io/docs/reference/access-authn-authz/admission-controllers/`).

Once we create the `MutatingWebhookConfiguration` in Kubernetes, it is easy to test the validation. All we need to do is create a Pod, Deployment, or ConfigMap as normal, and check whether our requests are denied or patched according to the logic in our server.

Let's assume for now that our server is set to deny any Pod with a name that includes the string `deny-me`. It is also set up to add an error response to the `AdmissionReviewResponse`.

Let's use a Pod spec as follows:

To-deny-pod.yaml

```
apiVersion: v1
kind: Pod
metadata:
  name: my-pod-to-deny
spec:
```

```
containers:
- name: nginx
    image: nginx
```

Now, we can create our Pod to check the admission controller. We can use the following command:

```
kubectl create -f to-deny-pod.yaml
```

This results in the following output:

```
Error from server (InternalError): error when creating
"to-deny-pod.yaml": Internal error occurred: admission webhook
"my-custom-webhook-server.default.svc" denied the request: Pod
name contains "to-deny"!
```

And that's it! Our custom admission controller has successfully denied a Pod that doesn't match the conditions we specified in our server. For resources that are patched (not denied, but altered), `kubectl` will not show any special response. You will need to fetch the resource in question to see the patch in action.

Now that we've explored custom admission controllers, let's look at another way to impose cluster security practices – Pod security policies.

Enabling Pod security policies

The basics of Pod security policies are that they allow a cluster administrator to create rules that Pods must follow in order to be scheduled onto a node. Technically, Pod security policies are just another type of admission controller. However, this feature is officially supported by Kubernetes and is worth an in-depth discussion, since many options are available.

Pod security policies can be used to prevent Pods from running as root, put limits on ports and volumes used, restrict privilege escalation, and much more. We will review a subset of Pod security policy capabilities now, but for a full list of Pod security policy configuration types, check the official PSP documentation at `https://kubernetes.io/docs/concepts/policy/pod-security-policy/`.

As a final note, Kubernetes also supports low-level primitives for controlling container permissions – namely *AppArmor*, *SELinux*, and *Seccomp*. These configurations are outside the scope of this book, but they can be useful for highly secure environments.

Steps to create a Pod security policy

There are several steps to implementing Pod security policies:

1. First, the Pod security policy admission controller must be enabled.

2. This will prevent all Pods from being created in your cluster since it requires a matched Pod security policy and role to be able to create a Pod. You will likely want to create your Pod security policies and roles before enabling the admission controller for this reason.

3. After the admission controller is enabled, the policy itself must be created.

4. Then, a `Role` or `ClusterRole` object must be created with access to the Pod security policy.

5. Finally, that role can be bound with a **ClusterRoleBinding** or **RoleBinding** to a user or service `accountService` account, allowing Pods created with that service account to use permissions available to the Pod security policy.

In some cases, you may not have the Pod security policy admission controller enabled by default on your cluster. Let's look at how to enable it.

Enabling the Pod security policy admission controller

In order to enable the PSP admission controller, the `kube-apiserver` must be started with a flag that specifies admission controllers to start with. On managed Kubernetes (EKS, AKS, and others), the PSP admission controller will likely be enabled by default, along with a privileged Pod security policy created for use by the initial admin user. This prevents the PSP from causing any issues with creating Pods in the new cluster.

If you're self-managing Kubernetes and you haven't yet enabled the PSP admission controller, you can do so by restarting the `kube-apiserver` component with the following flags:

```
kube-apiserver --enable-admission-plugins=PodSecurityPolicy,Ser
viceAccount...<all other desired admission controllers>
```

If your Kubernetes API server is run using a `systemd` file (as it would be if following *Kubernetes: The Hard Way*), you should update the flags there instead. Typically, `systemd` files are placed in the `/etc/systemd/system/` folder.

In order to find out which admission plugins are already enabled, you can run the following command:

```
kube-apiserver -h | grep enable-admission-plugins
```

This command will present a long list of admission plugins that are enabled. For instance, you will see the following admission plugins in the output:

```
NamespaceLifecycle, LimitRanger, ServiceAccount…
```

Now that we are sure the PSP admission controller is enabled, we can actually create a PSP.

Creating the PSP resource

Pod security policies themselves can be created using typical Kubernetes resource YAML. Here's a YAML file for a privileged Pod security policy:

Privileged-psp.yaml

```
apiVersion: policy/v1beta1
kind: PodSecurityPolicy
metadata:
  name: privileged-psp
  annotations:
    seccomp.security.alpha.kubernetes.io/allowedProfileNames:
'*'
spec:
  privileged: true
  allowedCapabilities:
  - '*'
  volumes:
  - '*'
  hostNetwork: true
  hostPorts:
  - min: 2000
    max: 65535
  hostIPC: true
  hostPID: true
  allowPrivilegeEscalation: true
  runAsUser:
```

```
      rule: 'RunAsAny'
    supplementalGroups:
      rule: 'RunAsAny'
    fsGroup:
      rule: 'RunAsAny'
```

This Pod security policy allows the user or service account (via a **RoleBinding** or **ClusterRoleBinding**) to create Pods that have privileged capabilities. For instance, the Pod using this `PodSecurityPolicy` would be able to bind to the host network on ports `2000-65535`, run as any user, and bind to any volume type. In addition, we have an annotation for a `seccomp` restriction on `allowedProfileNames` – to give you an idea of how `Seccomp` and `AppArmor` annotations work with `PodSecurityPolicies`.

As we mentioned previously, just creating the PSP does nothing. For any service account or user that will be creating privileged Pods, we need to give them access to the Pod security policy via a **Role** and **RoleBinding** (or `ClusterRole` and `ClusterRoleBinding`).

In order to create a `ClusterRole` that has access to this PSP, we can use the following YAML:

Privileged-clusterrole.yaml

```
apiVersion: rbac.authorization.k8s.io
kind: ClusterRole
metadata:
  name: privileged-role
rules:
- apiGroups: ['policy']
  resources: ['podsecuritypolicies']
  verbs:    ['use']
  resourceNames:
  - privileged-psp
```

Now, we can bind our newly created `ClusterRole` to the user or service account with which we intend to create privileged Pods. Let's do this with a `ClusterRoleBinding`:

Privileged-clusterrolebinding.yaml

```yaml
apiVersion: rbac.authorization.k8s.io/v1
kind: ClusterRoleBinding
metadata:
  name: privileged-crb
roleRef:
  kind: ClusterRole
  name: privileged-role
  apiGroup: rbac.authorization.k8s.io
subjects:
- kind: Group
  apiGroup: rbac.authorization.k8s.io
  name: system:authenticated
```

In our case, we want to let every authenticated user on the cluster create privileged Pods, so we bind to the `system:authenticated` group.

Now, it is likely that we do not want all our users or Pods to be privileged. A more realistic Pod security policy places restrictions on what Pods are capable of.

Let's take a look at some example YAML of a PSP that has these restrictions:

unprivileged-psp.yaml

```yaml
apiVersion: policy/v1beta1
kind: PodSecurityPolicy
metadata:
  name: unprivileged-psp
spec:
  privileged: false
  allowPrivilegeEscalation: false
  volumes:
    - 'configMap'
    - 'emptyDir'
    - 'projected'
```

```
  - 'secret'
  - 'downwardAPI'
  - 'persistentVolumeClaim'
hostNetwork: false
hostIPC: false
hostPID: false
runAsUser:
  rule: 'MustRunAsNonRoot'
supplementalGroups:
  rule: 'MustRunAs'
  ranges:
    - min: 1
      max: 65535
fsGroup:
  rule: 'MustRunAs'
  ranges:
    - min: 1
      max: 65535
readOnlyRootFilesystem: false
```

As you can tell, this Pod security policy is vastly different in the restrictions it imposes on created Pods. No Pods under this policy are allowed to run as root or escalate to root. They also have restrictions on the types of volumes they can bind to (this section has been highlighted in the preceding code snippet) – and they cannot use host networking or bind directly to host ports.

In this YAML, both the runAsUser and supplementalGroups sections control the Linux user ID and group IDs that can run or be added by the container, while the fsGroup key controls the filesystem groups that can be used by the container.

In addition to using rules like MustRunAsNonRoot, it is possible to directly specify which user ID a container can run with – and any Pods not running specifically with that ID in their spec will not be able to schedule onto a Node.

For a sample PSP that restricts users to a specific ID, look at the following YAML:

Specific-user-id-psp.yaml

```
apiVersion: policy/v1beta1
kind: PodSecurityPolicy
metadata:
  name: specific-user-psp
spec:
  privileged: false
  allowPrivilegeEscalation: false
  hostNetwork: false
  hostIPC: false
  hostPID: false
  runAsUser:
    rule: 'MustRunAs'
    ranges:
      - min: 1
        max: 3000
  readOnlyRootFilesystem: false
```

This Pod security policy, when applied, will prevent any Pods from running as user ID 0 or 3001, or higher. In order to create a Pod that satisfies this condition, we use the runAs option in the securityContext in a Pod spec.

Here is an example Pod that satisfies this constraint and would be successfully scheduled even with this Pod security policy in place:

Specific-user-pod.yaml

```
apiVersion: v1
kind: Pod
metadata:
  name: specific-user-pod
spec:
  securityContext:
    runAsUser: 1000
  containers:
  - name: test
```

```
  image: busybox
  securityContext:
    allowPrivilegeEscalation: false
```

As you can see, in this YAML, we give our Pod a specific user to run with, ID `1000`. We also disallowed our Pod from escalating to root. This Pod spec would successfully schedule even when `specific-user-psp` is in place.

Now that we've discussed how Pod security policies can secure Kubernetes by placing restrictions on how a Pod runs, we can move onto network policies, where we can restrict how Pods network.

Using network policies

Network policies in Kubernetes work similar to firewall rules or route tables. They allow users to specify a group of Pods via a selector and then determine how and where those Pods can communicate.

For network policies to work, your chosen Kubernetes network plugin (such as, *Weave*, *Flannel*, or *Calico*) must support the network policy spec. Network policies can be created as all other Kubernetes resources are – through a YAML file. Let's start with a very simple network policy.

Here is a network policy spec that restricts access to Pods with the label `app=server`:

Label-restriction-policy.yaml

```
apiVersion: networking.k8s.io/v1
kind: NetworkPolicy
metadata:
  name: frontend-network-policy
spec:
  podSelector:
    matchLabels:
      app: server
  policyTypes:
  - Ingress
  ingress:
  - from:
    - podSelector:
        matchLabels:
```

```
        app: frontend
    ports:
    - protocol: TCP
      port: 80
```

Now, let's pick apart this network policy YAML since it will help us explain some more complicated network policies as we progress.

First, in our spec, we have a `podSelector`, which works similarly to node selectors in functionality. Here, we are using `matchLabels` to specify that this network policy will only affect Pods with the label `app=server`.

Next, we specify a policy type for our network policy. There are two policy types: `ingress` and `egress`. A network policy can specify one or both types. `ingress` refers to making network rules that come into effect for connections to the matched Pods, and `egress` refers to network rules that come into effect for connections leaving the matched Pods.

In this specific network policy, we are simply dictating a single `ingress` rule: the only traffic that will be accepted by Pods with the label `app=server` is traffic that originates from Pods with the label `app:frontend`. Additionally, the only port that will accept traffic on Pods with the label `app=server` is `80`.

There can be multiple `from` blocks in an `ingress` policy set that correspond to multiple traffic rules. Similarly, with `egress`, there can be multiple `to` blocks.

It is important to note that network policies work by namespace. By default, if there isn't a single network policy in a namespace, there are no restrictions on Pod-to-Pod communication within that namespace. However, as soon as a specific Pod is selected by a single network policy, all traffic to and from that Pod must explicitly match a network policy rule. If it doesn't match a rule, it will be blocked.

With this in mind, we can easily create policies that enforce broad restrictions on Pod networking. Let's take a look at the following network policy:

Full-restriction-policy.yaml

```
apiVersion: networking.k8s.io/v1
kind: NetworkPolicy
metadata:
  name: full-restriction-policy
  namespace: development
spec:
```

```
policyTypes:
- Ingress
- Egress
podSelector: {}
```

In this `NetworkPolicy`, we specify that we will be including both an `Ingress` and `Egress` policy, but we don't write a block for either of them. This has the effect of automatically denying any traffic for both `Egress` and `Ingress` since there are no rules for traffic to match against.

Additionally, our { } Pod selector value corresponds to selecting every Pod in the namespace. The end result of this rule is that every Pod in the `development` namespace will not be able to accept ingress traffic or send egress traffic.

> **Important note**
> It is also important to note that network policies are interpreted by combining all the separate network policies that affect a Pod and then applying the combination of all those rules to Pod traffic.

This means that even though we have restricted all ingress and egress traffic in the `development` namespace in our preceding example, we can still enable it for specific Pods by adding another network policy.

Let's assume that now our `development` namespace has complete traffic restriction for Pods, we want to allow a subset of Pods to receive network traffic on port `443` and send traffic on port `6379` to a database Pod. In order to do this, we simply need to create a new network policy that, by the additive nature of policies, allows this traffic.

This is what the network policy looks like:

Override-restriction-network-policy.yaml

```
apiVersion: networking.k8s.io/v1
kind: NetworkPolicy
metadata:
  name: override-restriction-policy
  namespace: development
spec:
  podSelector:
    matchLabels:
```

```
      app: server
  policyTypes:
  - Ingress
  - Egress
  ingress:
  - from:
    - podSelector:
        matchLabels:
          app: frontend
    ports:
    - protocol: TCP
      port: 443
  egress:
  - to:
    - podSelector:
        matchLabels:
          app: database
    ports:
    - protocol: TCP
      port: 6379
```

In this network policy, we are allowing our server Pods in the development namespace to receive traffic from frontend Pods on port 443 and send traffic to database Pods on port 6379.

If instead, we wanted to open up all Pod-to-Pod communication without any restrictions, while still actually instituting a network policy, we could do so with the following YAML:

All-open-network-policy.yaml

```
apiVersion: networking.k8s.io/v1
kind: NetworkPolicy
metadata:
  name: allow-all-egress
spec:
  podSelector: {}
  egress:
  - {}
```

```
ingress:
- {}
policyTypes:
- Egress
- Ingress
```

Now we have discussed how we can use network policies to set rules on Pod-to-Pod traffic. However, it is also possible to use network policies as an external-facing firewall of sorts. To do this, we create network policy rules based not on Pods as origin or destination, but external IPs.

Let's look at an example network policy where we are restricting communication to and from a Pod, with a specific IP range as the target:

External-ip-network-policy.yaml

```
apiVersion: networking.k8s.io/v1
kind: NetworkPolicy
metadata:
  name: specific-ip-policy
spec:
  podSelector:
    matchLabels:
      app: worker
  policyTypes:
  - Ingress
  - Egress
  ingress:
  - from:
    - ipBlock:
        cidr: 157.10.0.0/16
        except:
        - 157.10.1.0/24
  egress:
  - to:
    - ipBlock:
        cidr: 157.10.0.0/16
```

```
      except:
      - 157.10.1.0/24
```

In this network policy, we are specifying a single `Ingress` rule and a single `Egress` rule. Each of these rules accepts or denies traffic based not on which Pod it is coming from but on the source IP of the network request.

In our case, we have selected a `/16` subnet mask range (with a specified `/24` CIDR exception) for both our `Ingress` and `Egress` rules. This has the side effect of preventing any traffic from within our cluster from reaching these Pods since none of our Pod IPs will match the rules in a default cluster networking setup.

However, traffic from outside the cluster in the specified subnet mask (and not in the exception range) will be able to both send traffic to the `worker` Pods and also be able to accept traffic from the `worker` Pods.

With the end of our discussion on network policies, we can move onto a completely different layer of the security stack – runtime security and intrusion detection.

Handling intrusion detection, runtime security, and compliance on Kubernetes

Once you have set your Pod security policies and network policies – and generally ensured that your configuration is as watertight as possible – there are still many attack vectors that are possible in Kubernetes. In this section, we will focus on attacks from within a Kubernetes cluster. Even with highly specific Pod security policies in place (which definitely do help, to be clear), it is possible for containers and applications running in your cluster to perform unexpected or malicious operations.

In order to solve this problem, many professionals look to runtime security tools, which allow constant monitoring and alerting of application processes. For Kubernetes, a popular open source tool that can accomplish this is *Falco*.

Installing Falco

Falco bills itself as a *behavioral activity monitor* for processes on Kubernetes. It can monitor both your containerized applications running on Kubernetes as well as the Kubernetes components themselves.

How does Falco work? In real time, Falco parses system calls from the Linux kernel. It then filters these system calls through rules – which are sets of configurations that can be applied to the Falco engine. Whenever a rule is broken by a system call, Falco triggers an alert. It's that simple!

Falco ships with an extensive set of default rules that add significant observability at the kernel level. Custom rules are of course supported by Falco – and we will show you how to write them.

First, however, we need to install Falco on our cluster! Luckily, Falco can be installed using Helm. However, it is very important to note that there are a few different ways to install Falco, and they differ significantly in how effective they can be in the event of a breach.

We're going to be installing Falco using the Helm chart, which is simple and works well for managed Kubernetes clusters, or any scenario where you may not have direct access to the worker nodes.

However, for the best possible security posture, Falco should be installed directly onto the Kubernetes nodes at the Linux level. The Helm chart, which uses a DaemonSet is great for ease of use but is inherently not as secure as a direct Falco installation. To install Falco directly to your nodes, check the installation instructions at `https://falco.org/docs/installation/`.

With that caveat out of the way, we can install Falco using Helm:

1. First, we need to add the `falcosecurity` repo to our local Helm:

    ```
    helm repo add falcosecurity https://falcosecurity.github.io/charts
    helm repo update
    ```

    Next, we can proceed with actually installing Falco using Helm.

    > **Important note**
    >
    > The Falco Helm chart has many possible variables that can be changed in the values file – for a full review of those, you can check the official Helm chart repo at `https://github.com/falcosecurity/charts/tree/master/falco`.

2. To install Falco, run the following:

```
helm install falco falcosecurity/falco
```

This command will install Falco using the default values, which you can see at `https://github.com/falcosecurity/charts/blob/master/falco/values.yaml`.

Next, let's dive into what Falco offers a security-conscious Kubernetes administrator.

Understanding Falco's capabilities

As mentioned previously, Falco ships with a set of default rules, but we can easily add more rules using new YAML files. Since we're using the Helm version of Falco, passing custom rules to Falco is as simple as either creating a new values file or editing the default one with custom rules.

Adding custom rules looks like this:

Custom-falco.yaml

```
customRules:
  my-rules.yaml: |-
    Rule1
    Rule2
    etc...
```

Now is a good time to discuss the structure of a Falco rule. To illustrate, let's borrow a few lines of rules from the `Default` Falco ruleset that ships with the Falco Helm chart.

When specifying Falco configuration in YAML, we can use three different types of keys to help compose our rules. These are macros, lists, and rules themselves.

The specific rule we're looking at in this example is called `Launch Privileged Container`. This rule will detect when a privileged container has been started and log some information about the container to `STDOUT`. Rules can do all sorts of things when it comes to alerts, but logging to `STDOUT` is a good way to increase observability when high-risk events happen.

First, let's look at the rule entry itself. This rule uses a few helper entries, several macros, and lists – but we'll get to those in a second:

```
- rule: Launch Privileged Container
  desc: Detect the initial process started in a privileged
container. Exceptions are made for known trusted images.
```

```
  condition: >
    container_started and container
    and container.privileged=true
    and not falco_privileged_containers
    and not user_privileged_containers
  output: Privileged container started (user=%user.name
command=%proc.cmdline %container.info image=%container.image.
repository:%container.image.tag)
  priority: INFO
  tags: [container, cis, mitre_privilege_escalation, mitre_
lateral_movement]
```

As you can see, a Falco rule has several parts. First, we have the rule name and description. Then, we specify the triggering condition for the rule – which acts as a filter for Linux system calls. If a system call matches all the logic filters in the `condition` block, the rule is triggered.

When a rule is triggered, the output key allows us to set a format for how the text of the output appears. The `priority` key lets us assign a priority, which can be one of `emergency`, `alert`, `critical`, `error`, `warning`, `notice`, `informational`, and `debug`.

Finally, the `tags` key applies tags to the rule in question, making it easier to categorize rules. This is especially important when using alerts that aren't simply plain text `STDOUT` entries.

The syntax for `condition` is especially important here, and we will focus on how this system of filtering works.

First off, since the filters are essentially logical statements, you will see some familiar syntax (if you have ever programmed or written pseudocode) – and, and not, and so on. This syntax is pretty simple to learn, and a full discussion of it – the *Sysdig* filter syntax – can be found at `https://github.com/draios/sysdig/wiki/sysdig-user-guide#filtering`.

As a note, the Falco open source project was originally created by *Sysdig*, which is why it uses the common *Sysdig* filter syntax.

Next, you will see reference to `container_started` and `container`, as well as `falco_privileged_containers` and `user_privileged_containers`. These are not plain strings but the use of macros – references to other blocks in the YAML that specify additional functionality, and generally make it much easier to write rules without repeating a lot of configuration.

To see how this rule really works, let's look at a full reference for all the macros that were referenced in the preceding rule:

```
- macro: container
  condition: (container.id != host)

- macro: container_started
  condition: >
    ((evt.type = container or
     (evt.type=execve and evt.dir=< and proc.vpid=1)) and
     container.image.repository != incomplete)

- macro: user_sensitive_mount_containers
  condition: (container.image.repository = docker.io/sysdig/
agent)

- macro: falco_privileged_containers
  condition: (openshift_image or
              user_trusted_containers or
              container.image.repository in (trusted_images) or
              container.image.repository in (falco_privileged_
images) or
              container.image.repository startswith istio/
proxy_ or
              container.image.repository startswith quay.io/
sysdig)

- macro: user_privileged_containers
  condition: (container.image.repository endswith sysdig/agent)
```

You will see in the preceding YAML that each macro is really just a reusable block of `Sysdig` filter syntax, often using other macros to accomplish the rule functionality. Lists, not pictured here, are like macros except that they do not describe filter logic. Instead, they include a list of string values that can be used as part of a comparison using the filter syntax.

For instance, `(trusted_images)` in the `falco_privileged_containers` macro references a list called `trusted_images`. Here's the source for that list:

```
- list: trusted_images
  items: []
```

As you can see, this particular list is empty in the default rules, but a custom ruleset could use a list of trusted images in this list, which would then automatically be consumed by all the other macros and rules that use the `trusted_image` list as part of their filter rules.

As mentioned previously, in addition to tracking Linux system calls, Falco can also track Kubernetes control plane events as of Falco v0.13.0.

Understanding Kubernetes audit event rules in Falco

Structurally, these Kubernetes audit event rules work the same way as Falco's Linux system call rules. Here's an example of one of the default Kubernetes rules in Falco:

```
- rule: Create Disallowed Pod
  desc: >
    Detect an attempt to start a pod with a container image
  outside of a list of allowed images.
    condition: kevt and pod and kcreate and not allowed_k8s_
  containers
    output: Pod started with container not in allowed list
  (user=%ka.user.name pod=%ka.resp.name ns=%ka.target.namespace
  images=%ka.req.pod.containers.image)
    priority: WARNING
    source: k8s_audit
    tags: [k8s]
```

This rule acts on Kubernetes audit events in Falco (essentially, control plane events) to alert when a Pod is created that isn't on the list `allowed_k8s_containers`. The default `k8s` audit rules contain many similar rules, most of which output formatted logs when triggered.

Now, we talked about Pod security policies a bit earlier in this chapter – and you may be seeing some similarities between PSPs and Falco Kubernetes audit event rules. For instance, take this entry from the default Kubernetes Falco rules:

```
- rule: Create HostNetwork Pod
  desc: Detect an attempt to start a pod using the host
```

```
network.
   condition: kevt and pod and kcreate and ka.req.pod.host_
network intersects (true) and not ka.req.pod.containers.image.
repository in (falco_hostnetwork_images)
   output: Pod started using host network (user=%ka.user.name
pod=%ka.resp.name ns=%ka.target.namespace images=%ka.req.pod.
containers.image)
   priority: WARNING
   source: k8s_audit
   tags: [k8s]
```

This rule, which is triggered when a Pod is attempting to start using the host network, maps directly to host network PSP settings.

Falco capitalizes on this similarity by letting us use Falco as a way to `trial` new Pod security policies without applying them cluster-wide and causing issues with running Pods.

For this purpose, `falcoctl` (the Falco command-line tool) comes with the `convert psp` command. This command takes in a Pod security policy definition and turns it into a set of Falco rules. These Falco rules will just output logs to `STDOUT` when triggered (instead of causing Pod scheduling failures like a PSP mismatch), which makes it much easier to test out new Pod security policies in an existing cluster.

To learn how to use the `falcoctl` conversion tool, check out the official Falco documentation at `https://falco.org/docs/psp-support/`.

Now that we have a good grounding on the Falco tool, let's discuss how it can be used to implement compliance controls and runtime security.

Mapping Falco to compliance and runtime security use cases

Because of its extensibility and ability to audit low-level Linux system calls, Falco is a great tool for continuous compliance and runtime security.

On the compliance side, it is possible to leverage Falco rulesets that map specifically to the requirements of a compliance standard – for instance, PCI or HIPAA. This allows users to quickly detect and act on any processes that do not comply with the standard in question. There are open and closed source Falco rulesets for several standards.

Similarly, for runtime security, Falco exposes an alerting/eventing system, which means that any runtime events that trigger an alert can also trigger automated intervention and remediation processes. This can work for both security and compliance. As an example, if a Pod triggers a Falco alert for non-compliance, a process can work off that alert and delete the offending Pod immediately.

Summary

In this chapter, we learned about security in the context of Kubernetes. First, we reviewed the basics of security on Kubernetes – which layers of the security stack are relevant to our cluster and some broad strokes of how to manage that complexity. Next, we learned about some of the major security issues that Kubernetes has encountered, as well as discussing the results of the 2019 security audit.

Then, we implemented security at two different levels of the stack in Kubernetes – first, in configuration with Pod security policies and network policies, and finally, runtime security with Falco.

In the next chapter, we will learn how to make Kubernetes your own by building custom resources. This will allow you to add significant new functionality to your cluster.

Questions

1. What are the names of the two webhook controllers that a custom admission controller can use?

2. What effect does a blank `NetworkPolicy` for ingress have?

3. What sort of Kubernetes control plane events would be valuable to track in order to prevent attackers from altering Pod functionality?

Further reading

*   Kubernetes CVE Database: `https://cve.mitre.org/cgi-bin/cvekey.cgi?keyword=kubernetes`

Section 4: Extending Kubernetes

In this section, you will take the knowledge you've gained in the previous sections and apply it to advanced patterns on Kubernetes. We'll extend default Kubernetes functionality using custom resource definitions, implement a service mesh and serverless patterns on your cluster, and run some stateful workloads.

This part of the book comprises the following chapters:

- *Chapter 13, Extending Kubernetes with CRDs*
- *Chapter 14, Service Meshes and Serverless*
- *Chapter 15, Stateful Workloads on Kubernetes*

13
Extending Kubernetes with CRDs

This chapter explains the many possibilities for extending the functionality of Kubernetes. It begins with a discussion of the **Custom Resource Definition (CRD)**, a Kubernetes-native way to specify custom resources that can be acted on by the Kubernetes API using familiar `kubectl` commands such as `get`, `create`, `describe`, and `apply`. It is followed by a discussion of the Operator pattern, an extension of the CRD. It then details some of the hooks that cloud providers attach to their Kubernetes implementations, and ends with a brief introduction to the greater cloud-native ecosystem. Using the concepts learned in this chapter, you will be able to architect and develop extensions to your Kubernetes cluster, unlocking advanced usage patterns.

The case study in this chapter will include creating two simple CRDs to support an example application. We'll begin with CRDs, which will give you a good base understanding of how extensions can build on the Kubernetes API.

In this chapter, we will cover the following topics:

- How to extend Kubernetes with **Custom Resource Definitions** (CRDs)
- Self-managing functionality with Kubernetes operators

- Using cloud-specific Kubernetes extensions

- Integrating with the ecosystem

Technical requirements

In order to run the commands detailed in this chapter, you will need a computer that supports the `kubectl` command-line tool along with a working Kubernetes cluster. See *Chapter 1*, *Communicating with Kubernetes*, for several methods for getting up and running with Kubernetes quickly, and for instructions on how to install the `kubectl` tool.

The code used in this chapter can be found in the book's GitHub repository at `https://github.com/PacktPublishing/Cloud-Native-with-Kubernetes/tree/master/Chapter13`.

How to extend Kubernetes with custom resource definitions

Let's start with the basics. What is a CRD? We know that Kubernetes has an API model where we can perform operations against resources. Some examples of Kubernetes resources (which you should be well acquainted with by now) are Pods, PersistentVolumes, Secrets, and others.

Now, what if we want to implement some custom functionality in our cluster, write our own controllers, and store the state of our controllers somewhere? We could, of course, store the state of our custom functionality in a SQL or NoSQL database running on Kubernetes or elsewhere (which is actually one of the strategies for extending Kubernetes) – but what if our custom functionality acts more as an extension of Kubernetes functionality, instead of a completely separate application?

In cases like this, we have two options:

- Custom resource definitions

- API aggregation

API aggregation allows advanced users to build their own resource APIs outside of the Kubernetes API server and use their own storage – and then aggregate those resources at the API layer so they can be queried using the Kubernetes API. This is obviously highly extensible and is essentially just using the Kubernetes API as a proxy to your own custom functionality, which may or may not actually integrate with Kubernetes.

The other option is CRDs, where we can use the Kubernetes API and underlying data store (`etcd`) instead of building our own. We can use the `kubectl` and `kube api` methods that we know to interact with our own custom functionality.

In this book, we will not discuss API aggregation. While definitely more flexible than CRDs, this is an advanced topic that deserves a thorough understanding of the Kubernetes API and a thorough perusal of the Kubernetes documentation to do it right. You can learn more about API aggregation in the Kubernetes documentation at `https://kubernetes.io/docs/concepts/extend-kubernetes/api-extension/apiserver-aggregation/`.

So, now that we know that we are using the Kubernetes control plane as our own stateful store for our new custom functionality, we need a schema. Similar to how the Pod resource spec in Kubernetes expects certain fields and configurations, we can tell Kubernetes what we expect for our new custom resources. Let's go through the spec for a CRD now.

Writing a custom resource definition

For CRDs, Kubernetes uses the OpenAPI V3 specification. For more information on OpenAPI V3, you can check the official documentation at `https://github.com/OAI/OpenAPI-Specification/blob/master/versions/3.0.0.md`, but we'll soon see how exactly this translates into Kubernetes CRD definitions.

Let's take a look at an example CRD spec. Now let's be clear, this is not how YAMLs of any specific record of this CRD would look. Instead, this is simply where we define the requirements for the CRD inside of Kubernetes. Once created, Kubernetes will accept resources matching the spec and we can start making our own records of this type.

Here's an example YAML for a CRD spec, which we are calling `delayedjob`. This highly simplistic CRD is intended to start a container image job on a delay, which prevents users from having to script in a delayed start for their container. This CRD is quite brittle, and we don't recommend anyone actually use it, but it does well to highlight the process of building a CRD. Let's start with a full CRD spec YAML, then break it down:

Custom-resource-definition-1.yaml

```yaml
apiVersion: apiextensions.k8s.io/v1
kind: CustomResourceDefinition
metadata:
  name: delayedjobs.delayedresources.mydomain.com
spec:
  group: delayedresources.mydomain.com
  versions:
    - name: v1
      served: true
      storage: true
      schema:
        openAPIV3Schema:
          type: object
          properties:
            spec:
              type: object
              properties:
                delaySeconds:
                  type: integer
                image:
                  type: string
  scope: Namespaced
  conversion:
    strategy: None
  names:
    plural: delayedjobs
    singular: delayedjob
    kind: DelayedJob
    shortNames:
      - dj
```

Let's review the parts of this file. At first glance, it looks like your typical Kubernetes
YAML spec – and that's because it is! In the `apiVersion` field, we have
`apiextensions.k8s.io/v1`, which is the standard since Kubernetes `1.16`
(before then it was `apiextensions.k8s.io/v1beta1`). Our `kind` will always be
`CustomResourceDefinition`.

The `metadata` field is when things start to get specific to our resource. We need to structure the `name` metadata field as the `plural` form of our resource, then a period, then its group. Let's take a quick diversion from our YAML file to discuss how groups work in the Kubernetes API.

Understanding Kubernetes API groups

Groups are a way that Kubernetes segments resources in its API. Each group corresponds to a different subpath of the Kubernetes API server.

By default, there is a legacy group called the core group – which corresponds to resources accessed on the `/api/v1` endpoint in the Kubernetes REST API. By extension, these legacy group resources have `apiVersion: v1` in their YAML specs. An example of one of the resources in the core group is the Pod.

Next, there is the set of named groups – which correspond to resources that can be accessed on REST URLs formed as `/apis/<GROUP NAME>/<VERSION>`. These named groups form the bulk of Kubernetes resources. However, the oldest and most basic resources, such as the Pod, Service, Secret, and Volume, are in the core group. An example of a resource that is in a named group is the `StorageClass` resource, which is in the `storage.k8s.io` group.

> **Important note**
> To see which resource is in which group, you can check the official Kubernetes API docs for whatever version of Kubernetes you are using. For example, the version `1.18` docs would be at `https://kubernetes.io/docs/reference/generated/kubernetes-api/v1.18`.

CRDs can specify their own named group, which means that the specific CRD will be available on a REST endpoint that the Kubernetes API server can listen on. With that in mind, let's get back to our YAML file, so we can talk about the main portion of the CRD – the versions spec.

Understanding custom resource definition versions

As you can see, we have chosen the group `delayedresources.mydomain.com`. This group would theoretically hold any other CRDs of the delayed kind – for instance, `DelayedDaemonSet` or `DelayedDeployment`.

Next, we have the main portion of our CRD. Under `versions`, we can define one or more CRD versions (in the `name` field), along with the API specification for that version of the CRD. Then, when you create an instance of your CRD, you can define which version you will be using for the version parameter in the `apiVersion` key of your YAML – for instance, `apps/v1`, or in this case, `delayedresources.mydomain.com/v1`.

Each version item also has a `served` attribute, which is essentially a way to define whether the given version is enabled or disabled. If `served` is `false`, the version will not be created by the Kubernetes API, and the API requests (or `kubectl` commands) for that version will fail.

In addition, it is possible to define a `deprecated` key on a specific version, which will cause Kubernetes to return a warning message when requests are made to the API using the deprecated version. This is how a CRD. `yaml` file with a deprecated version looks – we have removed some of the spec to keep the YAML short:

Custom-resource-definition-2.yaml

```yaml
apiVersion: apiextensions.k8s.io/v1
kind: CustomResourceDefinition
metadata:
  name: delayedjob.delayedresources.mydomain.com
spec:
  group: delayedresources.mydomain.com
  versions:
    - name: v1
      served: true
      storage: false
      deprecated: true
      deprecationWarning: "DelayedJob v1 is deprecated!"
      schema:
        openAPIV3Schema:
          ...
    - name: v2
      served: true
      storage: true
      schema:
        openAPIV3Schema:
```

```
        . . .
    scope: Namespaced
    conversion:
        strategy: None
    names:
        plural: delayedjobs
        singular: delayedjob
        kind: DelayedJob
        shortNames:
        - dj
```

As you can see, we have marked `v1` as deprecated, and also include a deprecation warning for Kubernetes to send as a response. If we do not include a deprecation warning, a default message will be used.

Moving further down, we have the `storage` key, which interacts with the `served` key. The reason this is necessary is that while Kubernetes supports multiple active (aka `served`) versions of a resource at the same time, only one of those versions can be stored in the control plane. However, the `served` attribute means that multiple versions of a resource can be served by the API. So how does that even work?

The answer is that Kubernetes will convert the CRD object from whatever the stored version is to the version you ask for (or vice versa, when creating a resource).

How is this conversion handled? Let's skip past the rest of the version attributes to the `conversion` key to see how.

The `conversion` key lets you specify a strategy for how Kubernetes will convert CRD objects between whatever your served version is and whatever the stored version is. If the two versions are the same – for instance, if you ask for a `v1` resource and the stored version is `v1`, then no conversion will happen.

The default value here as of Kubernetes 1.13 is `none`. With the `none` setting, Kubernetes will not do any conversion between fields. It will simply include the fields that are supposed to be present on the `served` (or stored, if creating a resource) version.

The other possible conversion strategy is `Webhook`, which allows you to define a custom webhook that will take in one version and do the proper conversion to your intended version. Here is an example of our CRD with a `Webhook` conversion strategy – we've cut out some of the version schema for conciseness:

Custom-resource-definition-3.yaml

```yaml
apiVersion: apiextensions.k8s.io/v1
kind: CustomResourceDefinition
metadata:
  name: delayedjob.delayedresources.mydomain.com
spec:
  group: delayedresources.mydomain.com
  versions:
    - name: v1
      served: true
      storage: true
      schema:
        openAPIV3Schema:

          ...
  scope: Namespaced
  conversion:
    strategy: Webhook
    webhook:
      clientConfig:
        url: "https://webhook-conversion.com/delayedjob"
  names:
    plural: delayedjobs
    singular: delayedjob
    kind: DelayedJob
    shortNames:
      - dj
```

As you can see, the Webhook strategy lets us define a URL that requests will be made to with information about the incoming resource object, its current version, and the version it needs to be converted to.

The idea is that our Webhook server will then handle the conversion and pass back the corrected Kubernetes resource object. The Webhook strategy is complex and can have many possible configurations, which we will not get into in depth in this book.

> **Important note**
>
> To see how conversion Webhooks can be configured, check the official Kubernetes documentation at `https://kubernetes.io/docs/tasks/extend-kubernetes/custom-resources/custom-resource-definition-versioning/`.

Now, back to our `version` entry in the YAML! Under the `served` and `storage` keys, we see the `schema` object, which contains the actual specification of our resource. As previously mentioned, this follows the OpenAPI Spec v3 schema.

The `schema` object, which was removed from the preceding code block for space reasons, is as follows:

Custom-resource-definition-3.yaml (continued)

```yaml
schema:
  openAPIV3Schema:
    type: object
    properties:
      spec:
        type: object
        properties:
          delaySeconds:
            type: integer
          image:
            type: string
```

As you can see, we support a field for `delaySeconds`, which will be an integer, and `image`, which is a string that corresponds to our container image. If we really wanted to make the `DelayedJob` production-ready, we would want to include all sorts of other options to make it closer to the original Kubernetes Job resource – but that isn't our intent here.

Moving further back in the original code block, outside the versions list, we see some other attributes. First is the `scope` attribute, which can be either `Cluster` or `Namespaced`. This tells Kubernetes whether to treat instances of the CRD object as namespace-specific resources (such as Pods, Deployments, and so on) or instead as cluster-wide resources – like namespaces themselves, since getting namespace objects within a namespace doesn't make any sense!

Finally, we have the `names` block, which lets you define both a plural and singular form of your resource name, to be used in various situations (for instance, `kubectl get pods` and `kubectl get pod` both work).

The `names` block also lets you define the camel-cased `kind` value, which will be used in the resource YAML, as well as one or more `shortNames`, which can be used to refer to the resource in the API or `kubectl` – for instance, `kubectl get po`.

With our CRD specification YAML explained, let's take a look at an instance of our CRD – as defined by the spec we just reviewed, the YAML will look like this:

Delayed-job.yaml

```yaml
apiVersion: delayedresources.mydomain.com/v1
kind: DelayedJob
metadata:
  name: my-instance-of-delayed-job
spec:
  delaySeconds: 6000
  image: "busybox"
```

As you can see, this is just like our CRD defined this object. Now, with all our pieces in place, let's test out our CRD!

Testing a custom resource definition

Let's go ahead and test out our CRD concept on Kubernetes:

1. First, let's create the CRD spec in Kubernetes – the same way we would create any other object:

    ```
    kubectl apply -f delayedjob-crd-spec.yaml
    ```

    This will result in the following output:

    ```
    customresourcedefinition "delayedjob.delayedresources.
    mydomain.com" has been created
    ```

2. Now, Kubernetes will accept requests for our `DelayedJob` resource. We can test this out by finally creating one using the preceding resource YAML:

    ```
    kubectl apply -f my-delayed-job.yaml
    ```

If we've defined our CRD properly, we will see the following output:

```
delayedjob "my-instance-of-delayed-job" has been created
```

As you can see, the Kubernetes API server has successfully created our instance of `DelayedJob`!

Now, you may be asking a very relevant question – now what? This is an excellent question, because the truth is that we have accomplished nothing more so far than essentially adding a new `table` to the Kubernetes API database.

Just because we gave our `DelayedJob` resource an application image and a `delaySeconds` field does not mean that any functionality like what we intend will actually occur. By creating our instance of `DelayedJob`, we have just added an entry to that `table`. We can fetch it, edit it, or delete it using the Kubernetes API or `kubectl` commands, but no application functionality has been implemented.

In order to actually get our `DelayedJob` resource to do something, we need a custom controller that will take our instance of `DelayedJob` and do something with it. In the end, we still need to implement actual container functionality using the official Kubernetes resources – Pods et al.

This is what we're going to discuss now. There are many ways to build custom controllers for Kubernetes, but a popular way is the **Operator pattern**. Let's move onto the next section to see how we can give our `DelayedJob` resource a life of its own.

Self-managing functionality with Kubernetes operators

No discussion of Kubernetes operators would be possible without first discussing the **Operator Framework**. A common misconception is that operators are specifically built via the Operator Framework. The Operator Framework is an open source framework originally created by Red Hat to make it easy to write Kubernetes operators.

In reality, an operator is simply a custom controller that interfaces with Kubernetes and acts on resources. The Operator Framework is one opinionated way to make Kubernetes operators, but there are many other open source frameworks you can use – or, you can make one from scratch!

When building an operator using frameworks, two of the most popular options are the aforementioned **Operator Framework** and **Kubebuilder**.

Both of these projects have a lot in common. They both make use of `controller-tools` and `controller-runtime`, which are two libraries for building Kubernetes controllers that are officially supported by the Kubernetes project. If you are building an operator from scratch, using these officially supported controller libraries will make things much easier.

Unlike the Operator Framework, Kubebuilder is an official part of the Kubernetes project, much like the `controller-tools` and `controller-runtime` libraries – but both projects have their pros and cons. Importantly, both these options, and the Operator pattern in general, have the controller running on the cluster. It may seem obvious that this is the best option, but you could run your controller outside of the cluster and have it work the same. To get started with the Operator Framework, check the official GitHub at `https://github.com/operator-framework`. For Kubebuilder, you can check `https://github.com/kubernetes-sigs/kubebuilder`.

Most operators, regardless of the framework, follow a control-loop paradigm – let's see how this idea works.

Mapping the operator control loop

A control loop is a control scheme in system design and programming that consists of a never-ending loop of logical processes. Typically, a control loop implements a measure-analyze-adjust approach, where it measures the current state of the system, analyzes what changes are required to bring it in line with the intended state, and then adjusts the system components to bring it in line with (or at least closer to) the intended state.

In Kubernetes operators or controllers specifically, this operation usually works like this:

1. First, a `watch` step – that is, watching the Kubernetes API for changes in the intended state, which is stored in `etcd`.

2. Then, an `analyze` step – which is the controller deciding what to do to bring the cluster state in line with the intended state.

3. And lastly, an `update` step – which is updating the cluster state to fulfill the intent of the cluster changes.

To help understand the control loop, here is a diagram showing how the pieces fit together:

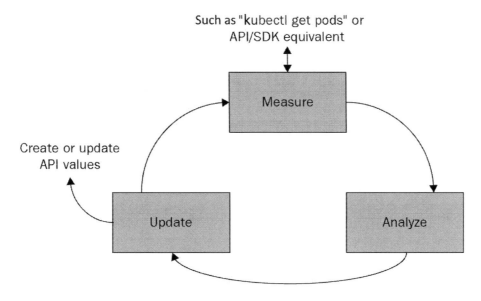

Figure 13.1 – Measure Analyze Update Loop

Let's use the Kubernetes scheduler – which is itself a control loop process – to illustrate this:

1. Let's start with a hypothetical cluster in a steady state: all Pods are scheduled, Nodes are healthy, and everything is operating normally.

2. Then, a user creates a new Pod.

We've discussed before that the kubelet works on a `pull` basis. This means that when a kubelet creates a Pod on its Node, that Pod was already assigned to that Node via the scheduler. However, when Pods are first created via a `kubectl create` or `kubectl apply` command, the Pod isn't scheduled or assigned anywhere. This is where our scheduler control loop starts:

1. The first step is **Measure**, where the scheduler reads the state of the Kubernetes API. When listing Pods from the API, it discovers that one of the Pods is not assigned to a Node. It now moves to the next step.

2. Next, the scheduler performs an analysis of the cluster state and Pod requirements in order to decide which Node the Pod should be assigned to. As we discussed in previous chapters, this takes into account Pod resource limits and requests, Node statuses, placement controls, and so on, which makes it a fairly complex process. Once this processing is complete, the update step can start.

3. Finally, **Update** – the scheduler updates the cluster state by assigning the Pod to the Node obtained from the *step 2* analysis. At this point, the kubelet takes over on its own control loop and creates the relevant container(s) for the Pod on its Node.

Next, let's take what we learned from the scheduler control loop and apply it to our very own `DelayedJob` resource.

Designing an operator for a custom resource definition

Actually, coding an operator for our `DelayedJob` CRD is outside the scope of our book since it requires knowledge of a programming language. If you're choosing a programming language to build an operator with, Go offers the most interoperability with the Kubernetes SDK, **controller-tools**, and **controller-runtime**, but any programming language where you can write HTTP requests will work, since that is the basis for all of the SDKs.

However, we will still walk through the steps of implementing an operator for our `DelayedJob` CRD with some pseudocode. Let's take it step by step.

Step 1: Measure

First comes the **Measure** step, which we will implement in our pseudocode as a `while` loop that runs forever. In a production implementation, there would be debouncing, error handling, and a bunch of other concerns, but we'll keep it simple for this illustrative example.

Take a look at the pseudo code for this loop, which is essentially the main function of our application:

Main-function.pseudo

```
// The main function of our controller
function main() {
  // While loop which runs forever
  while() {
    // fetch the full list of delayed job objects from the
cluster
    var currentDelayedJobs = kubeAPIConnector.
list("delayedjobs");
    // Call the Analysis step function on the list
```

```
      var jobsToSchedule =
analyzeDelayedJobs(currentDelayedJobs);
      // Schedule our Jobs with added delay
      scheduleDelayedJobs(jobsToSchedule);
      wait(5000);
  }
}
```

As you can see, the loop in our `main` function calls the Kubernetes API to find a list of the `delayedjobs` CRDs stored in `etcd`. This is the `measure` step. It then calls the analysis step, and with the results of that, calls the update step to schedule any `DelayedJobs` that need to be scheduled.

> **Important note**
>
> Keep in mind that the Kubernetes scheduler is still going to do the actual container scheduling in this example – but we need to boil down our `DelayedJob` into an official Kubernetes resource first.

After the update step, our loop waits for a full 5 seconds before performing the loop again. This sets the cadence of the control loop. Next, let's move on to the analysis step.

Step 2: Analyze

Next, let's review the **Analysis** step of our operator, which is the `analyzeDelayedJobs` function in our controller pseudocode:

Analysis-function.pseudo

```
// The analysis function
function analyzeDelayedJobs(listOfDelayedJobs) {
  var listOfJobsToSchedule = [];
  foreach(dj in listOfDelayedJobs) {
    // Check if dj has been scheduled, if not, add a Job object with
    // added delay command to the to schedule array
    if(dj.annotations["is-scheduled"] != "true") {
      listOfJobsToSchedule.push({
        Image: dj.image,
        Command: "sleep " + dj.delaySeconds + "s",
```

```
                originalDjName: dj.name
        });
    }
    }
    return listOfJobsToSchedule;
}
```

As you can see, the preceding function loops through the list of DelayedJob objects from the cluster as passed from the **Measure** loop. It then checks to see if the DelayedJob has been scheduled yet by checking the value of one of the object's annotations. If it hasn't been scheduled yet, it adds an object to an array called listOfJobsToSchedule, which contains the image specified in the DelayedJob object, a command to sleep for the number of seconds that was specified in the DelayedJob object, and the original name of the DelayedJob, which we will use to mark as scheduled in the **Update** step.

Finally, in the **Analyze** step the analyzeDelayedJobs function returns our newly created listOfJobsToSchedule array back to the main function. Let's wrap up our Operator design with the final update step, which is the scheduleDelayedJobs function in our main loop.

Step 3: Update

Finally, the **Update** part of our control loop will take the outputs from our analysis and update the cluster as necessary to create the intended state. Here's the pseudocode:

Update-function.pseudo

```
// The update function
function scheduleDelayedJobs(listOfJobs) {
    foreach(job in listOfDelayedJobs) {
        // First, go ahead and schedule a regular Kubernetes Job
        // which the Kube scheduler can pick up on.
        // The delay seconds have already been added to the job
spec
        // in the analysis step
        kubeAPIConnector.create("job", job.image, job.command);
        // Finally, mark our original DelayedJob with a "scheduled"
        // attribute so our controller doesn't try to schedule it
again
```

```
kubeAPIConnector.update("delayedjob", job.originalDjName,
annotations: {
    "is-scheduled": "true"
});
}
}
```

In this case, we are taking our regular Kubernetes object, which was derived from our `DelayedJob` object, and creating it in Kubernetes so the `Kube` scheduler can pick up on it, create the relevant Pod, and manage it. Once we create the regular Job object with the delay, we also update our `DelayedJob` CRD instance with an annotation that sets the `is-scheduled` annotation to `true`, preventing it from getting rescheduled.

This completes our control loop – from this point, the `Kube` scheduler takes over and our CRD is given life as a Kubernetes Job object, which controls a Pod, which is finally assigned to a Node and a container is scheduled to run our code!

This example is of course highly simplified, but you would be surprised how many Kubernetes operators perform a simple control loop to coordinate CRDs and boil them down to basic Kubernetes resources. Operators can get very complicated and perform application-specific functions such as backing up databases, emptying Persistent Volumes, and others – but this functionality is usually tightly coupled to whatever is being controlled.

Now that we've discussed the Operator pattern in a Kubernetes controller, we can talk about some of the open source options for cloud-specific Kubernetes controllers.

Using cloud-specific Kubernetes extensions

Usually available by default in managed Kubernetes services such as Amazon EKS, Azure AKS, and Google Cloud's GKE, cloud-specific Kubernetes extensions and controllers can integrate tightly with the cloud platform in question and make it easy to control other cloud resources from Kubernetes.

Even without adding any additional third-party components, a lot of this cloud-specific functionality is available in upstream Kubernetes via the **cloud-controller-manager (CCM)** component, which contains many options for integrating with the major cloud providers. This is the functionality that is usually enabled by default in the managed Kubernetes services on each public cloud – but they can be integrated with any cluster running on that specific cloud platform, managed or not.

In this section, we will review a few of the more common cloud extensions to Kubernetes, both in **cloud-controller-manager (CCM)** and functionality that requires the installation of other controllers such as **external-dns** and **cluster-autoscaler**. Let's start with some of the heavily used CCM functionality.

Understanding the cloud-controller-manager component

As reviewed in *Chapter 1, Communicating with Kubernetes*, CCM is an officially supported Kubernetes controller that provides hooks into the functionality of several public cloud services. To function, the CCM component needs to be started with access permissions to the cloud service in question – for instance, an IAM role in AWS.

For officially supported clouds such as AWS, Azure, and Google Cloud, CCM can simply be run as a DaemonSet within the cluster. We use a DaemonSet since CCM can perform tasks such as creating persistent storage in the cloud provider, and it needs to be able to attach storage to specific Nodes. If you're using a cloud that isn't officially supported, you can run CCM for that specific cloud, and you should follow the specific instructions in that project. These alternate types of CCM are usually open source and can be found on GitHub. For the specifics of installing CCM, let's move on to the next section.

Installing cloud-controller-manager

Typically, CCM is configured when the cluster is created. As mentioned in the previous section, managed services such as EKS, AKS, and GKE will already have this component enabled, but even Kops and Kubeadm expose the CCM component as a flag in the installation process.

Assuming you have not installed CCM any other way and plan to use one of the officially supported public clouds from the upstream version, you can install CCM as a DaemonSet.

First, you will need a `ServiceAccount`:

Service-account.yaml

```
apiVersion: v1
kind: ServiceAccount
metadata:
  name: cloud-controller-manager
  namespace: kube-system
```

This `ServiceAccount` will be used to give the necessary access to the CCM.

Next, we'll need a `ClusterRoleBinding`:

Clusterrolebinding.yaml

```
apiVersion: rbac.authorization.k8s.io/v1
kind: ClusterRoleBinding
metadata:
  name: system:cloud-controller-manager
subjects:
- kind: ServiceAccount
  name: cloud-controller-manager
  namespace: kube-system
roleRef:
  apiGroup: rbac.authorization.k8s.io
  kind: ClusterRole
  name: cluster-admin
```

As you can see, we need to give the `cluster-admin` role access to our CCM service account. The CCM will need to be able to edit Nodes, among other things.

Finally, we can deploy the CCM `DaemonSet` itself. You will need to fill in this YAML file with the proper settings for your specific cloud provider – check your cloud provider's documentation on Kubernetes for this information.

The `DaemonSet` spec is quite long, so we'll review it in two parts. First, we have the template for the `DaemonSet` with the required labels and names:

Daemonset.yaml

```
apiVersion: apps/v1
kind: DaemonSet
metadata:
  labels:
    k8s-app: cloud-controller-manager
  name: cloud-controller-manager
  namespace: kube-system
spec:
  selector:
```

```
        matchLabels:
            k8s-app: cloud-controller-manager
    template:
        metadata:
            labels:
                k8s-app: cloud-controller-manager
```

As you can see, to match our `ServiceAccount`, we are running the CCM in the `kube-system` namespace. We are also labeling the `DaemonSet` with the `k8s-app` label to distinguish it as a Kubernetes control plane component.

Next, we have the spec of the `DaemonSet`:

Daemonset.yaml (continued)

```
    spec:
        serviceAccountName: cloud-controller-manager
        containers:
        - name: cloud-controller-manager
            image: k8s.gcr.io/cloud-controller-manager:<current ccm
version for your version of k8s>
            command:
            - /usr/local/bin/cloud-controller-manager
            - --cloud-provider=<cloud provider name>
            - --leader-elect=true
            - --use-service-account-credentials
            - --allocate-node-cidrs=true
            - --configure-cloud-routes=true
            - --cluster-cidr=<CIDR of the cluster based on Cloud
Provider>
        tolerations:
        - key: node.cloudprovider.kubernetes.io/uninitialized
            value: "true"
            effect: NoSchedule
        - key: node-role.kubernetes.io/master
            effect: NoSchedule
        nodeSelector:
            node-role.kubernetes.io/master: ""
```

As you can see, there are a couple of places in this spec that you will need to review your chosen cloud provider's documentation or cluster networking setup to find the proper values. Particularly in the networking flags such as `--cluster-cidr` and `--configure-cloud-routes`, where values could change based on how you have set up your cluster, even on a single cloud provider.

Now that we have CCM running on our cluster one way or another, let's dive into some of the capabilities it provides.

Understanding the cloud-controller-manager capabilities

The default CCM provides capabilities in a few key areas. For starters, the CCM contains subsidiary controllers for Nodes, routes, and Services. Let's review each in turn to see what it affords us, starting with the Node/Node lifecycle controller.

The CCM Node/Node lifecycle controller

The CCM Node controller makes sure that the cluster state, as far as which Nodes are in the cluster, is equivalent to what is in the cloud provider's systems. A simple example of this is autoscaling groups in AWS. When using AWS EKS (or just Kubernetes on AWS EC2, though that requires additional configuration), it is possible to configure worker node groups in an AWS autoscaling group that will scale up or down depending on the CPU or memory usage of the nodes. When these nodes are added and initialized by the cloud provider, the CCM nodes controller will ensure that the cluster has a node resource for each Node presented by the cloud provider.

Next, let's move on to the routes controller.

The CCM routes controller

The CCM routes controller takes care of configuring your cloud provider's networking settings in a way that supports a Kubernetes cluster. This can include the allocation of IPs and setting routes between Nodes. The services controller also handles networking – but the external aspect.

The CCM services controller

The CCM services controller provides a lot of the "magic" of running Kubernetes on a public cloud provider. One such aspect that we reviewed in *Chapter 5, Services and Ingress – Communicating with the Outside World*, is the `LoadBalancer` service. For instance, on a cluster configured with AWS CCM, a Service of type `LoadBalancer` will automatically configure a matching AWS Load Balancer resource, providing an easy way to expose services in your cluster without dealing with `NodePort` settings or even Ingress.

Now that we understand what the CCM provides, we can venture further and talk about a couple of the other cloud provider extensions that are often used when running Kubernetes on the public cloud. First, let's look at `external-dns`.

Using external-dns with Kubernetes

The `external-dns` library is an officially supported Kubernetes add-on that allows the cluster to configure external DNS providers to provide DNS resolution for services and ingress in an automated fashion. The `external-dns` add-on supports a broad range of cloud providers such as AWS and Azure, and also other DNS services such as Cloudflare.

> **Important note**
>
> In order to install `external-dns`, you can check the official GitHub repository at `https://github.com/kubernetes-sigs/external-dns`.

Once `external-dns` is implemented on your cluster, it's simple to create new DNS records in an automated fashion. To test `external-dns` with a service, we simply need to create a service in Kubernetes with the proper annotation.

Let's see what this looks like:

service.yaml

```yaml
apiVersion: v1
kind: Service
metadata:
  name: my-service-with-dns
  annotations:
    external-dns.alpha.kubernetes.io/hostname: myapp.mydomain.com
```

```
spec:
  type: LoadBalancer
  ports:
  - port: 80
    name: http
    targetPort: 80
  selector:
    app: my-app
```

As you can see, we only need to add an annotation for the `external-dns` controller to check, with the domain record to be created in DNS. The domain and hosted zone must of course be accessible by your `external-dns` controller – for instance, on AWS Route 53 or Azure DNS. Check the specific documentation on the `external-dns` GitHub repository for specifics.

Once the Service is up and running, `external-dns` will pick up the annotation and create a new DNS record. This pattern is excellent for multi-tenancy or per-version deploys since with something like a Helm chart, variables can be used to change the domain depending on which version or branch of the application is deployed – for instance, `v1.myapp.mydomain.com`.

For Ingress, this is even easier – you just need to specify a host on your Ingress record, like so:

ingress.yaml

```
apiVersion: networking.k8s.io/v1beta1
kind: Ingress
metadata:
  name: my-domain-ingress
  annotations:
    kubernetes.io/ingress.class: "nginx".
spec:
  rules:
  - host: myapp.mydomain.com
    http:
      paths:
      - backend:
          serviceName: my-app-service
          servicePort: 80
```

This host value will automatically create a DNS record pointing to whatever method your Ingress is using – for instance, a Load Balancer on AWS.

Next, let's talk about how the **cluster-autoscaler** library works.

Using the cluster-autoscaler add-on

Similar to `external-dns`, `cluster-autoscaler` is an officially supported add-on for Kubernetes that supports some major cloud providers with specific functionality. The purpose of `cluster-autoscaler` is to trigger the scaling of the number of Nodes in a cluster. It performs this process by controlling the cloud provider's own scaling resources, such as AWS autoscaling groups.

The cluster autoscaler will perform an upward scaling action the moment any single Pod fails to schedule due to resource constraints on a Node, but only if a Node of the existing Node size (for instance, a `t3.medium` sized Node in AWS) would allow the Pod to be scheduled.

Similarly, the cluster autoscaler will perform a downward scaling action the moment any Node could be emptied of Pods without causing memory or CPU pressure on any of the other Nodes.

To install `cluster-autoscaler`, simply follow the correct instructions from your cloud provider, for the cluster type and intended version of the `cluster-autoscaler`. For instance, the AWS installation instructions for `cluster-autoscaler` on EKS are found at `https://aws.amazon.com/premiumsupport/knowledge-center/eks-cluster-autoscaler-setup/`.

Next, let's look at how you can find open and closed source extensions for Kubernetes by examining the Kubernetes ecosystem.

Integrating with the ecosystem

The Kubernetes (and more generally, cloud-native) ecosystem is massive, consisting of hundreds of popular open source software libraries, and thousands more fledgling ones. This can be tough to navigate since every month brings new technologies to vet, and acquisitions, rollups, and companies going out of business can turn your favorite open source library into an unmaintained mess.

Thankfully, there is some structure in this ecosystem, and it's worth knowing about it in order to help navigate the dearth of options in cloud-native open source. The first big structural component of this is the **Cloud Native Computing Foundation** or **CNCF**.

Introducing the Cloud Native Computing Foundation

The CNCF is a sub-foundation of the Linux Foundation, which is a non-profit entity that hosts open source projects and coordinates an ever-changing list of companies that contribute to and use open source software.

The CNCF was founded almost entirely to shepherd the future of the Kubernetes project. It was announced alongside the 1.0 release of Kubernetes and has since grown to encompass hundreds of projects in the cloud-native space – from Prometheus to Envoy to Helm, and many more.

The best way to see an overview of the CNCF's constituent projects is to check out the CNCF Cloud Native Landscape, which can be found at `https://landscape.cncf.io/`.

The CNCF Landscape is a good place to start if you are interested in possible solutions to a problem you are experiencing with Kubernetes or cloud-native. For every category (monitoring, logging, serverless, service mesh, and others), there are several open source options to vet and choose from.

This is both a strength and weakness of the current ecosystem of cloud-native technologies. There are a significant number of options available, which makes the correct path often unclear, but also means that you will likely be able to find a solution that is close to your exact needs.

The CNCF also operates an official Kubernetes forum, which can be joined from the Kubernetes official website at `kubernetes.io`. The URL of the Kubernetes forums is `https://discuss.kubernetes.io/`.

Finally, it is relevant to mention *KubeCon/CloudNativeCon*, a large conference that is run by the CNCF and encompasses topics including Kubernetes itself and many ecosystem projects. *KubeCon* gets larger every year, with almost 12,000 attendees for *KubeCon North America* in 2019.

Summary

In this chapter, we learned about extending Kubernetes. First, we talked about CRDs – what they are, some relevant use cases, and how to implement them in your cluster. Next, we reviewed the concept of an operator in Kubernetes and discussed how to use an operator, or custom controller, to give life to your CRD.

Then, we discussed cloud-provider-specific extensions to Kubernetes including `cloud-controller-manager`, `external-dns`, and `cluster-autoscaler`. Finally, we wrapped up with an introduction to the cloud-native open source ecosystem at large and some great ways to discover projects for your use case.

The skills you used in this chapter will help you extend your Kubernetes cluster to interface with your cloud provider as well as your own custom functionality.

In the next chapter, we'll talk about two nascent architectural patterns as applied to Kubernetes – serverless and service meshes.

Questions

1. What is the difference between a served version and a stored version of a CRD?

2. What are three typical parts of a custom controller or operator control loop?

3. How does `cluster-autoscaler` interact with existing cloud provider scaling solutions such as AWS autoscaling groups?

Further reading

- CNCF Landscape: `https://landscape.cncf.io/`

- Official Kubernetes Forums: `https://discuss.kubernetes.io/`

14
Service Meshes and Serverless

This chapter discusses advanced Kubernetes patterns. First, it details the in-vogue service mesh pattern, where observability and service-to-service discovery are handled by a sidecar proxy, as well as a guide to setting up Istio, a popular service mesh. Lastly, it describes the serverless pattern and how it can be applied in Kubernetes. The major case study in this chapter will include setting up Istio for an example application and service discovery, along with Istio ingress gateways.

Let's start with a discussion of the sidecar proxy, which builds the foundation of service-to-service connectivity for service meshes.

In this chapter, we will cover the following topics:

- Using sidecar proxies
- Adding a service mesh to Kubernetes
- Implementing serverless on Kubernetes

Technical requirements

In order to run the commands detailed in this chapter, you will need a computer that supports the `kubectl` command-line tool, along with a working Kubernetes cluster. See *Chapter 1, Communicating with Kubernetes*, for several methods for getting up and running with Kubernetes quickly, and for instructions on how to install the `kubectl` tool.

The code used in this chapter can be found in the book's GitHub repository at `https://github.com/PacktPublishing/Cloud-Native-with-Kubernetes/tree/master/Chapter14`.

Using sidecar proxies

As we mentioned earlier in this book, a sidecar is a pattern where a Pod contains another container in addition to the actual application container to be run. This additional "extra" container is the sidecar. Sidecars can be used for a number of different reasons. Some of the most popular uses for sidecars are monitoring, logging, and proxying.

For logging, a sidecar container can fetch application logs from the application container (since they can share volumes and communicate on localhost), before sending the logs to a centralized logging stack, or parsing them for the purpose of alerting. It's a similar story for monitoring, where the sidecar Pod can track and send metrics about the application Pod.

With a sidecar proxy, when requests come into the Pod, they first go to the proxy container, which then routes requests (after logging or performing other filtering) to the application container. Similarly, when requests leave the application container, they first go to the proxy, which can provide routing out of the Pod.

Normally, proxy sidecars such as NGINX only provide proxying for requests coming into a Pod. However, in the service mesh pattern, both requests coming into and leaving the Pod go through the proxy, which provides the foundation for the service mesh pattern itself.

Refer to the following diagram to see how a sidecar proxy can interact with an application container:

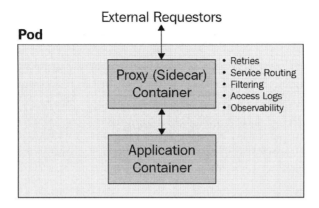

Figure 14.1 – Proxy sidecar

As you can see, the sidecar proxy is in charge of routing requests to and from the application container in the Pod, allowing for functionality such as service routing, logging, and filtering.

The sidecar proxy pattern is an alternative to a DaemonSet-based proxy, where a proxy Pod on each node handles proxying to other Pods on that node. The Kubernetes proxy itself is similar to a DaemonSet pattern. Using a sidecar proxy can provide more flexibility than using a DaemonSet proxy, at the expense of performance efficiency, since many extra containers need to be run.

Some popular proxy options for Kubernetes include the following:

- *NGINX*

- *HAProxy*

- *Envoy*

While NGINX and HAProxy are more traditional proxies, Envoy was built specifically for a distributed, cloud-native environment. For this reason, Envoy forms the core of popular service meshes and API gateways built for Kubernetes.

Before we get to Envoy, let's discuss the installation of other proxies as sidecars.

Using NGINX as a sidecar reverse proxy

Before we specify how NGINX can be used as a sidecar proxy, it is relevant to note that in an upcoming Kubernetes release, the sidecar will be a Kubernetes resource type that will allow easy injection of sidecar containers to large numbers of Pods. Currently however, sidecar containers must be specified at the Pod or controller (ReplicaSet, Deployment, and others) level.

Let's take a look at how we can configure NGINX as a sidecar, with the following Deployment YAML, which we will not create just yet. This process is a bit more manual than using the NGINX Ingress Controller.

We've split the YAML into two parts for space reasons and trimmed some of the fat, but you can see it in its entirety in the code repository. Let's start with the containers spec for our deployment:

Nginx-sidecar.yaml:

```
spec:
  containers:
  - name: myapp
    image: ravirdv/http-responder:latest
    imagePullPolicy: IfNotPresent
  - name: nginx-sidecar
    image: nginx
    imagePullPolicy: IfNotPresent
    volumeMounts:
      - name: secrets
        mountPath: /app/cert
      - name: config
        mountPath: /etc/nginx/nginx.conf
        subPath: nginx.conf
```

As you can see, we specify two containers, both our main app container, `myapp`, and the `nginx` sidecar, where we inject some configuration via volume mounts, as well as some TLS certificates.

Next, let's look at the `volumes` spec in the same file, where we inject some certs (from a secret) and `config` (from a `ConfigMap`):

```
volumes:
  - name: secrets
    secret:
      secretName: nginx-certificates
      items:
        - key: server-cert
          path: server.pem
        - key: server-key
          path: server-key.pem
  - name: config
    configMap:
      name: nginx-configuration
```

As you can see, we need both a cert and a secret key.

Next, we need to create the NGINX configuration using `ConfigMap`. The NGINX configuration looks like this:

nginx.conf:

```
http {
    sendfile        on;
    include         mime.types;
    default_type    application/octet-stream;
    keepalive_timeout  80;
    server {
        ssl_certificate        /app/cert/server.pem;
        ssl_certificate_key   /app/cert/server-key.pem;
        ssl_protocols TLSv1.2;
        ssl_ciphers
EECDH+AES128:RSA+AES128:EECDH+AES256:RSA+AES256:
!EECDH+3DES:!RSA+3DES:!MD5;
        ssl_prefer_server_ciphers on;
        listen        443 ssl;
        server_name  localhost;
        location / {
```

```
        proxy_set_header X-Forwarded-For $proxy_add_x_
forwarded_for;
        proxy_set_header Host $http_host;
        proxy_pass http://127.0.0.1:5000/;
      }
    }
  }
worker_processes  1;
events {
    worker_connections  1024;
}
```

As you can see, we have some basic NGINX configuration. Importantly, we have the proxy_pass field, which proxies requests to a port on 127.0.0.1, or localhost. Since containers in a Pod can share localhost ports, this acts as our sidecar proxy. We won't review all the other lines for the purposes of this book, but check the NGINX docs for more information about what each line means (https://nginx.org/en/docs/).

Now, let's create the ConfigMap from this file. Use the following command to imperatively create the ConfigMap:

```
kubectl create cm nginx-configuration --from-file=nginx.conf=./
nginx.conf
```

This will result in the following output:

```
Configmap "nginx-configuration" created
```

Next, let's make our certificates for TLS in NGINX, and embed them in a Kubernetes secret. You will need the CFSSL (CloudFlare's PKI/TLS open source toolkit) library installed to follow these instructions, but you can use any other method to create your cert.

First, we need to create the **Certificate Authority** (**CA**). Start with the JSON configuration for the CA:

nginxca.json:

```
{
    "CN": "mydomain.com",
    "hosts": [
```

```
            "mydomain.com",
            "www.mydomain.com"
    ],
    "key": {
            "algo": "rsa",
            "size": 2048
    },
    "names": [
        {
                "C": "US",
                "ST": "MD",
                "L": "United States"
        }
    ]
}
```

Now, use CFSSL to create the CA certificate:

```
cfssl gencert -initca nginxca.json | cfssljson -bare nginxca
```

Next, we will require the CA config:

Nginxca-config.json:

```
{
    "signing": {
        "default": {
            "expiry": "20000h"
        },
        "profiles": {
            "client": {
                "expiry": "43800h",
                "usages": [
                    "signing",
                    "key encipherment",
                    "client auth"
                ]
            },
```

```
        "server": {
            "expiry": "20000h",
            "usages": [
                "signing",
                "key encipherment",
                "server auth",
                "client auth"
            ]
        }
    }
}
```

And we'll also need a cert request config:

Nginxcarequest.json:

```
{
    "CN": "server",
    "hosts": [
        ""
    ],
    "key": {
        "algo": "rsa",
        "size": 2048
    }
}
```

Now, we can actually make our certs! Use the following command:

```
cfssl gencert -ca=nginxca.pem -ca-key=nginxca-key.
pem -config=nginxca-config.json -profile=server
-hostname="127.0.0.1" nginxcarequest.json | cfssljson -bare
server
```

As the final step for our cert secrets, create the Kubernetes secret from the certificate files' output by means of the last `cfssl` command:

```
kubectl create secret generic nginx-certs --from-file=server-
cert=./server.pem --from-file=server-key=./server-key.pem
```

Now, we can finally create our deployment:

```
kubectl apply -f nginx-sidecar.yaml
```

This produces the following output:

```
deployment "myapp" created
```

In order to check the NGINX proxy functionality, let's create a service to direct to our deployment:

Nginx-sidecar-service.yaml:

```
apiVersion: v1
kind: Service
metadata:
 name:myapp
 labels:
   app: myapp
spec:
 selector:
   app: myapp
 type: NodePort
 ports:
 - port: 443
   targetPort: 443
   protocol: TCP
   name: https
```

Now, accessing any node of the cluster using `https` should result in a working HTTPS connection! However, since our cert is self-signed, browsers will display an *insecure* message.

Now that you've seen how NGINX can be used as a sidecar proxy with Kubernetes, let's move on to a more modern, cloud-native proxy sidecar – Envoy.

Using Envoy as a sidecar proxy

Envoy is a modern proxy built for cloud-native environments. In the Istio service mesh, which we'll review later in this chapter, Envoy acts as both a reverse and forward proxy. Before we get to Istio, however, let's try our hand at deploying Envoy as a proxy.

We will tell Envoy where to route various requests using routes, listeners, clusters, and endpoints. This functionality is what forms the core of Istio, which we will review later in this chapter.

Let's go through each of the Envoy configuration pieces to see how it all works.

Envoy listeners

Envoy allows the configuration of one or more listeners. With each listener, we specify a port for Envoy to listen on, as well as any filters we want to apply to the listener.

Filters can provide complex functionality, including caching, authorization, **Cross-Origin Resource Sharing** (**CORS**) configuration, and more. Envoy supports the chaining of multiple filters together.

Envoy routes

Certain filters have route configuration, which specifies domains from which requests should be accepted, route matching, and forwarding rules.

Envoy clusters

A Cluster in Envoy represents a logical service where requests can be routed to based-on routes in listeners. A cluster likely contains more than one possible IP address in a cloud-native setting, so it supports load balancing configurations such as *round robin*.

Envoy endpoints

Finally, endpoints are specified within a cluster as one logical instance of a service. Envoy supports fetching a list of endpoints from an API (this is essentially what happens in the Istio service mesh) and load balancing between them.

In a production Envoy deployment on Kubernetes, it is likely that some form of dynamic, API-driven Envoy configuration is going to be used. This feature of Envoy is called xDS, and is used by Istio. Additionally, there are other open source products and solutions that use Envoy along with xDS, including the Ambassador API gateway.

For the purposes of this book, we will look at some static (non-dynamic) Envoy configuration; that way, we can pick apart each piece of the config, and you'll have a good idea of how everything works when we review Istio.

Let's now dive into an Envoy configuration for a setup where a single Pod needs to be able to route requests to two services, *Service 1* and *Service 2*. The setup looks like this:

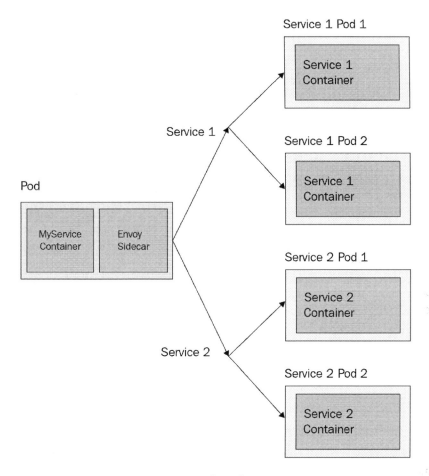

Figure 14.2 – Outbound envoy proxy

As you can see, the Envoy sidecar in our application Pod will have configurations to route to two upstream services, *Service 1* and *Service 2*. Both services have two possible endpoints.

In a dynamic setting with Envoy xDS, the Pod IPs for the endpoints would be loaded from the API, but for the purposes of our review, we will show the static Pod IPs in the endpoints. We will completely ignore Kubernetes Services and instead directly access Pod IPs in a round robin configuration. In a service mesh scenario, Envoy would also be deployed on all of the destination Pods, but we'll keep it simple for now.

Now, let's look at how this network map is configured in an envoy configuration YAML (which you can find in its entirety in the code repository). This is, of course, very different from a Kubernetes resource YAML – we will get to that part later. The entire configuration has a lot of YAML involved, so let's take it piece by piece.

Understanding Envoy configuration files

First off, let's look at the first few lines of our config—some basic information about our Envoy setup:

Envoy-configuration.yaml:

```yaml
admin:
  access_log_path: "/dev/null"
  address:
    socket_address:
      address: 0.0.0.0
      port_value: 8001
```

As you can see, we specify a port and address for Envoy's admin. As with the following configuration, we are running Envoy as a sidecar so the address will always be local – 0.0.0.0. Next, we start our list of listeners with an HTTPS listener:

```yaml
static_resources:
  listeners:
  - address:
      socket_address:
        address: 0.0.0.0
        port_value: 8443
    filter_chains:
    - filters:
      - name: envoy.filters.network.http_connection_manager
        typed_config:
          "@type": type.googleapis.com/envoy.config.filter.network.http_connection_manager.v2.HttpConnectionManager
          stat_prefix: ingress_https
          codec_type: auto
          route_config:
            name: local_route
            virtual_hosts:
            - name: backend
              domains:
              - "*"
              routes:
```

```
        - match:
            prefix: "/service/1"
          route:
            cluster: service1
        - match:
            prefix: "/service/2"
          route:
            cluster: service2
      http_filters:
      - name: envoy.filters.http.router
        typed_config: {}
```

As you can see, for each Envoy listener, we have a local address and port for the listener (this listener is an HTTPS listener). Then, we have a list of filters – though in this case, we only have one. Each envoy filter type has slightly different configuration, and we won't review it line by line (check the Envoy docs for more information at `https://www.envoyproxy.io/docs`), but this particular filter matches two routes, `/service/1` and `/service/2`, and routes them to two envoy clusters. Still under our first HTTPS listener section of the YAML, we have the TLS configuration, including certs:

```
      transport_socket:
        name: envoy.transport_sockets.tls
        typed_config:
          "@type": type.googleapis.com/envoy.extensions.
transport_sockets.tls.v3.DownstreamTlsContext
          common_tls_context:
            tls_certificates:
              certificate_chain:
                inline_string: |
                  <INLINE CERT FILE>
              private_key:
                inline_string: |
                  <INLINE PRIVATE KEY FILE>
```

As you can see, this configuration passes in a `private_key` and a `certificate_chain`. Next, we have our second and final listener, an HTTP listener:

```
  - address:
      socket_address:
        address: 0.0.0.0
        port_value: 8080
    filter_chains:
    - filters:
      - name: envoy.filters.network.http_connection_manager
        typed_config:
          "@type": type.googleapis.com/envoy.config.filter.
network.http_connection_manager.v2.HttpConnectionManager
          codec_type: auto
          stat_prefix: ingress_http
          route_config:
            name: local_route
            virtual_hosts:
            - name: backend
              domains:
              - "*"
              routes:
              - match:
                  prefix: "/service1"
                route:
                  cluster: service1
              - match:
                  prefix: "/service2"
                route:
                  cluster: service2
          http_filters:
          - name: envoy.filters.http.router
            typed_config: {}
```

As you can see, this configuration is quite similar to that of our HTTPS listener, except that it listens on a different port, and does not include certificate information. Next, we move into our cluster configuration. In our case, we have two clusters, one for `service1` and one for `service2`. First off, `service1`:

```
clusters:
- name: service1
  connect_timeout: 0.25s
  type: strict_dns
  lb_policy: round_robin
  http2_protocol_options: {}
  load_assignment:
    cluster_name: service1
    endpoints:
    - lb_endpoints:
      - endpoint:
          address:
            socket_address:
              address: service1
              port_value: 5000
```

And next, `Service 2`:

```
- name: service2
  connect_timeout: 0.25s
  type: strict_dns
  lb_policy: round_robin
  http2_protocol_options: {}
  load_assignment:
    cluster_name: service2
    endpoints:
    - lb_endpoints:
      - endpoint:
          address:
            socket_address:
              address: service2
              port_value: 5000
```

For each of these clusters, we specify where requests should be routed, and to which port. For instance, for our first cluster, requests are routed to `http://service1:5000`. We also specify a load balancing policy (in this case, round robin) and a timeout for the connections. Now that we have our Envoy configuration, we can go ahead and create our Kubernetes Pod and inject our sidecar along with the envoy configuration. We'll also split this file into two since it is a bit too big to understand as is:

Envoy-sidecar-deployment.yaml:

```yaml
apiVersion: apps/v1
kind: Deployment
metadata:
  name: my-service
spec:
  replicas: 1
  template:
    metadata:
      labels:
        app: my-service
    spec:
      containers:
      - name: envoy
        image: envoyproxy/envoy:latest
        ports:
          - containerPort: 9901
            protocol: TCP
            name: envoy-admin
          - containerPort: 8786
            protocol: TCP
            name: envoy-web
```

As you can see, this is a typical deployment YAML. In this case, we actually have two containers. First off is the Envoy proxy container (or sidecar). It listens on two ports. Next up, moving further down the YAML, we have a volume mount for that first container (to hold the Envoy config) as well as a start command and arguments:

```yaml
        volumeMounts:
          - name: envoy-config-volume
```

```
      mountPath: /etc/envoy-config/
   command: ["/usr/local/bin/envoy"]
      args: ["-c", "/etc/envoy-config/config.yaml", "--v2-
config-only", "-l", "info","--service-cluster","myservice","--
service-node","myservice", "--log-format", "[METADATA][%Y-%m-%d
%T.%e][%t][%l][%n] %v"]
```

Finally, we have our second container in the Pod, which is an application container:

```
- name: my-service
      image: ravirdv/http-responder:latest
      ports:
      - containerPort: 5000
         name: svc-port
         protocol: TCP
   volumes:
      - name: envoy-config-volume
        configMap:
           name: envoy-config
           items:
              - key: envoy-config
                path: config.yaml
```

As you can see, this application responds on port 5000. Lastly, we also have our Pod-level volume definition to match the Envoy config volume mounted in the Envoy container. Before we create our deployment, we need to create a ConfigMap with our Envoy configuration. We can do this using the following command:

```
kubectl create cm envoy-config
--from-file=config.yaml=./envoy-config.yaml
```

This will result in the following output:

```
Configmap "envoy-config" created
```

Now we can create our deployment with the following command:

```
kubectl apply -f deployment.yaml
```

This will result in the following output:

```
Deployment "my-service" created
```

Finally, we need our downstream services, `service1` and `service2`. For this purpose, we will continue to use the `http-responder` open source container image, which will respond on port `5000`. The deployment and service specs can be found in the code repository, and we can create them using the following commands:

```
kubectl create -f service1-deployment.yaml
kubectl create -f service1-service.yaml
kubectl create -f service2-deployment.yaml
kubectl create -f service2-service.yaml
```

Now, we can test our Envoy configuration! From our `my-service` container, we can make a request to localhost on port `8080`, with the `/service1` path. This should direct to one of our `service1` Pod IPs. To make this request we use the following command:

```
Kubectl exec <my-service-pod-name> -it -- curl localhost:8080/
service1
```

We've set up out services to echo their names on a `curl` request. Look at the following output of our `curl` command:

```
Service 1 Reached!
```

Now that we've looked at how Envoy works with a static configuration, let's move on to a dynamic service mesh based on Envoy – Istio.

Adding a service mesh to Kubernetes

A *service mesh* pattern is a logical extension of the sidecar proxy. By attaching sidecar proxies to every Pod, a service mesh can control functionality for service-to-service requests, such as advanced routing rules, retries, and timeouts. In addition, by having every request pass through a proxy, service meshes can implement mutual TLS encryption between services for added security and can give administrators incredible observability into requests in their cluster.

There are several service mesh projects that support Kubernetes. The most popular are as follows:

- *Istio*
- *Linkerd*
- *Kuma*
- *Consul*

Each of these service meshes has different takes on the service mesh pattern. *Istio* is likely the single most popular and comprehensive solution, but is also quite complex. *Linkerd* is also a mature project, but is easier to configure (though it uses its own proxy instead of Envoy). *Consul* is an option that supports Envoy in addition to other providers, and not just on Kubernetes. Finally, *Kuma* is an Envoy-based option that is also growing in popularity.

Exploring all the options is beyond the scope of this book, so we will stick with Istio, as it is often considered the default solution. That said, all of these meshes have strengths and weaknesses, and it is worth looking at each one when planning to adopt the service mesh.

Setting up Istio on Kubernetes

Although Istio can be installed with Helm, the Helm installation option is no longer the officially supported installation method.

Instead, we use the `Istioctl` CLI tool to install Istio with configuration onto our clusters. This configuration can be completely customized, but for the purposes of this book, we will just use the "demo" configuration:

1. The first step to installing Istio on a cluster is to install the Istio CLI tool. We can do this with the following command, which installs the newest version of the CLI tool:

```
curl -L https://istio.io/downloadIstio | sh -
```

2. Next, we'll want to add the CLI tool to our path for ease of use:

```
cd istio-<VERSION>
export PATH=$PWD/bin:$PATH
```

3. Now, let's install Istio! Istio configurations are called *profiles* and, as mentioned previously, they can be completely customized using a YAML file.

    For this demonstration, we'll use the inbuilt `demo` profile with Istio, which provides some basic setup. Install profile using the following command:

    ```
    istioctl install --set profile=demo
    ```

    This will result in the following output:

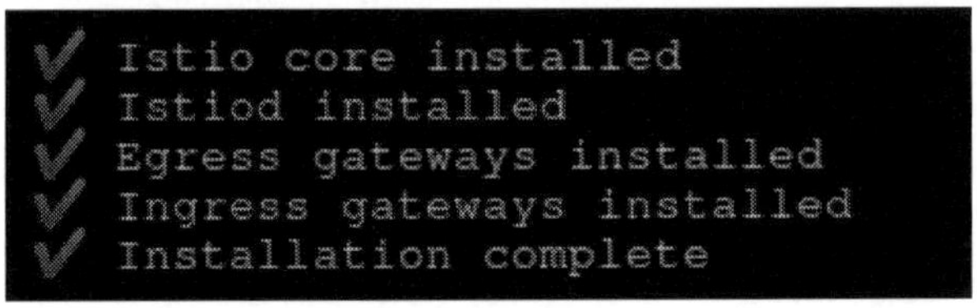

    ```
    ✓ Istio core installed
    ✓ Istiod installed
    ✓ Egress gateways installed
    ✓ Ingress gateways installed
    ✓ Installation complete
    ```

    Figure 14.3 – Istioctl profile installation output

4. Since the sidecar resource has not been released yet as of Kubernetes 1.19, Istio will itself inject Envoy proxies into any namespace that is labeled with `istio-injection=enabled`.

    To label any namespace with this, run the following command:

    ```
    kubectl label namespace my-namespace istio-
    injection=enabled
    ```

5. To test easily, label the `default` namespace with the preceding `label` command. Once the Istio components come up, any Pods in that namespace will automatically be injected with the Envoy sidecar, just like we created manually in the previous section.

    In order to remove Istio from the cluster, run the following command:

    ```
    istioctl x uninstall --purge
    ```

    This should result in a confirmation message telling you that Istio has been removed.

6. Now, let's deploy a little something to test our new mesh with! We will deploy three different application services, each with a deployment and a service resource:

a. Service Frontend

b. Service Backend A

c. Service Backend B

Here's the Deployment for *Service Frontend*:

Istio-service-deployment.yaml:

```yaml
apiVersion: apps/v1
kind: Deployment
metadata:
  name: service-frontend
spec:
  replicas: 1
  template:
    metadata:
      labels:
        app: service-frontend
        version: v2
    spec:
      containers:
      - name: service-frontend
        image: ravirdv/http-responder:latest
        ports:
        - containerPort: 5000
          name: svc-port
          protocol: TCP
```

And here's the Service for *Service Frontend*:

Istio-service-service.yaml:

```yaml
apiVersion: v1
kind: Service
metadata:
  name: service-frontend
spec:
```

```
  selector:
    name: service-frontend
  ports:
    - protocol: TCP
      port: 80
      targetPort: 5000
```

The YAML for Service Backends A and B will be the same as *Service Frontend*, apart from swapping the names, image names, and selector labels.

7. Now that we have a couple of services to route to (and between), let's start setting up some Istio resources!

    First thing's first, we need a `Gateway` resource. In this case, we are not using the NGINX Ingress Controller, but that's fine because Istio provides a `Gateway` resource that can be used for ingress and egress. Here's what an Istio `Gateway` definition looks like:

Istio-gateway.yaml:

```
apiVersion: networking.istio.io/v1alpha3
kind: Gateway
metadata:
  name: myapplication-gateway
spec:
  selector:
    istio: ingressgateway
  servers:
  - port:
      number: 80
      name: http
      protocol: HTTP
    hosts:
    - "*"
```

These `Gateway` definitions look pretty similar to ingress records. We have `name`, and `selector`, which Istio uses to decide which Istio Ingress Controller to use. Next, we have one or more servers, which are essentially ingress points on our gateway. In this case, we do not restrict the host, and we accept requests on port `80`.

8. Now that we have a gateway for getting requests into our cluster, we can start setting up some routes. We do this in Istio using `VirtualService`. `VirtualService` in Istio is a set of routes that should be followed when requests to a particular hostname are made. In addition, we can use a wildcard host to make global rules for requests from anywhere in the mesh. Let's take a look at an example `VirtualService` configuration:

Istio-virtual-service-1.yaml:

```
apiVersion: networking.istio.io/v1alpha3
kind: VirtualService
metadata:
  name: myapplication
spec:
  hosts:
  - "*"
  gateways:
  - myapplication-gateway
  http:
  - match:
    - uri:
        prefix: /app
    - uri:
        prefix: /frontend
    route:
    - destination:
        host: service-frontend
        subset: v1
```

In this `VirtualService`, we route requests to any host to our entry point at *Service Frontend* if it matches one of our `uri` prefixes. In this case, we are matching on the prefix, but you can use exact matching as well by swapping out `prefix` with `exact` in the URI matcher.

9. So, now we have a setup fairly similar to what we would expect with an NGINX Ingress, with entry into the cluster dictated by a route match.

    However, what's that v1 in our route? This actually represents a version of our *Frontend Service*. Let's go ahead and specify this version using a new resource type – the Istio `DestinationRule`. Here's what a `DestinationRule` config looks like:

Istio-destination-rule-1.yaml:

```
apiVersion: networking.istio.io/v1alpha3
kind: DestinationRule
metadata:
  name: service-frontend
spec:
  host: service-frontend
  subsets:
  - name: v1
    labels:
      version: v1
  - name: v2
    labels:
      version: v2
```

As you can see, we specify two different versions of our frontend service in Istio, each looking at a label selector. From our previous Deployment and Service, you see that our current frontend service version is v2, but we could be running both in parallel! By specifying our v2 version in the ingress virtual service, we tell Istio to route all requests to v2 of the service. In addition, we have our v1 version also configured, which is referenced in the previous `VirtualService`. This hard rule is only one possible way to route requests to different subsets in Istio.

Now, we've managed to route traffic into our cluster via a gateway, and to a virtual service subset based on a destination rule. At this point, we are effectively "inside" our service mesh!

10. Now, from our *Service Frontend*, we want to be able to route to *Service Backend A* and *Service Backend B*. How do we do this? More virtual services is the answer! Let's take a look at a virtual service for *Backend Service A*:

Istio-virtual-service-2.yaml:

```yaml
apiVersion: networking.istio.io/v1alpha3
kind: VirtualService
metadata:
  name: myapplication-a
spec:
  hosts:
  - service-a
  http:
    route:
    - destination:
        host: service-backend-a
        subset: v1
```

As you can see, this `VirtualService` routes to a v1 subset for our service, `service-backend-a`. We'll also need another `VirtualService` for `service-backend-b`, which we won't include in full (but looks nearly identical). To see the full YAML, check the code repository for `istio-virtual-service-3.yaml`.

11. Once our virtual services are ready, we require some destination rules! The `DestinationRule` for *Backend Service A* is as follows:

Istio-destination-rule-2.yaml:

```yaml
apiVersion: networking.istio.io/v1alpha3
kind: DestinationRule
metadata:
  name: service-backend-a
spec:
  host: service-backend-a
  trafficPolicy:
    tls:
      mode: ISTIO_MUTUAL
```

```
    subsets:
    - name: v1
      labels:
        version: v1
```

And the `DestinationRule` for *Backend Service B* is similar, just with different subsets. We won't include the code, but check `istio-destination-rule-3.yaml` in the code repository for the exact specifications.

These destination rules and virtual services add up to make the following routing diagram:

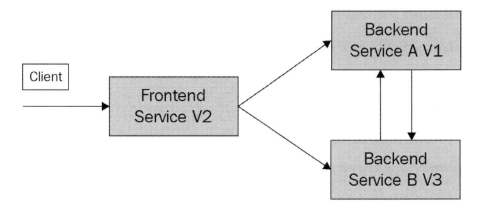

Figure 14.4 – Istio routing diagram

As you can see, requests from *Frontend Service* Pods can route to *Backend Service A version 1* or *Backend Service B version 3*, and each backend service can route to the other as well. These requests to Backend Service A or B additionally engage one of the most valuable features of Istio – mutual (two-way) TLS. In this setup, TLS security is maintained between any two points in the mesh, and this all happens automatically!

Next, let's take a look at using serverless patterns with Kubernetes.

Implementing serverless on Kubernetes

Serverless patterns on cloud providers have quickly been gaining in popularity. Serverless architectures consist of compute that can automatically scale up and down, even scaling all the way to zero (where zero compute capacity is being used to serve a function or other application). **Function-as-a-Service** (**FaaS**) is an extension of the serverless pattern, where function code is the only input, and the serverless system takes care of routing requests to compute and scale as necessary. AWS Lambda, Azure Functions, and Google Cloud Run are some of the more popular FaaS/serverless options officially supported by cloud providers. Kubernetes also has many different serverless frameworks and libraries that can be used to run serverless, scale-to-zero workloads as well as FaaS on Kubernetes. Some of the most popular ones are as follows:

- *Knative*
- *Kubeless*
- *OpenFaaS*
- *Fission*

A full discussion of all serverless options on Kubernetes is beyond the scope of this book, so we'll focus on two different ones, which aim to serve two vastly different use cases: *OpenFaaS* and *Knative*.

While Knative is highly extensible and customizable, it uses multiple coupled components that add complexity. This means that some added configuration is necessary to get started with an FaaS solution, since functions are just one of many other patterns that Knative supports. OpenFaaS, on the other hand, makes getting up and running with serverless and FaaS on Kubernetes extremely easy. Both technologies are valuable for different reasons.

For this chapter's tutorial, we will look at Knative, one of the most popular serverless frameworks, and one that also supports FaaS via its eventing feature.

Using Knative for FaaS on Kubernetes

As mentioned previously, Knative is a modular set of building blocks for serverless patterns on Kubernetes. For this reason, it requires a bit of configuration before we can get to the actual functions. Knative can also be installed with Istio, which it uses as a substrate for routing and scaling serverless applications. Other non-Istio routing options are also available.

To use Knative for FaaS, we will need to install both *Knative Serving* and *Knative Eventing*. While Knative Serving will allow us to run our serverless workloads, Knative Eventing will provide the pathway to make FaaS requests to these scale-to-zero workloads. Let's accomplish this by following these steps:

1. First, let's install the Knative Serving components. We will begin by installing the CRDs:

    ```
    kubectl apply --filename https://github.com/knative/
    serving/releases/download/v0.18.0/serving-crds.yaml
    ```

2. Next, we can install the serving components themselves:

    ```
    kubectl apply --filename https://github.com/knative/
    serving/releases/download/v0.18.0/serving-core.yaml
    ```

3. At this point, we'll need to install a networking/routing layer for Knative to use. Let's use Istio:

    ```
    kubectl apply --filename https://github.com/knative/
    net-istio/releases/download/v0.18.0/release.yaml
    ```

4. We'll need the gateway IP address from Istio. Depending on where you're running this (in other words, AWS or locally), this value may differ. Pull it using the following command:

    ```
    Kubectl get service -n istio-system istio-ingressgateway
    ```

5. Knative requires a specific DNS setup for enabling the serving component. The easiest way to do this in a cloud setting is to use xip.io "Magic DNS," though this will not work for Minikube-based clusters. If you're running one of these (or just want to see all the options available), check out the Knative docs at https://knative.dev/docs/install/any-kubernetes-cluster/.

    To set up Magic DNS, use the following command:

    ```
    kubectl apply --filename https://github.com/knative/
    serving/releases/download/v0.18.0/serving-default-domain.
    yaml
    ```

6. Now that we've installed Knative Serving, let's install Knative Eventing to deliver our FaaS requests. First, we'll need more CRDs. Install them using the following command:

```
kubectl apply --filename https://github.com/knative/
eventing/releases/download/v0.18.0/eventing-crds.yaml
```

7. Now, install the eventing components just like we did with serving:

```
kubectl apply --filename https://github.com/knative/
eventing/releases/download/v0.18.0/eventing-core.yaml
```

At this point, we need to add a queue/messaging layer for our eventing system to use. Did we mention that Knative supports lots of modular components?

> **Important note**
>
> To make things easy, let's just use the basic in-memory messaging layer, but it's good to know all the options available to you. As regards modular options for messaging channels, check the docs at `https://knative.dev/docs/eventing/channels/channels-crds/`. For event source options, you can look at `https://knative.dev/docs/eventing/sources/`.

8. To install the `in-memory` messaging layer, use the following command:

```
kubectl apply --filename https://github.com/knative/
eventing/releases/download/v0.18.0/in-memory-channel.yaml
```

9. Thought we were done? Nope! One last thing. We need to install a broker, which will take events from the messaging layer and get them processed in the right place. Let's use the default broker layer, the MT-Channel broker layer. You can install it using the following command:

```
kubectl apply --filename https://github.com/knative/
eventing/releases/download/v0.18.0/mt-channel-broker.yaml
```

With that, we are finally done. We have installed an end-to-end FaaS implementation via Knative. As you can tell, this was not an easy task. What makes Knative amazing is the same thing that makes it a pain – it offers so many different modular options and configurations that even when selecting the most basic options for each step, we've still taken a lot of time to explain the install. There are other options available, such as OpenFaaS, which are a bit easier to get up and running with, and we'll look into that in the next section! On the Knative side, however, now that we have our setup finally ready, we can add in our FaaS.

Implementing an FaaS pattern in Knative

Now that we have Knative set up, we can use it to implement an FaaS pattern where events will trigger some code running in Knative through a trigger. To set up a simple FaaS, we will require three things:

- A broker to route our events from an entry point

- A consumer service to actually process our events

- A trigger definition that specifies when to route events to the consumer for processing

First thing's first, our broker needs to be created. This is simple and similar to creating an ingress record or gateway. Our `broker` YAML looks like this:

Knative-broker.yaml:

```
apiVersion: eventing.knative.dev/v1
kind: broker
metadata:
  name: my-broker
  namespace: default
```

Next, we can create a consumer service. This component is really just our application that is going to process events – our function itself! Rather than showing you even more YAML than you've already seen, let's assume our consumer service is just a regular old Kubernetes Service called `service-consumer`, which routes to a four-replica deployment of Pods running our application.

Finally, we're going to need a trigger. This determines how and which events will be routed from the broker. The YAML for a trigger looks like this:

Knative-trigger.yaml:

```
apiVersion: eventing.knative.dev/v1
kind: Trigger
metadata:
  name: my-trigger
spec:
  broker: my-broker
  filter:
    attributes:
      type: myeventtype
  subscriber:
    ref:
      apiVersion: v1
      kind: Service
      name: service-consumer
```

In this YAML, we create a `Trigger` rule that any event that comes through our broker, `my-broker`, and has a type of `myeventtype`, will automatically be routed to our consumer, `service-consumer`. For full documentation on trigger filters in Knative, check out the docs at `https://knative.dev/development/eventing/triggers/`.

So, how do we create some events? First, check the broker URL using the following command:

```
kubectl get broker
```

This should result in the following output:

```
NAME         READY    REASON    URL
AGE
my-broker    True               http://broker-ingress.knative-
eventing.svc.cluster.local/default/my-broker      1m
```

We can now finally test our FaaS solution. Let's spin up a quick Pod from which we can make requests to our trigger:

```
kubectl run -i --tty --rm debug --image=radial/busyboxplus:curl
--restart=Never -- sh
```

Now, from inside this Pod, we can go ahead and test our trigger, using `curl`. The request we need to make needs to have a `Ce-Type` header that equals `myeventtype`, since this is what our trigger requires. Knative uses headers in the form `Ce-Id`, `Ce-Type`, as shown in the following code block, to do the routing.

The `curl` request will look like the following:

```
curl -v "http://broker-ingress.knative-eventing.svc.cluster.
local/default/my-broker" \
  -X POST \
  -H "Ce-Id: anyid" \
  -H "Ce-Specversion: 1.0" \
  -H "Ce-Type: myeventtype" \
  -H "Ce-Source: any" \
  -H "Content-Type: application/json" \
  -d '{"payload":"Does this work?"}'
```

As you can see, we are sending a `curl http` request to the broker URL. Additionally, we are passing some special headers along with the HTTP request. Importantly, we are passing `type=myeventtype`, which our filter on our trigger requires in order to send the request for processing.

In this example, our consumer service echoes back the payload key of the body JSON, along with a `200` HTTP response, so running this `curl` request gives us the following:

```
> HTTP/1.1 200 OK
> Content-Type: application/json
{
  "Output": "Does this work?"
}
```

Success! We have tested our FaaS and it returns what we are expecting. From here, our solution will scale up and down to zero along with the number of events, and, as with everything Knative, there are many more customizations and configuration options to tailor our solution precisely to what we need.

Next up, we'll look at the same pattern with OpenFaaS instead of Knative in order to highlight the differences between the two approaches.

Using OpenFaaS for FaaS on Kubernetes

Now that we've discussed getting started with Knative, let's do the same with OpenFaaS. First, to install OpenFaaS itself, we are going to use the Helm charts from the `faas-netes` repository, found at `https://github.com/openfaas/faas-netes`.

Installing OpenFaaS components with Helm

First, we will create two namespaces to hold our OpenFaaS components:

- `openfaas` to hold the actual service components of OpenFaas
- `openfaas-fn` to hold our deployed functions

We can add these two namespaces using a nifty YAML file from the `faas-netes` repository using the following command:

```
kubectl apply -f https://raw.githubusercontent.com/openfaas/
faas-netes/master/namespaces.yml
```

Next, we need to add the `faas-netes Helm repository` with the following Helm command:

```
helm repo add openfaas https://openfaas.github.io/faas-netes/
helm repo update
```

Finally, we actually deploy OpenFaaS!

The Helm chart for OpenFaaS at the preceding `faas-netes` repository has several possible variables, but we will use the following configuration to ensure that an initial set of authentication credentials are created, and that ingress records are deployed:

```
helm install openfaas openfaas/openfaas \
    --namespace openfaas \
    --set functionNamespace=openfaas-fn \
    --set ingress.enabled=true \
    --set generateBasicAuth=true
```

Now, that our OpenFaaS infrastructure has been deployed to our cluster, we'll want to fetch the credentials that were generated as part of the Helm install. The Helm chart will create these as part of a hook and store them in a secret, so we can get them by running the following command:

```
OPENFAASPWD=$(kubectl get secret basic-auth -n openfaas -o
jsonpath="{.data.basic-auth-password}" | base64 --decode)
```

That is all the Kubernetes setup we require!

Moving on, let's install the OpenFaas CLI, which will make it extremely easy to manage our OpenFaas functions.

Installing the OpenFaaS CLI and deploying functions

To install the OpenFaaS CLI, we can use the following command (for Windows, check the preceding OpenFaaS documents):

```
curl -sL https://cli.openfaas.com | sudo sh
```

Now, we can get started with building and deploying some functions. This is easiest to do via the CLI.

When building and deploying functions for OpenFaaS, the OpenFaaS CLI provides an easy way to generate boilerplates, and build and deploy functions for specific languages. It does this via "templates," and supports various flavors of Node, Python, and more. For a full list of the template types, check the templates repository at https://github.com/openfaas/templates.

The templates created using the OpenFaaS CLI are similar to what you would expect from a hosted serverless platform such as AWS Lambda. Let's create a brand-new Node.js function using the following command:

```
faas-cli new my-function -lang node
```

This results in the following output:

```
Folder: my-function created.
Function created in folder: my-function
Stack file written: my-function.yml
```

As you can see, the new command generates a folder, and within it some boilerplate for the function code itself, and an OpenFaaS YAML file.

The OpenFaaS YAML file will appear as follows:

My-function.yml:

```
provider:
  name: openfaas
  gateway: http://localhost:8080

functions:
  my-function:
    lang: node
    handler: ./my-function
    image: my-function
```

The actual function code (inside the my-function folder) consists of a function file – handler.js – and a dependencies manifest, package.json. For other languages, these files will be different, and we won't delve into the specifics of dependencies in Node. However, we will edit the handler.js file to return some text. This is what the edited file looks like:

Handler.js:

```
"use strict"

module.exports = (context, callback) => {
    callback(undefined, {output: "my function succeeded!"});
}
```

This JavaScript code will return a JSON response with our text.

Now that we have our function and handler, we can move on to building and deploying our function. The OpenFaaS CLI makes it simple to build the function, which we can do with the following command:

```
faas-cli build -f /path/to/my-function.yml
```

The output of this command is long, but when it is complete, we will have a new container image built locally with our function handler and dependencies embedded!

Next, we push our container image to a container repository as we would for any other container. The OpenFaaS CLI has a neat wrapper command for this, which will push the image to Docker Hub or an alternate container image repository:

```
faas-cli push -f my-function.yml
```

Now, we can deploy our function to OpenFaaS. Once again, this is made easy by the CLI. Deploy it using the following command:

```
faas-cli deploy -f my-function.yml
```

Everything is now set up for us to test our function, deployed on OpenFaaS! We used an ingress setting when deploying OpenFaaS so requests can go through that ingress. However, our generated YAML file from our new function is set to make requests on `localhost:8080` for development purposes. We could edit that file to the correct URL for our ingress gateway (refer to the docs at `https://docs.openfaas.com/deployment/kubernetes/` for how to do that), but instead, let's just do a shortcut to get OpenFaaS open on our localhost.

Let's use a `kubectl port-forward` command to open our OpenFaaS service on localhost port `8080`. We can do this as follows:

```
export OPENFAAS_URL=http://127.0.0.1:8080
kubectl port-forward -n openfaas svc/gateway 8080:8080
```

Now, let's add our previously generated auth credentials to the OpenFaaS CLI, as follows:

```
echo -n $OPENFAASPWD | faas-cli login -g $OPENFAAS_URL -u admin
--password-stdin
```

Finally, all we need to do in order to test our function is to run the following command:

```
faas-cli invoke -f my-function.yml my-function
```

This results in the following output:

```
Reading from STDIN - hit (Control + D) to stop.
This is my message
{ output: "my function succeeded!"});}
```

As you can see, we've successfully received our intended response!

Finally, if we want to delete this specific function, we can do so with the following command, similar to how we would use `kubectl delete -f`:

```
faas-cli rm -f my-function.yml
```

And that's it! Our function has been removed.

Summary

In this chapter, we learned about service mesh and serverless patterns on Kubernetes. In order to set the stage for these, we first discussed running sidecar proxies on Kubernetes, specifically with the Envoy proxy.

Then, we moved on to service mesh, and learned how to install and configure the Istio service mesh for service-to-service routing with mutual TLS.

Finally, we moved on to serverless patterns on Kubernetes, where you learned how to configure and install Knative, and an alternative, OpenFaaS, for serverless eventing, and FaaS on Kubernetes.

The skills you used in this chapter will help you to build service mesh and serverless patterns on Kubernetes, setting you up for fully automated service-to-service discovery and FaaS eventing.

In the next (and final) chapter, we'll discuss running stateful applications on Kubernetes.

Questions

1. What is the difference between static and dynamic Envoy configurations?
2. What are the four major pieces of Envoy configuration?
3. What are some of the downsides to Knative, and how does OpenFaaS compare?

Further reading

- CNCF landscape: `https://landscape.cncf.io/`
- Official Kubernetes forums: `https://discuss.kubernetes.io/`

15

Stateful Workloads on Kubernetes

This chapter details the current state of the industry when it comes to running stateful workloads in databases. We will discuss the use of Kubernetes (and popular open source projects) for running databases, storage, and queues on Kubernetes. Case study tutorials will include running object storage, a database, and a queue system on Kubernetes.

In this chapter, we will first understand how stateful applications run on Kubernetes and then learn how to use Kubernetes storage for stateful applications. We will then learn how to run databases on Kubernetes, as well as covering messaging and queues. Let's start with a discussion of why stateful applications are much more complex than stateless applications on Kubernetes.

In this chapter, we will cover the following topics:

- Understanding stateful applications on Kubernetes
- Using Kubernetes storage for stateful applications
- Running databases on Kubernetes
- Implementing messaging and queues on Kubernetes

Technical requirements

In order to run the commands detailed in this chapter, you will need a computer that supports the `kubectl` command-line tool along with a working Kubernetes cluster. See *Chapter 1, Communicating with Kubernetes*, for several methods for getting up and running with Kubernetes quickly, and for instructions on how to install the kubectl tool.

The code used in this chapter can be found in the book's GitHub repository:

```
https://github.com/PacktPublishing/Cloud-Native-with-
Kubernetes/tree/master/Chapter15
```

Understanding stateful applications on Kubernetes

Kubernetes provides excellent primitives for running both stateless and stateful applications, but stateful workloads have taken longer to mature on Kubernetes. However, in recent years, some high-profile Kubernetes-based stateful application frameworks and projects have proven the increasing maturity of stateful applications on Kubernetes. Let's review some of these first in order to set the stage for the rest of the chapter.

Popular Kubernetes-native stateful applications

There are many types of stateful applications. Though most applications are stateful, only certain components in those applications store *state* data. We can remove these specific stateful components from applications and focus on those components in our review. In this book, we'll talk about databases, queues, and object storage, leaving out persistent storage components such as those we reviewed in *Chapter 7, Storage on Kubernetes*. We'll also go over a few, less generic components as honorable mentions. Let's start with databases!

Kubernetes-compatible databases

In addition to typical **databases** (**DBs**) and key-value stores such as **Postgres**, **MySQL**, and **Redis** that can be deployed on Kubernetes with StatefulSets or community operators, there are some major made-for-Kubernetes options:

- **CockroachDB**: A distributed SQL database that can be deployed seamlessly on Kubernetes
- **Vitess**: A MySQL sharding orchestrator that allows global scalability for MySQL, also installable on Kubernetes via an operator
- **YugabyteDB**: A distributed SQL database similar to **CockroachDB** that also supports Cassandra-like querying

Next, let's look at queuing and messaging on Kubernetes.

Queues, streaming, and messaging on Kubernetes

Again, there are industry-standard options such as **Kafka** and **RabbitMQ** that can be deployed on Kubernetes using community Helm charts and operators, in addition to some purpose-made open- and closed-source options:

- **NATS**: Open source messaging and streaming system
- **KubeMQ**: Kubernetes-native message broker

Next, let's look at object storage on Kubernetes.

Object storage on Kubernetes

Object storage takes volume-based persistent storage from Kubernetes and adds on an object storage layer, similar to (and in many cases compatible with the API of) Amazon S3:

- **Minio**: S3-compatible object storage built for high performance.
- **Open IO**: Similar to *Minio*, this has high performance and supports S3 and Swift storage.

Next, let's look at a few honorable mentions.

Honorable mentions

In addition to the preceding generic components, there are some more specialized (but still categorical) stateful applications that can be run on Kubernetes:

- **Key and auth management**: **Vault**, **Keycloak**

- **Container registries**: **Harbor**, **Dragonfly**, **Quay**

- **Workflow management**: **Apache Airflow** with a Kubernetes Operator

Now that we've reviewed a few categories of stateful applications, let's talk about how these state-heavy applications are typically implemented on Kubernetes.

Understanding strategies for running stateful applications on Kubernetes

Though there is nothing inherently wrong with deploying a stateful application on Kubernetes with a ReplicaSet or Deployment, you will find that the majority of stateful applications on Kubernetes use StatefulSets. We talked about StatefulSets in *Chapter 4, Scaling and Deploying Your Application*, but why are they so useful for applications? We will review and answer this question in this chapter.

The main reason is Pod identity. Many distributed stateful applications have their own clustering mechanism or consensus algorithm. In order to smooth over the process for these types of applications, StatefulSets provide static Pod naming based on an ordinal system, starting from 0 to n. This, in combination with a rolling update and creation method, makes it much easier for applications to cluster themselves, which is extremely important for cloud-native databases such as CockroachDB.

To illustrate how and why StatefulSets can help run stateful applications on Kubernetes, let's look at how we might run MySQL on Kubernetes with StatefulSets.

Now, to be clear, running a single Pod of MySQL on Kubernetes is extremely simple. All we need to do is find a MySQL container image and ensure that it has the proper configuration and `startup` command.

However, when we look to scale our database, we start to run into issues. Unlike a simple stateless application, where we can scale our deployment without creating new state, MySQL (like many other DBs) has its own method of clustering and consensus. Each member of a MySQL cluster knows about the other members, and most importantly, it knows which member of the cluster is the leader. This is how databases like MySQL can offer consistency guarantees and **Atomicity, Consistency, Isolation, Durability** (**ACID**) compliance.

Therefore, since each member in a MySQL cluster needs to know about the other members (and most importantly, the master), we need to run our DB Pods in a way that means they have a common way to find and communicate with the other members of the DB cluster.

The way that StatefulSets offer this is, as we mentioned at the beginning of the section, via ordinal Pod numbering. This way, applications that need to self-cluster while running on Kubernetes know that a common naming scheme starting from 0 to n will be used. In addition, when a Pod at a specific ordinal restarts – for instance, `mysql-pod-2` – the same PersistentVolume will be mounted to the new Pod that starts in that ordinal spot. This allows for stateful consistency between restarts for a single Pod in a StatefulSet, which makes it much easier for applications to form a stable cluster.

To see how this works in practice, let's look at a StatefulSet specification for MySQL.

Running MySQL on StatefulSets

The following YAML spec is adapted from the Kubernetes documentation version. It shows how we can run MySQL clusters on StatefulSets. We will review each part of the YAML spec separately, so we can understand exactly how the mechanisms interact with StatefulSet guarantees.

Let's start with the first part of the spec:

statefulset-mysql.yaml

```yaml
apiVersion: apps/v1
kind: StatefulSet
metadata:
  name: mysql
spec:
  selector:
    matchLabels:
      app: mysql
  serviceName: mysql
  replicas: 3
  template:
    metadata:
      labels:
        app: mysql
```

As you can see, we are going to be creating a MySQL cluster with three `replicas`.

There isn't much else exciting about this piece, so let's move onto the start of `initContainers`. There will be quite a few containers running in this Pod between `initContainers` and regular containers, so we will explain each separately. What follows is the first `initContainer` instance:

```
  spec:
    initContainers:
    - name: init-mysql
      image: mysql:5.7
      command:
      - bash
      - "-c"
      - |
        set -ex
        [[ `hostname` =~ -([0-9]+)$ ]] || exit 1
        ordinal=${BASH_REMATCH[1]}
        echo [mysqld] > /mnt/conf.d/server-id.cnf
        echo server-id=$((100 + $ordinal)) >> /mnt/conf.d/
server-id.cnf
        if [[ $ordinal -eq 0 ]]; then
          cp /mnt/config-map/master.cnf /mnt/conf.d/
        else
          cp /mnt/config-map/slave.cnf /mnt/conf.d/
        fi
      volumeMounts:
      - name: conf
        mountPath: /mnt/conf.d
      - name: config-map
        mountPath: /mnt/config-map
```

This first `initContainer`, as you can see, is the MySQL container image. Now, this doesn't mean that we won't have the MySQL container running constantly in the Pod. This is a pattern you will tend to see fairly often with complex applications. Sometimes the same container image is used as both an `initContainer` instance and a normally running container in a Pod. This is because that container has the correct embedded scripts and tools to do common setup tasks programmatically.

In this example, the MySQL initContainer creates a file, /mnt/conf.d/
server-id.cnf, and adds a server ID, corresponding to the Pod's ordinal ID in
the StatefulSet, to the file. When writing the ordinal ID, it adds 100 as an offset, to get
around the reserved value in MySQL of a server-id ID of 0.

Then, depending on whether the Pod ordinal D is 0 or not, it copies configuration for
either a master or slave MySQL server to the volume.

Next, let's look at the second initContainer in the following section (we've left out
some code with volume mount information for brevity, but the full code is available in the
GitHub repository of the book):

```
- name: clone-mysql
  image: gcr.io/google-samples/xtrabackup:1.0
  command:
  - bash
  - "-c"
  - |
    set -ex
    [[ -d /var/lib/mysql/mysql ]] && exit 0
    [[ `hostname` =~ -([0-9]+)$ ]] || exit 1
    ordinal=${BASH_REMATCH[1]}
    [[ $ordinal -eq 0 ]] && exit 0          ncat --recv-
only mysql-$(($ordinal-1)).mysql 3307 | xbstream -x -C /var/
lib/mysql
    xtrabackup --prepare --target-dir=/var/lib/mysql
```

As you can see, this initContainer isn't MySQL at all! Instead, the container image is
a tool called Xtra Backup. Why do we need this container?

Consider a situation where a brand-new Pod, with a brand-new, empty PersistentVolume
joins the cluster. In this scenario, the data replication processes will need to copy all of the
data via replication from the other members in the MySQL cluster. With large databases,
this process could be exceedingly slow.

For this reason, we have an initContainer instance that loads in data from another
MySQL Pod in the StatefulSet, so that the data replication capabilities of MySQL have
something to start with. In a case where there is already data in the MySQL Pod, this
loading of data does not occur. The [[-d /var/lib/mysql/mysql]] && exit
0 line is the one that checks to see whether there is existing data.

Once these two `initContainer` instances have successfully completed their tasks, we have all our MySQL configuration courtesy of the first `initContainer`, and we have a somewhat recent set of data from another member in the MySQL StatefulSet.

Now, let's move on to the actual containers in the StatefulSet definition, starting with MySQL itself:

```
containers:
- name: mysql
  image: mysql:5.7
  env:
  - name: MYSQL_ALLOW_EMPTY_PASSWORD
    value: "1"
  ports:
  - name: mysql
    containerPort: 3306
  volumeMounts:
  - name: data
    mountPath: /var/lib/mysql
    subPath: mysql
  - name: conf
    mountPath: /etc/mysql/conf.d
```

As you can see, this MySQL container setup is fairly basic. In addition to an environment variable, we mount the previously created configuration. This pod also has some liveness and readiness probe configuration – check the GitHub repository of this book for those.

Now, let's move on and check out our final container, which will look familiar – it's actually another instance of Xtra Backup! Let's see how it is configured:

```
- name: xtrabackup
  containerPort: 3307
  command:
  - bash
  - "-c"
  - |
    set -ex
    cd /var/lib/mysql
    if [[ -f xtrabackup_slave_info && "x$(<xtrabackup_slave_info)"
    != "x" ]]; thencat xtrabackup_slave_info | sed -E 's/;$//g' >
```

```
change_master_to.sql.inrm -f xtrabackup_slave_info xtrabackup_
binlog_info
elif [[ -f xtrabackup_binlog_info ]]; then[[ `cat xtrabackup_
binlog_info` =~ ^(.*?)[[:space:]]+(.*?)$ ]] || exit 1
rm -f xtrabackup_binlog_info xtrabackup_slave_info
echo "CHANGE MASTER TO MASTER_LOG_FILE='${BASH_REMATCH[1]}',\
MASTER_LOG_POS=${BASH_REMATCH[2]}" > change_master_to.sql.in
fi
if [[ -f change_master_to.sql.in ]]; then
echo "Waiting for mysqld to be ready (accepting connections)"
until mysql -h 127.0.0.1 -e "SELECT 1"; do sleep 1; done
echo "Initializing replication from clone position"
mysql -h 127.0.0.1 \
-e "$(<change_master_to.sql.in), \
MASTER_HOST='mysql-0.mysql', \
MASTER_USER='root', \
MASTER_PASSWORD='', \
MASTER_CONNECT_RETRY=10; \
START SLAVE;" || exit 1
mv change_master_to.sql.in change_master_to.sql.orig
fi
exec ncat --listen --keep-open --send-only --max-conns=1 3307
-c \
"xtrabackup --backup --slave-info --stream=xbstream
--host=127.0.0.1 --user=root"
```

This container setup is a bit complex, so let's review it section by section.

We know from our `initContainers` that Xtra Backup loads in data from another Pod in the StatefulSet in order to get the Pod somewhat ready for replicating, to and from other members in the StatefulSet.

The Xtra Backup container in this case is the one that actually starts that replication! This container will first check to see whether the Pod it is running on is supposed to be a slave Pod in the MySQL cluster. If so, it will start a data replication process from the master.

Finally, the Xtra Backup container will also open a listener on port `3307`, which will send a clone of the data in the Pod, if requested. This is the setup that sends clone data to the other Pods in the StatefulSet when they request a clone. Remember that the first `initContainer` looks at other Pods in the StatefulSet, in order to get a clone. In the end, each Pod in the StatefulSet is able to request clones in addition to running a process that can send data clones to other Pods.

Finally, to wrap up our spec, let's look at `volumeClaimTemplate`. This section of the spec also lists volume mounts for the previous container and the volume setup for the Pod (but we've left that out for brevity. Check the GitHub repository of this book for the rest):

```
volumeClaimTemplates:
- metadata:
    name: data
  spec:
    accessModes: ["ReadWriteOnce"]
    resources:
      requests:
        storage: 10Gi
```

As you can see, there's nothing especially interesting about the volume setup for the last container or the volume list. However, it's worthwhile to note the `volumeClaimTemplates` section, because the data will remain the same as long as a Pod restarts at the same ordinal spot. A new Pod added to the cluster will instead start with a blank PersistentVolume, which will trigger the initial data clone.

All together, these features of StatefulSets, in combination with the correct configuration of Pods and tooling, allow for the easy scaling of a stateful DB on Kubernetes.

Now that we've talked about why stateful Kubernetes applications may use StatefulSets, let's go ahead and implement some to prove it! We'll start with an object storage application.

Deploying object storage on Kubernetes

Object storage is different from filesystem or block storage. It presents a higher-level abstraction that encapsulates a file, gives it an identifier, and often includes versioning. The file can then be accessed via its specific identifier.

The most popular object storage service is probably AWS S3, but Azure Blob Storage and Google Cloud Storage are similar alternatives. In addition, there are several self-hosted object storage technologies that can be run on Kubernetes, which we reviewed in the previous section.

For this book, we will review the configuration and usage of **Minio** on Kubernetes. Minio is an object storage engine that emphasizes high performance and can be deployed on Kubernetes, in addition to other orchestration technologies such as **Docker Swarm** and **Docker Compose**.

Minio supports Kubernetes deployments using both an operator and a Helm chart. In this book, we will focus on the operator, but for more information on the Helm chart, check out the Minio docs at `https://docs.min.io/docs`. Let's get started with the Minio Operator, which will let us review some cool community extensions to kubectl.

Installing the Minio Operator

Installing the Minio Operator will be quite different from anything we have done so far. Minio actually provides a `kubectl` plugin in order to manage the installation and configuration of the operator and Minio as a whole.

We haven't spoken much about `kubectl` plugins in this book, but they are a growing part of the Kubernetes ecosystem. `kubectl` plugins can provide additional functionality in the form of new `kubectl` commands.

In order to install the `minio` kubectl plugin, we use Krew, which is a plugin manager for `kubectl` that makes it easy to search and add `kubectl` plugins with a single command.

Installing Krew and the Minio kubectl plugin

So first, let's install Krew. The installation process varies depending on your OS and environment, but for macOS, it looks like the following (check out the Krew docs at `https://krew.sigs.k8s.io/docs` for more information):

1. First, let's install the Krew CLI tool with the following Terminal commands:

```
(
    set -x; cd "$(mktemp -d)" &&
    curl -fsSLO "https://github.com/kubernetes-sigs/krew/
releases/latest/download/krew.tar.gz" &&
    tar zxvf krew.tar.gz &&
    KREW=./krew-"$(uname | tr '[:upper:]'
'[:lower:]')_$(uname -m | sed -e 's/x86_64/amd64/' -e 's/
```

```
arm.*$/arm/')" &&
    "$KREW" install krew
)
```

2. Now, we can add Krew to our PATH variable with the following command:

```
export PATH="${KREW_ROOT:-$HOME/.krechw}/bin:$PATH"
```

In a new shell, we can now start using Krew! Krew is accessed using kubectl krew commands.

3. To install the Minio kubectl plugin, you can run the following krew command:

```
kubectl krew install minio
```

Now, with the Minio kubectl plugin installed, let's look at getting Minio set up on our cluster.

Starting the Minio Operator

First off, we need to actually install the Minio Operator on our cluster. This deployment will control all the Minio tasks that we need to do later:

1. We can install the Minio Operator using the following command:

```
kubectl minio init
```

This will result in the following output:

```
CustomResourceDefinition tenants.minio.min.io: created
ClusterRole minio-operator-role: created
ServiceAccount minio-operator: created
ClusterRoleBinding minio-operator-binding: created
MinIO Operator Deployment minio-operator: created
```

2. To check whether the Minio Operator is ready to go, let's check on our Pods with the following command:

```
kubectl get pods
```

You should see the Minio Operator Pod running in the output:

```
NAMESPACE        NAME                                    READY     STATUS
RESTARTS    AGE
default          minio-operator-85ccdcfb6-r8g8b          1/1
Running     0           5m37s
```

We now have the Minio Operator running properly on Kubernetes. Next up, we can create a Minio tenant.

Creating a Minio tenant

The next step is to create a **tenant**. Since Minio is a multi-tenant system, each tenant has its own namespace separation for buckets and objects, in addition to separate PersistentVolumes. Additionally, the Minio Operator starts Minio in Distributed Mode with a highly available setup and data replication.

Before creating our Minio tenant, we need to install a **Container Storage Interface** (**CSI**) driver for Minio. CSI is a standardized way to interface between storage providers and containers – and Kubernetes implements CSI in order to allow third-party storage providers to write their own drivers for seamless integration to Kubernetes. Minio recommends the Direct CSI driver in order to manage PersistentVolumes for Minio.

To install the Direct CSI driver, we need to run a `kubectl apply` command with Kustomize. However, the Direct CSI driver installation requires some environment variables to be set in order to create the Direct CSI configuration with the proper configuration, as shown:

1. First, let's go ahead and create this environment file based on the Minio recommendations:

default.env

```
DIRECT_CSI_DRIVES=data{1...4}
DIRECT_CSI_DRIVES_DIR=/mnt
KUBELET_DIR_PATH=/var/lib/kubelet
```

As you can see, this environment file determines where the Direct CSI driver will mount volumes.

2. Once we've created `default.env`, let's load these variables into memory using the following command:

```
export $(cat default.env)
```

3. Finally, let's install the Direct CSI driver with the following command:

```
kubectl apply -k github.com/minio/direct-csi
```

This should result in the following output:

```
kubenamespace/direct-csi created
storageclass.storage.k8s.io/direct.csi.min.io created
serviceaccount/direct-csi-min-io created
clusterrole.rbac.authorization.k8s.io/direct-csi-min-io
created
clusterrolebinding.rbac.authorization.k8s.io/direct-csi-
min-io created
configmap/direct-csi-config created
secret/direct-csi-min-io created
service/direct-csi-min-io created
deployment.apps/direct-csi-controller-min-io created
daemonset.apps/direct-csi-min-io created
csidriver.storage.k8s.io/direct.csi.min.io created
```

4. Before we go ahead and create our Minio tenant, let's check to see whether our CSI Pods started up properly. Run the following command to check:

```
kubectl get pods -n direct-csi
```

You should see output similar to the following if the CSI Pods have started:

NAME	READY
STATUS	RESTARTS	AGE	
direct-csi-controller-min-io-cd598c4b-hn9ww	2/2
Running	0	9m	
direct-csi-controller-min-io-cd598c4b-knvbn	2/2
Running	0	9m	
direct-csi-controller-min-io-cd598c4b-tth6q	2/2
Running	0	9m	
direct-csi-min-io-4qlt7	3/3
Running	0	9m	
direct-csi-min-io-kt7bw	3/3

```
Running    0              9m
direct-csi-min-io-vzdkv                        3/3
Running    0              9m
```

5. Now with our CSI driver installed, let's create our Minio tenant – but first, let's take a look at the YAML that the `kubectl minio tenant create` command generates:

```
kubectl minio tenant create --name my-tenant --servers 2
--volumes 4 --capacity 1Gi -o > my-minio-tenant.yaml
```

If you want to directly create the Minio tenant without examining the YAML, use the following command instead:

```
kubectl minio tenant create --name my-tenant --servers 2
--volumes 4 --capacity 1Gi
```

This command will just create the tenant without showing you the YAML first. However, since we are using the Direct CSI implementation, we will need to update the YAML. So, using just the command will not work. Let's take a look at the generated YAML file now.

We won't look at the file in its entirety for space reasons, but let's look at some parts of the Tenant **Custom Resource Definition (CRD)**, which the Minio Operator will use to create the necessary resources to host our Minio tenant. First, let's look at the upper portion of the spec, which should look like this:

my-minio-tenant.yaml

```
apiVersion: minio.min.io/v1
kind: Tenant
metadata:
  creationTimestamp: null
  name: my-tenant
  namespace: default
scheduler:
  name: ""
spec:
  certConfig:
    commonName: ""
    organizationName: []
    dnsNames: []
```

```
console:
  consoleSecret:
    name: my-tenant-console-secret
  image: minio/console:v0.3.14
  metadata:
    creationTimestamp: null
    name: my-tenant
  replicas: 2
  resources: {}
credsSecret:
  name: my-tenant-creds-secret
image: minio/minio:RELEASE.2020-09-26T03-44-56Z
imagePullSecret: {}
```

As you can see, this file specifies an instance of the Tenant CRD. This first part of our spec has two containers specified, a container for the Minio console and one for the Minio `server` itself. In addition, the `replicas` value mirrors what we specified in our `kubectl minio tenant create` command. Finally, it specifies the name of a secret for the Minio `console`.

Next, let's look at the bottom portion of the Tenant CRD:

```
liveness:
  initialDelaySeconds: 10
  periodSeconds: 1
  timeoutSeconds: 1
mountPath: /export
requestAutoCert: true
zones:
- resources: {}
  servers: 2
  volumeClaimTemplate:
    apiVersion: v1
    kind: persistentvolumeclaims
    metadata:
      creationTimestamp: null
    spec:
      accessModes:
        - ReadWriteOnce
```

```
          resources:
             requests:
               storage: 256Mi
       status: {}
     volumesPerServer: 2
  status:
    availableReplicas: 0
    currentState: ""
```

As you can see, the `Tenant` resource specifies a number of servers (also specified by the `creation` command) that matches the number of replicas. It also specifies the name of the internal Minio Service, as well as a `volumeClaimTemplate` instance to be used.

This spec, however, does not work for our purposes, since we are using the Direct CSI. Let's update the `zones` key with a new `volumeClaimTemplate` that uses the Direct CSI, as follows (save this file as `my-updated-minio-tenant.yaml`). Here's just the `zones` portion of that file, which we updated:

my-updated-minio-tenant.yaml

```
zones:
  - resources: {}
    servers: 2
    volumeClaimTemplate:
      metadata:
        name: data
      spec:
        accessModes:
          - ReadWriteOnce
        resources:
          requests:
            storage: 256Mi
        storageClassName: direct.csi.min.io
```

6. Let's now go ahead and create our Minio tenant! We can do this using the following command:

```
kubectl apply -f my-updated-minio-tenant.yaml
```

This should result in the following output:

```
tenant.minio.min.io/my-tenant created
secret/my-tenant-creds-secret created
secret/my-tenant-console-secret created
```

At this point, the Minio Operator will start creating the necessary resources for our new Minio tenant, and after a couple of minutes, you should see some Pods start up in addition to the operator, which will look similar to the following:

```
NAMESPACE   NAME                                    READY   STATUS    RESTARTS   AGE
default     minio-operator-85ccdcfb6-r8g8b          1/1     Running   0          74m
default     my-tenant-console-8696cd7d84-6dwxq      1/1     Running   0          30s
default     my-tenant-console-8696cd7d84-gkv7t      1/1     Running   0          30s
default     my-tenant-zone-0-0                      1/1     Running   0          50s
default     my-tenant-zone-0-1                      1/1     Running   0          50s
```

Figure 15.1 – Minio Pods output

We now have our Minio tenant completely up and running! Next, let's take a look at the Minio console to see how our tenant looks.

Accessing the Minio console

First, in order to get the login information for the console, we will need to fetch the content of two keys, which are kept in the autogenerated `<TENANT NAME>-console-secret` secret.

To fetch the `access` key and the `secret` key (which in our case will be autogenerated) for the console, let's use the two following commands. In our case, we use our `my-tenant` tenant to get the `access` key:

```
echo $(kubectl get secret my-tenant-console-secret
-o=jsonpath='{.data.CONSOLE_ACCESS_KEY}' | base64 --decode)
```

And to get the `secret` key, we use this:

```
echo $(kubectl get secret my-tenant-console-secret
-o=jsonpath='{.data.CONSOLE_SECRET_KEY}' | base64 --decode)
```

Now, our Minio console will be available on a service, `<TENANT NAME>-console`.

Let's access this console using a `port-forward` command. In our case, this will be as follows:

```
kubectl port-forward service/my-tenant-console 8081:9443
```

Our Minio console will then be available at `https://localhost:8081` on your browser. You will need to accept the browser security warning since we haven't set up TLS certificates for the console for localhost in this example. Put in the `access` key and `secret` key you got from the previous steps to log in!

Now that we're logged into the console, we can start adding to our Minio tenant. First, let's create a bucket. To do this, click **Buckets** on the left sidebar, then click the **Create Bucket** button.

In the popup, enter the name of the bucket (in our case, we will use `my-bucket`) and submit the form. You should see a new bucket in the list – see the following screenshot for an example:

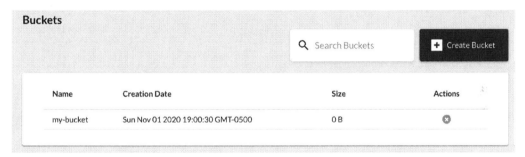

Figure 15.2 – Bucket

We now have our distributed Minio setup ready, together with a bucket to upload to. Let's wrap this example up by uploading a file to our brand-new object storage system!

We're going to do this upload using the Minio CLI, which makes the process of interacting with S3-compatible storage such as Minio much easier. Instead of using the Minio CLI from our local machine, we will run a container image preloaded with the Minio CLI from within Kubernetes, since the TLS setup will only work when accessing Minio from within the cluster.

First, we'll need to fetch the Minio `access` key and `secret`, which are different from the console `access` key and `secret` we fetched earlier. To get these keys, run the following console commands (in our case, our tenant is `my-tenant`). First, get the `access` key:

```
echo $(kubectl get secret my-tenant-creds-secret
-o=jsonpath='{.data.accesskey}' | base64 --decode)
```

Then, get the `secret` key:

```
echo $(kubectl get secret my-tenant-creds-secret
-o=jsonpath='{.data.secretkey}' | base64 --decode)
```

Now, let's start up that pod with the Minio CLI. To do this, let's use this Pod spec:

minio-mc-pod.yaml

```yaml
apiVersion: v1
kind: Pod
metadata:
  name: minio-mc
spec:
  containers:
  - name: mc
    image: minio/mc
    command: ["/bin/sh", "-c", "sleep 10000000s"]
  restartPolicy: OnFailure
```

Create this Pod using this:

```
kubectl apply -f minio-mc-pod.yaml
```

Then, to `exec` into this `minio-mc` Pod, we run the usual `exec` command:

```
Kubectl exec -it minio-mc -- sh
```

Now, let's configure access for our newly created Minio distributed cluster in the Minio CLI. We can do this with the following command (the `--insecure` flag is required in this config):

```
mc config host add my-minio https://<MINIO TENANT POD IP>:9000
--insecure
```

The Pod IP for this command can be the IP for either of our tenant Minio Pods – in our case, these are `my-tenant-zone-0-0` and `my-tenant-zone-0-1`. Once you run this command, you will be prompted for the access key and secret key. Enter them, and you will see a confirmation message if successful, which will look like this:

```
Added `my-minio` successfully.
```

Now, to test that the CLI configuration is working, we can create another test bucket using the following command:

```
mc mb my-minio/my-bucket-2 --insecure
```

This should result in the following output:

```
Bucket created successfully `my-minio/my-bucket-2`.
```

As a final test of our setup, let's upload a file to our Minio bucket!

First, still on the `minio-mc` Pod, create a text file named `test.txt`. Fill the file with whatever text you'd like.

Now, let's upload it to our recently created bucket using this:

```
mc mv test.txt my-minio/my-bucket-2 --insecure
```

You should see a loading bar with the upload, which should end with the entire file size as uploaded.

As one last check, go to the **Dashboard** page on the Minio console and see whether the object shows up, as shown in the following figure:

Figure 15.3 – Dashboard

As you can see, our file was successfully uploaded!

That's it for Minio – there is a lot more you can do in terms of configuration, but that is outside the scope of this book. Check the docs at `https://docs.min.io/` for more information.

Next up, let's look at running DBs on Kubernetes.

Running DBs on Kubernetes

Now that we've taken a look at object storage workloads on Kubernetes, we can move on to databases. As we've discussed previously in this chapter and elsewhere in the book, many databases support running on Kubernetes, with varying levels of maturity.

First off, there are several legacy and existing DB engines that support deploying to Kubernetes. Often, these engines will have supported Helm charts or operators. For instance, SQL databases such as PostgreSQL and MySQL have Helm charts and operators supported by various different organizations. NoSQL databases such as MongoDB also have supported ways to deploy to Kubernetes.

In addition to these previously existing database engines, container orchestrators such as Kubernetes have lead to the creation of a new category – the **NewSQL** database.

These databases offer the incredible scalability of NoSQL databases in addition to SQL-compliant APIs. They can be thought of as a way to easily scale SQL on Kubernetes (and other orchestrators). CockroachDB is a popular choice here, as is **Vitess**, which isn't so much a replacement NewSQL database as it is a way to easily scale the MySQL engine.

In this chapter, we will focus on deploying CockroachDB, which is a modern NewSQL database built for distributed environments and perfect for Kubernetes.

Running CockroachDB on Kubernetes

To run CockroachDB on our cluster, we will use the official CockroachDB Helm chart:

1. The first thing we need to do is to add the CockroachDB Helm chart repository, using the following command:

   ```
   helm repo add cockroachdb https://charts.cockroachdb.com/
   ```

   This should result in the following output:

   ```
   "cockroachdb" has been added to your repositories
   ```

2. Before we install the chart, let's create a custom `values.yaml` file in order to tweak some of the default settings for CockroachDB. Our file for this demo looks like the following:

Cockroach-db-values.yaml

```
storage:
  persistentVolume:
    size: 2Gi
statefulset:
  resources:
    limits:
      memory: "1Gi"
    requests:
      memory: "1Gi"
conf:
  cache: "256Mi"
  max-sql-memory: "256Mi"
```

As you can see, we are specifying a PersistentVolume size of 2 GB, Pod memory limits and requests of 1 GB, and the contents of a configuration file for CockroachDB. This configuration file includes settings for `cache` and max `memory`, which are set to 25% of the size of the memory limits at 256 MB. This ratio is a CockroachDB best practice. Keep in mind that these are not all production-ready settings, but they will work for our demo.

3. At this point, let's go ahead and create our CockroachDB cluster using the following Helm command:

```
helm install cdb --values cockroach-db-values.yaml
cockroachdb/cockroachdb
```

If successful, you will see a lengthy deploy message from Helm, which we will not reproduce here. Let's check to see exactly what was deployed on our cluster using the following command:

```
kubectl get po
```

You will see output similar to the following:

```
NAMESPACE        NAME
READY     STATUS          RESTARTS     AGE
default           cdb-cockroachdb-0
0/1       Running          0           57s
default           cdb-cockroachdb-1
0/1       Running          0           56s
default           cdb-cockroachdb-2
1/1       Running          0           56s
default           cdb-cockroachdb-init-8p2s2
0/1       Completed        0           57s
```

As you can see, we have three Pods in a StatefulSet in addition to a setup Pod that was used for some initialization tasks.

4. In order to check to see whether our cluster is functional, we can use a command that is handily given to us in the CockroachDB Helm chart output (it will vary depending on your Helm release name):

```
kubectl run -it --rm cockroach-client \
       --image=cockroachdb/cockroach \
       --restart=Never \
       --command -- \
       ./cockroach sql --insecure --host=cdb-
cockroachdb-public.default
```

If successful, a console will be opened with a prompt similar to the following:

```
root@cdb-cockroachdb-public.default:26257/defaultdb>
```

In the next section, we will test CockroachDB with SQL.

Testing CockroachDB with SQL

Now, we can run SQL commands to our new CockroachDB database!

1. First, let's create a database with the following command:

```
CREATE DATABASE mydb;
```

2. Next, let's create a simple table:

```
CREATE TABLE mydb.users (
    id UUID PRIMARY KEY DEFAULT gen_random_uuid(),
    first_name STRING,
    last_name STRING,
    email STRING
);
```

3. Then, let's add some data with this command:

```
INSERT INTO mydb.users (first_name, last_name, email)
  VALUES
      ('John', 'Smith', 'jsmith@fake.com');
```

4. Finally, let's confirm the data using this:

```
SELECT * FROM mydb.users;
```

That should give you the following output:

```
                  id                  | first_name | last_name
  |      email
--------------------------------------+------------+-----------
-+------------------
  e6fa342f-8fe5-47ad-adde-e543833ffd28 | John       | Smith
  | jsmith@fake.com
(1 row)
```

Success!

As you can see, we have a fully functional distributed SQL database. Let's move on to the final stateful workload type that we will review: messaging.

Implementing messaging and queues on Kubernetes

For messaging, we will be implementing RabbitMQ, an open source message queue system that supports Kubernetes. Messaging systems are typically used in applications to decouple various components of the application in order to support the scale and throughput, as well as asynchronous patterns such as retries and service worker fleets. For instance, instead of one service calling another service directly, a service could place a message onto a persistent message queue, at which point it would be picked up by a worker container that is listening to the queue. This allows for easy horizontal scaling and greater tolerance of entire component downtime as compared to a load balancing approach.

RabbitMQ is one of many options for message queues. As we mentioned in the first section of the chapter, RabbitMQ is an industry-standard option for message queues, not necessarily a queue system built for Kubernetes specifically. However, it's still a great choice and very easy to deploy, as we will see shortly.

Let's start with implementing RabbitMQ on Kubernetes!

Deploying RabbitMQ on Kubernetes

Installing RabbitMQ on Kubernetes can be easily done via an operator or via a Helm chart. For the purposes of this tutorial, we will use the Helm chart:

1. First, let's add the proper `helm` repository (provided by **Bitnami**):

    ```
    helm repo add bitnami https://charts.bitnami.com/bitnami
    ```

2. Next, let's create a custom values file to tweak some parameters:

    Values-rabbitmq.yaml

    ```
    auth:
      user: user
      password: test123
    persistence:
      enabled: false
    ```

    As you can see, in this case, we are disabling persistence, which is great for a quick demo.

3. Then, RabbitMQ can easily be installed on the cluster using the following command:

```
helm install rabbitmq bitnami/rabbitmq --values values-
rabbitmq.yaml
```

Once successful, you will see a confirmation message from Helm. The RabbitMQ Helm chart also includes a management UI, so let's use that to validate that our installation worked.

4. First, let's start a port forward to the `rabbitmq` service:

```
kubectl port-forward --namespace default svc/rabbitmq
15672:15672
```

Then, we should be able to access the RabbitMQ management UI on `http://localhost:15672`. It will look like the following:

Figure 15.4 – RabbitMQ management console login

5. Now, we should be able to log in to the dashboard using the username and password specified in the values file. Upon login, you will see the RabbitMQ dashboard main view.

Importantly, you will see a list of the nodes in your RabbitMQ cluster. In our case, we only have a single node, which will display as follows:

▼ Nodes	
Name	File descriptors ?
rabbit@rabbitmq-0.rabbitmq-headless.default.svc.cluster.local	99
	1048576 available

Figure 15.5 – RabbitMQ management console node item

For each node, you can see the name and some metadata, including memory, uptime, and more.

6. In order to add a new queue navigate to **Queues** on the top bar, click **Add a new queue** toward the bottom of the screen. Fill out the form as follows, then click **Add queue**:

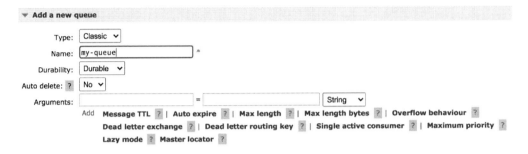

Figure 15.6 – RabbitMQ management console queue creation

If successful, the screen should refresh with your new queue added to the list. This means our RabbitMQ setup is working properly!

7. Finally, now that we have a queue, we can publish a message to it. To do this, click on your newly created queue on the **Queues** page, then click **Publish Message**.

8. Write any text in the **Payload** text box and click **Publish Message**. You should see a confirmation popup telling you that your message has been published successfully, and the screen should refresh, showing your message on the queue, as shown in the following figure:

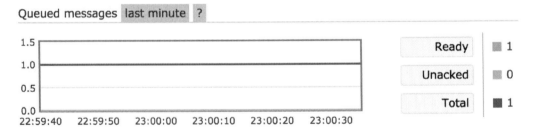

Figure 15.7 – RabbitMQ management console queue status

9. Finally, to emulate fetching messages from the queue, click on **Get messages** near the bottom of the page, which should expand to show a new section, and then click the **Get Message(s)** button. You should see an output of the message you sent, proving that the queue system works!

Summary

In this chapter, we learned about running stateful workloads on Kubernetes. First, we reviewed a high-level overview of some of the types of stateful workloads and some examples of each. Then, we moved on to actually deploying one of these workloads – an object storage system – on Kubernetes. Next, we did the same with a NewSQL database, CockroachDB, showing you how to easily deploy a CockroachDB cluster on Kubernetes.

Finally, we showed you how to deploy the RabbitMQ message queue on Kubernetes using a Helm chart. The skills you used in this chapter will help you deploy and use popular stateful application patterns on Kubernetes.

If you've made it this far, thanks for sticking with us through all 15 chapters of this book! I hope that you have learned how to use a broad spectrum of Kubernetes functionality and that you now have all the tools you need in order to build and deploy complex applications on Kubernetes.

Questions

1. What cloud storage offering is Minio's API compatible with?
2. What are the benefits of a StatefulSet for a distributed database?
3. In your words, what makes stateful applications difficult to run on Kubernetes?

Further reading

- Minio Quickstart Documentation: `https://docs.min.io/docs/minio-quickstart-guide.html`
- CockroachDB Kubernetes Guide: `https://www.cockroachlabs.com/docs/v20.2/orchestrate-a-local-cluster-with-kubernetes`

Assessments

Chapter 1 – Communicating with Kubernetes

1. Container orchestration is a software pattern where multiple containers are controlled and scheduled in order to serve an application.

2. The Kubernetes API server (`kube-apiserver`) handles requests to update Kubernetes resources. The scheduler (`kube-scheduler`) decides where to place (schedule) containers. The controller manager (`kube-controller-manager`) ensures that the desired configuration of Kubernetes resources is reflected in the cluster. `etcd` provides a data store for the cluster configuration.

3. The `kube-apiserver` must be started with the `--authorization-mode=ABAC` and `--authorization-policy-file=filename` parameters.

4. For high availability of the control plane, in case of a failure of one of the master nodes.

5. In the event that a resource has already been created, `kubectl create` will fail because the resource already exists, while `kubectl apply` will attempt to apply any YAML changes to the resource.

6. The `kubectl use-context` command can be used to switch between multiple contexts within a `kubeconfig` file. To change between `kubeconfig` files, the `KUBECONFIG` environment variable can be set to the path of the new file.

7. Imperative commands do not provide a history of changes to a resource.

Chapter 2 – Setting Up Your Kubernetes Cluster

1. Minikube makes it easy to set up a local Kubernetes cluster for development.

2. In some cases, there may be a fixed minimum cost for the cluster that is larger than a self-provisioned cluster. Some managed options also have license costs in addition to the cost of compute.

3. Kubeadm is agnostic to infrastructure providers, while Kops supports only several major providers with deeper integration and compute provisioning.

4. As of the writing of this book, AWS, Google Cloud Platform, Digital Ocean, VMware, and OpenStack, in various levels of production readiness.

5. Typically, the cluster components are defined in the `systemd` service definitions, which allows the automatic restart of services if a node shuts down and restarts at the OS level.

Chapter 3 – Running Application Containers on Kubernetes

1. If you had development, staging, and production environments, you could make one namespace for each.

2. The Node that the Pod is running in could be in a *broken* state where the control plane cannot reach it. Typically, when a Node gracefully exits the cluster, the Pod will simply be rescheduled instead of showing an *Unknown* status.

3. To prevent memory-hungry Pods from taking over the entire Node and causing indeterminate behavior in other Pods on the Node.

4. You should add more delay to the *Startup* probe if you have one. If not, you will need to add one, or add a delay to the *Readiness* probe.

Chapter 4 – Scaling and Deploying Your Application

1. ReplicationControllers have less flexibility in how the selector is configured – only key-value selectors are allowed.

2. Deployments allow you to specify how updates are rolled out.

3. Jobs work well for batch tasks, or tasks that can be scaled horizontally with a clear completion target.

4. StatefulSets provide an ordinal Pod identity that stays the same when those Pods restart.

5. In addition to an existing version, a new Deployment can be created with the canary version. Then, both versions can be accessed in parallel.

Chapter 5 – Services and Ingress – Communicating with the Outside World

1. You would use a ClusterIP service.

2. You can use the `kubectl describe` command to see what port on the Nodes a NodePort service is active on.

3. In a cloud environment where you often have to pay per load balancer, Ingress allows you to specify multiple routing rules while only having to pay for one load balancer.

4. ExternalName services can be used to easily route to other pieces of infrastructure in your cloud environment – such as managed databases and object storage.

Chapter 6 – Kubernetes Application Configuration

1. Secrets are stored encoded and optionally encrypted in `etcd`. ConfigMaps are stored in plain text.

2. They are Base64-encoded.

3. The data will be more visible when describing the ConfigMap. The key-value pattern is also easier to use when mounting the ConfigMap as an environment variable.

4. Depending on how you set up your cluster, your secrets may not be encrypted at all. If a cluster's EncryptionConfiguration is not set, secrets will only be Base64-encoded – and they can easily be decoded. By creating your cluster with an EncryptionConfiguration, your secrets will be stored encrypted in `etcd`. This is not a security panacea, but encryption at rest is certainly necessary to improve security for secrets.

Chapter 7 – Storage on Kubernetes

1. Volumes are tied to the life cycle of a Pod and are deleted when the Pod is deleted. Persistent Volumes will remain until a cluster is deleted, or they are specifically deleted themselves.

2. StorageClasses define the *type* of a Persistent Volume. They can be used to distinguish between different types of storage, such as between faster SSD storage and slower hard drives – or different types of cloud storage. StorageClasses determine where a PersistentVolumeClaim and Persistent Volume will go to get provisioned storage.

3. Use a managed Kubernetes service with integrated storage provisioning or add a **cloud-controller-manager** configuration to your cluster.

4. Any application that needs to store state for longer than the life of an individual Pod would not work with Volumes. Any application that needs to have state that is tolerant to Pod failure needs a Persistent Volume.

Chapter 8 – Pod Placement Controls

1. Node Selectors can be used to match against Node labels and multiple Nodes can fulfill the requirements. Using a Node name means that you specify the single Node where the Pod must be placed.

2. Kubernetes implements some default taints to ensure that Pods do not get scheduled on Nodes that are malfunctioning or lack resources. In addition, Kubernetes taints the master Nodes to prevent scheduling of user applications on the masters.

3. Too many affinities and anti-affinities can slow down the scheduler or cause it to become unresponsive. Determining Pod placement in cases with a lot of affinities or anti-affinities is very compute-heavy.

4. Using anti-affinities, you could prevent Pods from co-existing with like Pods in the same failure domain. Nodes in the same failure domain would be labeled with a failure domain or zone identifier. Anti-affinity would look for Pods matching the specific tier of the application level in the same failure domain, and prevent scheduling on Nodes matching that domain. The end result would be each tier of the three-tier application being spread out among multiple failure domains.

Chapter 9 – Observability on Kubernetes

1. Metrics correspond to numerical values that present application/compute performance and/or usage across many categories, including disk, CPU, memory, latency, and so on. Logs correspond to the application, Node, or control plane text logs.

2. The Grafana UI is highly customizable and can be used to present complex Prometheus (or another data source's) queries in an elegant, flexible way.

3. FluentD would need to run on the production cluster in order to collect logs. Elasticsearch and Kibana could run on a separate cluster or other infrastructure.

Chapter 10 – Troubleshooting Kubernetes

1. One of the strengths of Kubernetes is the ability to scale the cluster easily by adding nodes or changing Pod placement by using controls such as taints and tolerations. In addition, Pod restarts can result in completely different IPs for the same application. This means that both the compute and network topologies can be ever-changing.

2. The `kubelet` is typically run as a Linux service with `systemd`, with control available using `systemctl` and logs in `journalctl`.

3. There are a few different methodologies to use, but generally, you would want to check whether all Nodes are ready and schedulable; whether there are any Pod Placement Controls precluding scheduling of the Pod; and whether there is any dependent storage, ConfigMaps, or secrets that do not exist.

Chapter 11 – Template Code Generation and CI/CD on Kubernetes

1. Helm Charts use templates and variables, while Kustomize uses a patch-based strategy. Kustomize is built into recent versions of kubectl, while Helm uses a separate CLI tool.

2. The configuration should emphasize security, since deploy credentials could be used to deploy attacker workloads to your cluster. Using either secure environment variables or access management controls on your cloud provider are two good strategies. The credentials should absolutely not be placed in any Git repository.

3. In-cluster setups can be preferable since Kubernetes credentials are not required to be provided by an external system. Out-of-cluster setups are usually simpler, and more synchronous than in-cluster setups, where a control loop determines when changes are made to the resource configuration.

Chapter 12 – Kubernetes Security and Compliance

1. MutatingAdmissionWebhook and ValidatingAdmissionWebhook.

2. A NetworkPolicy with a blank Pod Selector has the effect of selecting all Pods. A NetworkPolicy with all Pods selected, and Ingress and Egress types added without any rules, will have the effect of automatically denying all ingress and egress to all Pods in the namespace of the NetworkPolicy.

3. We would want to track any API requests where resources are patched or updated, because attackers could update a Deployment, Pod, or another resource with malicious containers.

Chapter 13 – Extending Kubernetes with CRDs

1. The stored version is the version that is actually stored in the data store. Served versions are any versions that are accepted by the API for read or write operations. The served versions are converted into the stored version when stored in `etcd`.

2. Measure, Analyze, and Update (typically).

3. Depending on the cloud provider, the **cluster-autoscaler** addon will directly update autoscaling groups in order to add or remove Nodes.

Chapter 14 – Service Meshes and Serverless

1. A static Envoy configuration refers to an Envoy configuration that is manually created or written by a user. A dynamic Envoy configuration (like those provided by Istio) will constantly adapt to new containers, as well as new routing and filter rules, from an external controller or data plane.

2. Listeners, Routes, Clusters, and Endpoints.

3. Knative requires many components in order to run. This allows for plenty of customization but makes it more difficult to set up and operate than OpenFaaS.

Chapter 15 – Stateful Workloads on Kubernetes

1. Minio is an AWS S3-compatible storage tool.

2. StatefulSets assist self-clustering applications such as distributed databases by providing stable, ordinal Pod identities, in addition to Persistent Volume stability.

3. In Kubernetes, Pods can be short-lived, and stateful applications can be distributed. This means that the process of maintaining state between Pods (for instance, the database consensus) can become difficult if Pods change identity and storage needs to be replicated from scratch.

Other Books You May Enjoy

If you enjoyed this book, you may be interested in these other books by Packt:

Mastering Kubernetes

Gigi Sayfan

ISBN: 978-1-83921-125-6

- Master the fundamentals of Kubernetes architecture and design
- Build and run stateful applications and complex microservices on Kubernetes
- Use tools like Kubectl, secrets, and Helm to manage resources and storage
- Master Kubernetes Networking with load balancing options like Ingress
- Achieve high-availability Kubernetes clusters
- Improve Kubernetes observability with tools like Prometheus, Grafana, and Jaeger
- Extend Kubernetes working with Kubernetes API, plugins, and webhooks

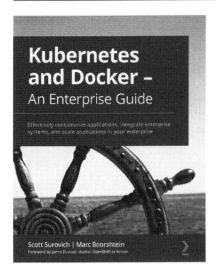

Kubernetes and Docker - An Enterprise Guide

Scott Surovich, Marc Boorshtein

ISBN: 978-1-83921-340-3

- Create a multinode Kubernetes cluster using kind

- Implement Ingress, MetalLB, and ExternalDNS

- Configure a cluster OIDC using impersonation

- Map enterprise authorization to Kubernetes

- Secure clusters using PSPs and OPA

- Enhance auditing using Falco and EFK

- Back up your workload for disaster recovery and cluster migration

- Deploy to a platform using Tekton, GitLab, and ArgoCD

Leave a review - let other readers know what you think

Please share your thoughts on this book with others by leaving a review on the site that you bought it from. If you purchased the book from Amazon, please leave us an honest review on this book's Amazon page. This is vital so that other potential readers can see and use your unbiased opinion to make purchasing decisions, we can understand what our customers think about our products, and our authors can see your feedback on the title that they have worked with Packt to create. It will only take a few minutes of your time, but is valuable to other potential customers, our authors, and Packt. Thank you!

Index

Made in the USA
Coppell, TX
07 September 2021